CROCK·POT

◆ THE ORIGINAL SLOW COOKER ◆

RECIPE COLLECTION

Publications International, Ltd.

Contents

Page 32

Slow Cooking Tips

Sizes of CROCK-POT® Slow Cookers

Smaller **CROCK-POT®** slow cookers—such as 1- to 3-quart models—are the perfect size for cooking for singles, a couple or empty nesters (and also for serving dips).

While medium-size **CROCK-POT®** slow cookers (those holding somewhere between 3 quarts and 5 quarts) will easily cook enough food at a time to feed a small family. They are also convenient for holiday side dishes or appetizers.

Large **CROCK-POT®** slow cookers are great for large family dinners, holiday entertaining and potluck suppers. A 6- to 7-quart model is ideal if you like to make meals in advance, or have dinner tonight and store leftovers for another day.

Types of CROCK-POT® Slow Cookers

Current **CROCK-POT®** slow cookers come equipped with many different features and benefits, from auto cook programs to oven-safe stoneware to timed programming. Please visit **WWW.CROCK-POT.COM** to find the **CROCK-POT®** slow cooker that best suits your needs.

How you plan to use a **CROCK-POT®** slow cooker may affect the model you choose to purchase. For everyday cooking, choose a size large enough to serve your family. If you plan to use the **CROCK-POT®** slow cooker primarily for entertaining, choose one of the larger sizes. Basic **CROCK-POT®** slow cookers can hold as little as 16 ounces or as much as 7 quarts. The smallest sizes are great for keeping dips warm on a buffet, while the larger sizes can more readily fit large quantities of food and larger roasts.

Cooking, Stirring and Food Safety

CROCK-POT® slow cookers are safe to leave unattended. The outer heating base may get hot as it cooks, but it should not pose a fire hazard. The heating element in the heating base functions at a low wattage and is safe for your countertops.

Your **CROCK-POT®** slow cooker should be filled about one-half to three-fourths full for most recipes unless otherwise instructed. Lean meats such as chicken or pork tenderloin will cook faster than meats with more connective tissue and fat such as beef chuck or pork shoulder. Bone-in meats will take longer than boneless cuts. Typical **CROCK-POT®** slow cooker dishes take approximately 7 to 8 hours to reach the simmer point on LOW and about 3 to 4 hours on HIGH. Once the vegetables and meat start to simmer and braise, their flavors will fully blend and meat will become fall-off-the-bone tender.

According to the U.S. Department of Agriculture, all bacteria are killed at a temperature of 165°F. It's important to follow the recommended cooking times and not to open the lid often, especially early in the cooking process when heat is building up inside the unit. If you need to open the lid to check on your food or are adding additional ingredients, remember to allow additional cooking time if necessary to ensure food is cooked through and tender.

Large **CROCK-POT®** slow cookers, the 6- to 7-quart sizes, may benefit from a quick stir halfway through cook time to help distribute heat and promote even cooking. It's usually unnecessary to stir at all, as even ½ cup liquid will help to distribute heat and the stoneware is the perfect medium for holding food at an even temperature throughout the cooking process.

Oven-Safe Stoneware

All **CROCK-POT®** slow cooker removable stoneware inserts may (without their lids) be used safely in ovens at up to 400°F. In addition, all **CROCK-POT®** slow cookers are microwavable without their lids. If you own another slow cooker brand, please refer to your owner's manual for specific stoneware cooking medium tolerances.

Frozen Food

Frozen food can be successfully cooked in a **CROCK-POT®** slow cooker. However, it will require longer cooking time than the same recipe made with fresh food. It's almost always preferable to thaw frozen food prior to placing it in the **CROCK-POT®** slow cooker. Using an instant-read thermometer is recommended to ensure meat is fully cooked through.

Pasta and Rice

If you are converting a recipe for a **CROCK-POT®** slow cooker that calls for uncooked pasta, first cook the pasta on the stovetop just until slightly tender.

Then add the pasta to the **CROCK-POT**® slow cooker. If you are converting a recipe for the **CROCK-POT**® slow cooker that calls for cooked rice, stir in raw rice with the other recipe ingredients plus ¼ cup extra liquid per ¼ cup of raw rice.

Beans

Beans must be softened completely before combining with sugar and/or acidic foods in the **CROCK-POT**® slow cooker. Sugar and acid have a hardening effect on beans and will prevent softening. Fully cooked canned beans may be used as a substitute for dried beans.

Vegetables

Root vegetables often cook more slowly than meat. Cut vegetables accordingly to cook at the same rate as meat—large or small or lean versus marbled—and place near the sides or bottom of the stoneware to facilitate cooking.

Herbs

Fresh herbs add flavor and color when added at the end of the cooking cycle; if added at the beginning, many fresh herbs' flavor will dissipate over long cook times. Ground and/or dried herbs and spices work well in slow cooking and may be added at the beginning of cook time. For dishes with shorter cook times, hearty fresh herbs such as rosemary and thyme hold up well. The flavor power of all herbs and spices can vary greatly depending on their particular strength and shelf life. Use chili powders and garlic powder sparingly, as these can sometimes intensify over the long cook times. Always taste the finished dish and correct seasonings including salt and pepper.

Thickeners

It's not necessary to use more than ½ to 1 cup liquid in most instances since juices in meats and vegetables are retained more in slow cooking than in conventional cooking. Excess liquid can be cooked down and concentrated after slow cooking on the stovetop or by removing meat and vegetables from stoneware, stirring in one of the following thickeners and setting the **CROCK-POT**® slow cooker to HIGH. Cover; cook on HIGH for approximately 15 minutes or until juices are thickened.

FLOUR: All-purpose flour is often used to thicken soups or stews. Stir cold water into the flour in a small bowl until smooth. With the **CROCK-POT**® slow cooker on HIGH, whisk the flour mixture into the liquid in the **CROCK-POT**® slow cooker. Cover; cook on HIGH 15 minutes or until the mixture is thickened.

CORNSTARCH: Cornstarch gives sauces a clear, shiny appearance; it's used most often for sweet dessert sauces and stir-fry sauces. Stir cold water into the cornstarch in a small bowl until the cornstarch dissolves. Quickly stir this mixture into the liquid in the **CROCK-POT®** slow cooker; the sauce will thicken as soon as the liquid simmers. Cornstarch breaks down with too much heat, so never add it at the beginning of the slow cooking process and turn off the heat as soon as the sauce thickens.

ARROWROOT: Arrowroot (or arrowroot flour) comes from the root of a tropical plant that is dried and ground to a powder; it produces a thick, clear sauce. Those who are allergic to wheat often use it in place of flour. Place arrowroot in a small bowl or cup and stir in cold water until the mixture is smooth. Quickly stir this mixture into the liquid in the **CROCK-POT®** slow cooker. Arrowroot thickens below the boiling point, so it even works well in a **CROCK-POT®** slow cooker on LOW. Too much stirring can break down an arrowroot mixture.

TAPIOCA: Tapioca is a starchy substance extracted from the root of the cassava plant. Its greatest advantage is that it withstands long cooking, making it an ideal choice for slow cooking. Add it at the beginning of cooking and you'll get a clear, thickened sauce in the finished dish. Dishes using tapioca as a thickener are best cooked on the LOW setting; tapioca may become stringy when boiled for a long time.

Dairy

Milk, cream and sour cream break down during extended cooking. When possible, add them during the last 15 to 30 minutes of slow cooking, until just heated through. Condensed soups may be substituted for milk and may cook for extended times.

Fish

Fish is delicate and should be stirred into the **CROCK-POT®** slow cooker gently during the last 15 to 30 minutes of cooking time. Cover; cook just until cooked through and serve immediately.

Baked Goods

If you wish to prepare bread, cakes or pudding cakes in a **CROCK-POT®** slow cooker, you may want to purchase a covered, vented metal cake pan accessory for your **CROCK-POT®** slow cooker. You can also use any straight-sided soufflé dish or deep cake pan that will fit into the stoneware of your unit. Baked goods can be prepared directly in the stoneware; however, they can be a little difficult to remove from the insert, so follow the recipe directions carefully.

BREAKFAST AND BRUNCH

Overnight Breakfast Porridge

¾ cup steel-cut oats

¼ cup uncooked quinoa, rinsed and drained

¼ cup dried cranberries, plus additional for serving

¼ cup raisins

3 tablespoons ground flax seeds

2 tablespoons chia seeds

¼ teaspoon ground cinnamon

2½ cups almond milk, plus additional for serving

Maple syrup (optional)

¼ cup sliced almonds, toasted*

To toast almonds, spread in single layer in heavy skillet. Cook over medium heat 1 to 2 minutes or until nuts are lightly browned, stirring frequently.

1. Combine oats, quinoa, ¼ cup cranberries, raisins, flax seeds, chia seeds and cinnamon in heat-safe bowl that fits inside a 5- or 6-quart **CROCK-POT**® slow cooker. Stir in 2½ cups almond milk.

2. Place bowl into **CROCK-POT**® slow cooker; pour enough water to come halfway up side of bowl.

3. Cover; cook on LOW 8 hours. Carefully remove bowl from **CROCK-POT**® slow cooker. Stir in additional almond milk. Top with syrup, almonds and additional cranberries, if desired.

Makes 4 servings

Maple, Bacon and Raspberry Pancake

5 slices bacon	1 cup fresh raspberries
2 cups pancake mix	3 tablespoons chopped pecans, toasted*
1 cup water	
½ cup maple syrup, plus additional for serving	*To toast pecans, spread in single layer in heavy skillet. Cook over medium heat 1 to 2 minutes or until nuts are lightly browned, stirring frequently.

1. Heat large skillet over medium heat. Add bacon; cook and stir until crisp. Remove to paper towel-lined plate using slotted spoon; crumble.

2. Brush inside of 4- to 5-quart oval **CROCK-POT**® slow cooker with 1 to 2 tablespoons bacon fat from skillet. Combine pancake mix, water and ½ cup syrup in large bowl; stir to blend. Pour half of batter into **CROCK-POT**® slow cooker; top with half of raspberries, half of bacon and half of pecans. Pour remaining half of batter over top; sprinkle with remaining raspberries, bacon and pecans.

3. Cover; cook on HIGH 1½ to 2 hours or until pancake has risen and is cooked through. Turn off heat. Let stand, uncovered, 10 to 15 minutes. Remove pancake from **CROCK-POT**® slow cooker; cut into eight pieces. Serve with additional syrup.

Makes 8 servings

Spiced Vanilla Applesauce

5 pounds (about 10 medium) sweet apples (such as Fuji or Gala), peeled and cut into 1-inch pieces

½ cup water

2 teaspoons vanilla

1 teaspoon ground cinnamon

¼ teaspoon ground nutmeg

¼ teaspoon ground cloves

1. Combine apples, water, vanilla, cinnamon, nutmeg and cloves in **CROCK-POT**® slow cooker; stir to blend. Cover; cook on HIGH 3 to 4 hours or until apples are very tender.

2. Turn off heat. Mash mixture with potato masher to smooth out any large lumps. Let cool completely before serving.

Makes 6 cups

Egg and Sausage Strata

8 to 10 slices multigrain bread, torn into 1-inch pieces

2 cups (8 ounces) shredded mozzarella cheese

4 ounces cream cheese, cut into small cubes

8 ounces precooked maple pork breakfast sausage, cut into ¾-inch pieces

3 cups milk

8 eggs

1 tablespoon hot pepper sauce

½ teaspoon salt

¼ teaspoon black pepper

1. Coat inside of **CROCK-POT**® slow cooker with nonstick cooking spray. Place half of bread in **CROCK-POT**® slow cooker. Top with 1 cup mozzarella cheese, cream cheese and sausage. Top with remaining bread and mozzarella cheese.

2. Combine milk, eggs, hot pepper sauce, salt and black pepper in large bowl; mix well. Pour egg mixture over bread mixture in **CROCK-POT**® slow cooker. Cover; cook on LOW 3 to 4 hours or on HIGH 1½ to 2 hours or until strata is puffed and eggs are set.

Makes 6 to 8 servings

Triple Delicious Hot Chocolate

3 cups milk, divided

⅓ cup sugar

¼ cup unsweetened cocoa powder

¼ teaspoon salt

¾ teaspoon vanilla

1 cup whipping cream

1 square (1 ounce) bittersweet chocolate, chopped

1 square (1 ounce) white chocolate, chopped

Whipped cream

6 teaspoons mini semisweet chocolate chips or shaved bittersweet chocolate

1. Combine ½ cup milk, sugar, cocoa and salt in **CROCK-POT**® slow cooker; whisk until smooth. Stir in remaining 2½ cups milk and vanilla. Cover; cook on LOW 2 hours.

2. Stir in cream. Cover; cook on LOW 10 minutes. Stir in bittersweet and white chocolate until melted.

3. Pour hot chocolate into mugs. Top each serving with whipped cream and 1 teaspoon chocolate chips.

Makes 6 servings

Pear Crunch

1   can (8 ounces) crushed pineapple in juice, undrained

¼   cup pineapple or apple juice

3   tablespoons dried cranberries

1½   teaspoons quick-cooking tapioca

¼   teaspoon vanilla

2   pears, cored and halved

¼   cup granola with almonds

1. Combine pineapple, pineapple juice, cranberries, tapioca and vanilla in **CROCK-POT®** slow cooker; stir to blend. Top with pears, cut sides down.

2. Cover; cook on LOW 3½ to 4½ hours. Arrange pear halves on serving plates. Spoon pineapple mixture over pear halves. Sprinkle with granola.

Makes 4 servings

Savory Sausage Bread Pudding

4 eggs

2 cups milk *or* 1 cup *each* half-and-half and milk

¼ teaspoon salt

¼ teaspoon black pepper

¼ teaspoon dried thyme

⅛ teaspoon red pepper flakes

1 package (10 ounces) smoked breakfast sausage links, cut into ½-inch pieces

¾ cup (3 ounces) shredded Cheddar cheese

2 cups day-old bread, cut into ½-inch cubes

1. Beat eggs in large bowl. Stir in milk, salt, black pepper, thyme and red pepper flakes. Add sausage, cheese and bread; press bread into egg mixture. Let stand 10 minutes or until liquid is absorbed.

2. Generously butter 2-quart baking dish that fits inside **CROCK-POT**® slow cooker. Pour sausage mixture into baking dish. Cover dish with buttered foil, butter side down.

3. Pour 1 inch hot water into **CROCK-POT**® slow cooker. Add baking dish. Cover; cook on LOW 4 to 5 hours or until toothpick inserted into center comes out clean.

Makes 4 to 6 servings

Apple and Granola Breakfast Cobbler

4 Granny Smith apples, peeled, cored and sliced

½ cup packed light brown sugar

1 tablespoon lemon juice

1 teaspoon ground cinnamon

2 cups granola cereal, plus additional for garnish

2 tablespoons butter, cut into small pieces

Whipping cream, half-and-half or vanilla yogurt (optional)

1. Place apples in **CROCK-POT®** slow cooker. Sprinkle brown sugar, lemon juice and cinnamon over apples. Stir in 2 cups granola and butter.

2. Cover; cook on LOW 6 hours or on HIGH 2 to 3 hours. Serve warm with additional granola sprinkled on top. Serve with cream, if desired.

Makes 4 servings

Cherry-Orange Oatmeal

4 cups water

2 cups old-fashioned oats

4 tablespoons sugar substitute

2 tablespoons unsweetened cocoa powder

2 cups fresh pitted cherries or frozen dark sweet cherries

2 cans (11 ounces *each*) mandarin orange segments in light syrup, rinsed and drained

1. Combine water, oats, sugar substitute and cocoa in **CROCK-POT®** slow cooker; stir to blend. Cover; cook on LOW 8 hours.

2. Divide mixture evenly among eight serving bowls. Top with cherries and oranges.

Makes 8 servings

Bran Muffin Bread

¼ cup (½ stick) unsalted butter, melted, plus additional for mold

2 cups whole wheat flour, plus additional for dusting*

2 cups all-bran cereal

2 teaspoons baking powder

1 teaspoon baking soda

½ teaspoon salt

¼ teaspoon ground cinnamon

1 egg

1½ cups buttermilk

¼ cup molasses

1 cup chopped walnuts

½ cup raisins

Honey butter or cream cheese (optional)

*For proper texture of finished bread, spoon flour into measuring cup and level off. Do not dip into bag, pack down flour or tap on counter to level when measuring.

1. Butter and flour an 8-cup mold that fits inside 6-quart **CROCK-POT**® slow cooker; set aside. Combine cereal, 2 cups flour, baking powder, baking soda, salt and cinnamon in large bowl; stir to blend well.

2. Beat egg in medium bowl. Add buttermilk, molasses and ¼ cup melted butter; mix well to blend. Add buttermilk mixture to flour mixture; stir just until combined. Stir in walnuts and raisins. Spoon batter into prepared mold. Cover with buttered foil, butter side down.

3. Place rack in **CROCK-POT**® slow cooker or prop up mold with a few equal-size potatoes. Pour 1 inch hot water into **CROCK-POT**® slow cooker (water should not come to top of rack). Place mold on rack. Cover; cook on LOW 3½ to 4 hours.

4. To check for doneness, lift foil. Bread should just start to pull away from sides of mold and toothpick inserted into center of bread should come out clean. If necessary, replace foil and continue cooking on LOW 45 minutes.

5. Remove mold from **CROCK-POT**® slow cooker. Let stand 10 minutes. Remove foil and run rubber spatula around outer edges, lifting bottom slightly to loosen. Invert bread onto wire rack. Cool until lukewarm. Slice and serve with honey butter, if desired.

Makes 1 loaf

Tip: Cooking times are guidelines. **CROCK-POT**® slow cookers, just like ovens, cook differently depending on the recipe size and the individual **CROCK-POT**® slow cooker. Always check for doneness before serving.

Apple-Cinnamon Breakfast Risotto

¼ cup (½ stick) butter

4 medium Granny Smith apples (about
1½ pounds), peeled, cored and diced
into ½-inch cubes

1½ teaspoons ground cinnamon

¼ teaspoon ground allspice

¼ teaspoon salt

1½ cups uncooked Arborio rice

½ cup packed dark brown sugar

4 cups unfiltered apple juice, at room
temperature*

1 teaspoon vanilla

Optional toppings: dried cranberries, sliced
almonds, milk

*If unfiltered apple juice is unavailable, use any apple
juice.

1. Coat **CROCK-POT**® slow cooker with nonstick cooking spray; set aside. Melt butter in large skillet over medium-high heat. Add apples, cinnamon, allspice and salt. Cook and stir 3 to 5 minutes or until apples begin to release juices. Remove to **CROCK-POT**® slow cooker.

2. Add rice and stir to coat. Sprinkle brown sugar evenly over top. Add apple juice and vanilla. Cover; cook on HIGH 1½ to 2 hours or until all liquid is absorbed. Ladle risotto into bowls; top with cranberries, almonds and milk.

Makes 6 servings

Tip: Keep the lid on! The **CROCK-POT**® slow cooker can take as long as 30 minutes to regain heat lost when the cover is removed.

Whole-Grain Banana Bread

¼ cup plus 2 tablespoons wheat germ, divided

1 cup sugar

⅔ cup butter, softened

2 eggs

1 cup mashed bananas (2 to 3 bananas)

1 teaspoon vanilla

1 cup all-purpose flour

1 cup whole wheat pastry flour

1 teaspoon baking soda

½ teaspoon salt

½ cup chopped walnuts or pecans (optional)

1. Coat inside of 1-quart soufflé dish that fits inside **CROCK-POT®** slow cooker with nonstick cooking spray. Sprinkle dish with 2 tablespoons wheat germ.

2. Beat sugar and butter in large bowl with electric mixer until fluffy. Add eggs, one at a time; beat until blended. Add bananas and vanilla; beat until smooth.

3. Gradually stir in flours, remaining ¼ cup wheat germ, baking soda and salt. Stir in walnuts, if desired. Pour batter into prepared dish; place in 5-quart **CROCK-POT®** slow cooker. Cover; cook on LOW 4 to 6 hours or on HIGH 2 to 3 hours or until edges begin to brown and toothpick inserted into center comes out clean.

4. Remove dish from **CROCK-POT®** slow cooker. Cool on wire rack 10 minutes. Remove bread from dish; cool completely on wire rack.

Makes 1 loaf

Four Fruit Oatmeal

4¼ cups water

1 cup steel-cut oats

⅓ cup golden raisins

⅓ cup dried cranberries

⅓ cup dried cherries

2 tablespoons honey

1 teaspoon vanilla

¼ teaspoon salt

1 cup fresh sliced strawberries

Combine water, oats, raisins, cranberries, cherries, honey, vanilla and salt in **CROCK-POT®** slow cooker; stir well. Cover; cook on LOW 7 to 7½ hours. Top each serving evenly with strawberries.

Makes 4 servings

Raisin-Oat Quick Bread

1½ cups all-purpose flour, plus additional for dusting

⅔ cup old-fashioned oats

⅓ cup milk

4 teaspoons baking powder

1 teaspoon ground cinnamon

½ teaspoon salt

½ cup packed raisins

1 cup sugar

2 eggs, slightly beaten

½ cup (1 stick) unsalted butter, melted plus additional for serving

1 teaspoon vanilla

1. Spray inside of ovenproof glass or ceramic loaf pan that fits inside **CROCK-POT®** slow cooker with nonstick cooking spray; dust with flour.

2. Combine oats and milk in small bowl; let stand 10 minutes.

3. Meanwhile, combine 1½ cups flour, baking powder, cinnamon and salt in large bowl; stir in raisins. Whisk sugar, eggs, ½ cup butter and vanilla in separate medium bowl; stir in oat mixture. Pour sugar mixture into flour mixture; stir just until moistened. Pour into prepared pan. Place in **CROCK-POT®** slow cooker. Cover; cook on HIGH 2½ to 3 hours or until toothpick inserted into center comes out clean.

4. Remove bread from **CROCK-POT®** slow cooker; let cool in pan 10 minutes. Remove bread from pan; let cool on wire rack 3 minutes before slicing. Serve with additional butter, if desired.

Makes 1 loaf

Fresh Berry Compote

2 cups fresh blueberries

4 cups fresh sliced strawberries

2 tablespoons orange juice

½ cup sugar

4 slices (1½×½ inches) lemon peel with no white pith

1 cinnamon stick *or* ½ teaspoon ground cinnamon

1. Place blueberries in **CROCK-POT®** slow cooker. Cover; cook on HIGH 45 minutes or until blueberries begin to soften.

2. Add strawberries, orange juice, sugar, lemon peel and cinnamon stick; stir to blend. Cover; cook on HIGH 1 to 1½ hours or until berries soften and sugar dissolves.

3. Remove stoneware from **CROCK-POT®** slow cooker; let cool before serving.

Makes 4 servings

Tip: To turn this compote into a fresh-fruit topping for cake, ice cream, waffles or pancakes, carefully spoon out fruit, leaving cooking liquid in **CROCK-POT®** slow cooker. Stir ¼ cup cold water into 1 to 2 tablespoons cornstarch in small bowl until smooth. Whisk into cooking liquid. Cover; cook on HIGH 15 minutes or until thickened. Return fruit to sauce; stir to blend.

Zucchini Bread

1⅔ cups all-purpose flour, plus additional for dusting

1¼ teaspoons ground cinnamon

1 teaspoon baking powder

½ teaspoon salt

½ teaspoon ground allspice

¼ teaspoon baking soda

1 cup sugar

2 eggs, lightly beaten

½ cup canola oil

1 tablespoon vanilla

1 large zucchini, trimmed and shredded

½ cup chopped walnuts

1. Spray inside of 8½×4½×2¾-inch ovenproof glass or ceramic loaf pan* that fits inside **CROCK-POT®** slow cooker with nonstick cooking spray; dust with flour.

2. Combine 1⅔ cups flour, cinnamon, baking powder, salt, allspice and baking soda in medium bowl; stir to blend. Whisk sugar, eggs, oil and vanilla in another medium bowl. Pour sugar mixture into flour mixture; stir until just moistened. Gently fold in zucchini and walnuts. Pour into prepared loaf pan. Place in **CROCK-POT®** slow cooker. Cover; cook on HIGH 3½ to 3¾ hours or until toothpick inserted into center comes out clean.

3. Remove bread from **CROCK-POT®** slow cooker; let cool in pan 10 minutes. Remove bread from pan; let cool on wire rack 30 minutes before slicing.

*You may also use a glass bowl that fits inside **CROCK-POT®** slow cooker.*

Makes 1 loaf

Minted Hot Cocoa

6 cups milk

¾ cup semisweet chocolate pieces

½ cup sugar

½ cup unsweetened cocoa powder

1 teaspoon vanilla

½ teaspoon mint extract

10 sprigs fresh mint, tied together with
    kitchen string, plus additional for garnish

Whipped cream (optional)

1. Stir milk, chocolate, sugar, cocoa, vanilla and mint extract into **CROCK-POT®** slow cooker until combined. Add 10 mint sprigs. Cover; cook on LOW 3 to 4 hours.

2. Uncover; remove and discard mint sprigs. Whisk cocoa mixture well. Cover until ready to serve. Garnish with whipped cream and additional mint sprigs.

Makes 6 to 8 servings

Wheat and Walnut Loaf

2 cups warm water (100° to 110°F), divided

¼ cup sugar

2 tablespoons vegetable oil

1 packet (¼ ounce) active dry yeast

2 cups all-purpose flour

1 cup whole wheat flour

⅔ cup walnut halves and pieces

1½ teaspoons salt

1. Combine 1 cup water, sugar, oil and yeast in small bowl; mix well. Let stand 5 minutes.

2. Combine flours, walnuts and salt in large bowl; stir to blend. Pour yeast mixture over flour mixture; stir until rough dough forms. Turn dough out onto floured surface; knead 6 to 7 minutes or until smooth and elastic. Place in 2½-quart ceramic baking dish. Cover with plastic wrap; let stand in warm place 30 minutes.

3. Place crumpled foil in bottom of 6-quart oval **CROCK-POT®** slow cooker. Pour in remaining 1 cup water. Remove plastic wrap from baking dish. Carefully place baking dish in **CROCK-POT®** slow cooker.

4. Cover; cook on HIGH 2¾ to 3 hours or until bread is cooked through and pulls away from sides. Remove bread from baking dish; let cool on wire rack 30 minutes.

Makes 1 loaf

Hash Brown and Sausage Breakfast Casserole

4 **cups frozen southern-style hash browns**	1 **package (10 ounces) frozen chopped spinach, thawed and squeezed dry**
3 **tablespoons unsalted butter**	8 **eggs**
1 **large onion, chopped**	1 **cup milk**
8 **ounces (about 2 cups) sliced mushrooms**	1 **teaspoon salt**
3 **cloves garlic, minced**	¼ **teaspoon black pepper**
2 **precooked apple chicken sausages, cut into 1-inch slices**	1½ **cups (6 ounces) shredded sharp Cheddar cheese, divided**

1. Coat inside of **CROCK-POT®** slow cooker with nonstick cooking spray. Place hash browns in **CROCK-POT®** slow cooker.

2. Melt butter in large nonstick skillet over medium-high heat. Add onion, mushrooms and garlic; cook 4 to 5 minutes or until just starting to brown, stirring occasionally. Stir in sausage; cook 2 minutes. Add spinach; cook 2 minutes or until mushrooms are tender. Stir sausage mixture into **CROCK-POT®** slow cooker with hash browns until combined.

3. Combine eggs, milk, salt and pepper in large bowl; mix well. Pour over hash brown mixture in **CROCK-POT®** slow cooker. Top with 1 cup cheese. Cover; cook on LOW 4 to 4½ hours or on HIGH 1½ to 2 hours or until eggs are set. Top with remaining ½ cup cheese. Cut into wedges to serve.

Makes 6 to 8 servings

Blueberry-Banana Pancakes

2 cups all-purpose flour

⅓ cup sugar

1 tablespoon baking powder

½ teaspoon baking soda

½ teaspoon salt

½ teaspoon ground cinnamon

1¾ cups milk

2 eggs, lightly beaten

¼ cup (½ stick) unsalted butter, melted

1 teaspoon vanilla

1 cup fresh blueberries

2 small bananas, sliced

Maple syrup

1. Combine flour, sugar, baking powder, baking soda, salt and cinnamon in large bowl. Combine milk, eggs, butter and vanilla in separate medium bowl. Pour milk mixture into flour mixture; stir until moistened. Gently fold in blueberries until mixed.

2. Coat inside of **CROCK-POT**® slow cooker with nonstick cooking spray. Remove batter to **CROCK-POT**® slow cooker. Cover; cook on HIGH 2 hours or until puffed and toothpick inserted into center comes out clean. Cut into wedges; top with sliced bananas and syrup.

Makes 4 to 6 servings

Apple-Cranberry Crêpes

1 baking apple, such as Gala or Jonathan, peeled, cored and cut into 6 wedges

1 tart apple, such as Granny Smith, peeled, cored and cut into 6 wedges

¼ cup dried sweetened cranberries or cherries

2 tablespoons lemon juice

½ teaspoon plus ⅛ teaspoon ground cinnamon, divided

⅛ teaspoon ground nutmeg

⅛ teaspoon ground cloves or allspice

1 tablespoon butter

¼ cup orange juice

1 tablespoon sugar

¾ teaspoon cornstarch

¼ teaspoon almond extract

4 prepared crêpes

1 cup vanilla ice cream

1. Coat inside of **CROCK-POT®** slow cooker with nonstick cooking spray. Place apples, cranberries, lemon juice, ½ teaspoon cinnamon, nutmeg and cloves in **CROCK-POT®** slow cooker; toss to coat. Cover; cook on LOW 2 hours. Stir butter into apple mixture just until melted.

2. Stir orange juice, sugar, cornstarch and almond extract in small bowl until cornstarch dissolves. Stir into apple mixture in **CROCK-POT®** slow cooker. Turn **CROCK-POT®** slow cooker to HIGH. Cover; cook on HIGH 15 minutes or until sauce thickens slightly.

3. Place 1 crêpe on each of four dessert plates. Spoon apple mixture evenly down center of each crêpe. Fold edges over; turn crêpes with seam side down on plates. Sprinkle with remaining ⅛ teaspoon cinnamon. Microwave filled crêpes according to package directions, if desired. Serve with ice cream.

Makes 4 servings

Tip: Look for prepared crêpes in the produce section of the supermarket.

Orange Date-Nut Bread

2 cups unbleached all-purpose flour,
plus additional for dusting

½ cup chopped pecans

1 teaspoon baking powder

½ teaspoon baking soda

¼ teaspoon salt

1 cup chopped dates or cranberries

2 teaspoons dried orange peel

⅔ cup boiling water

¾ cup sugar

1 egg, lightly beaten

2 tablespoons shortening

1 teaspoon vanilla

1. Coat inside of 1-quart soufflé dish with nonstick cooking spray; dust with flour. Set aside.

2. Combine 2 cups flour, pecans, baking powder, baking soda and salt in medium bowl; set aside. Combine dates and orange peel in separate medium bowl; pour boiling water over date mixture. Add sugar, egg, shortening and vanilla; stir just until blended.

3. Add flour mixture to date mixture; stir just until blended. Pour batter into prepared dish; place in 5-quart **CROCK-POT®** slow cooker. Cover; cook on HIGH 2½ hours or until edges begin to brown.

4. Remove dish from **CROCK-POT®** slow cooker. Cool on wire rack 10 minutes. Remove bread from dish; cool completely.

Makes 1 loaf

Warm Spiced Apples and Pears

2 tablespoons unsalted butter

1 cup packed brown sugar

½ cup water

½ lemon, sliced

1 teaspoon vanilla

1 cinnamon stick, broken in half

½ teaspoon ground cloves

5 pears, quartered and cored

5 small Granny Smith apples, cored and quartered

1. Melt butter in saucepan over medium heat. Add brown sugar, water, lemon slices, vanilla, cinnamon stick halves and cloves. Bring to a boil; cook and stir 1 minute. Remove from heat.

2. Combine pears, apples and butter mixture in **CROCK-POT**® slow cooker; mix well. Cover; cook on LOW 3½ to 4 hours or on HIGH 2 hours, stirring every 45 minutes. Remove and discard cinnamon stick halves.

Makes 8 servings

Tip: Simmer a sweet treat in your **CROCK-POT**® slow cooker during dinner, so you can delight your family and guests with a delicious warm dessert.

Cinnamon Roll-Topped Mixed Berry Cobbler

2 bags (12 ounces *each*) frozen
   mixed berries, thawed

1 cup sugar

¼ cup quick-cooking tapioca

¼ cup water

2 teaspoons vanilla

1 package (about 12 ounces)
   refrigerated cinnamon rolls
   with icing

Combine berries, sugar, tapioca, water and vanilla in **CROCK-POT®** slow cooker; top with cinnamon rolls. Cover; cook on LOW 4 to 5 hours. Serve warm, drizzled with icing.

Makes 8 servings

Note: This recipe was designed to work best in a 4-quart **CROCK-POT®** slow cooker. Double the ingredients for larger **CROCK-POT®** slow cookers, but always place cinnamon rolls in a single layer.

Hot Mulled Cider

½ gallon apple cider

½ cup packed brown sugar

1½ teaspoons balsamic or cider vinegar
   (optional)

1 teaspoon vanilla

1 cinnamon stick

6 whole cloves

½ cup applejack or bourbon (optional)

1. Combine cider, brown sugar, vinegar, if desired, vanilla, cinnamon stick and cloves in **CROCK-POT®** slow cooker. Cover; cook on LOW 5 to 6 hours.

2. Remove and discard cinnamon stick and cloves. Stir in applejack just before serving, if desired. Serve warm in mugs.

Makes 16 servings

Mediterranean Frittata

Butter, softened

3 tablespoons extra virgin olive oil

1 large onion, chopped

8 ounces (about 2 cups) sliced mushrooms

6 cloves garlic, sliced

1 teaspoon dried basil

1 medium red bell pepper, chopped

1 package (10 ounces) frozen chopped spinach, thawed and squeezed dry

¼ cup sliced kalamata olives

8 eggs, beaten

4 ounces feta cheese, crumbled

½ teaspoon salt

¼ teaspoon black pepper

1. Coat inside lower third of 5- to 6-quart **CROCK-POT®** slow cooker with butter. Heat oil in large skillet over medium-high heat. Add onion, mushrooms, garlic and basil; cook 2 to 3 minutes or until slightly softened, stirring occasionally. Add bell pepper; cook 4 to 5 minutes or until vegetables are tender. Stir in spinach; cook 2 minutes. Stir in olives. Remove onion mixture to **CROCK-POT®** slow cooker.

2. Combine eggs, cheese, salt and black pepper in large bowl. Pour over vegetables in **CROCK-POT®** slow cooker. Cover; cook on LOW 2½ to 3 hours or on HIGH 1¼ to 1½ hours or until eggs are set. Cut into wedges to serve.

Makes 4 to 6 servings

Spiced Citrus Tea

4 tea bags
  Peel of 1 orange
4 cups boiling water
2 cans (6 ounces *each*) orange-
    pineapple juice
3 tablespoons honey
3 cinnamon sticks
3 whole star anise

1. Place tea bags, orange peel and boiling water in **CROCK-POT**® slow cooker; cover and let steep 10 minutes. Remove and discard tea bags and orange peel. Add juice, honey, cinnamon sticks and star anise.

2. Cover; cook on LOW 3 hours. Remove and discard cinnamon sticks and star anise.

Makes 6 servings

Oatmeal with Maple-Glazed Apples and Cranberries

3 cups water
2 cups quick-cooking or old-fashioned oats
¼ teaspoon salt
1 teaspoon unsalted butter

2 medium red or Golden Delicious apples, unpeeled and cut into ½-inch pieces
¼ teaspoon ground cinnamon
2 tablespoons maple syrup
4 tablespoons dried cranberries

1. Combine water, oats and salt in **CROCK-POT**® slow cooker. Cover; cook on LOW 8 hours.

2. Melt butter in large nonstick skillet over medium heat. Add apples and cinnamon; cook and stir 4 to 5 minutes or until tender. Stir in syrup; heat through.

3. Serve oatmeal with apple mixture and dried cranberries.

Makes 4 servings

SIMMERING SOUPS

Chicken and Vegetable Soup

1 tablespoon olive oil

2 medium parsnips, cut into ½-inch pieces

2 medium carrots, cut into ½-inch pieces

2 medium onions, chopped

2 stalks celery, cut into ½-inch pieces

1 whole chicken (3 to 3½ pounds)

4 cups chicken broth

10 sprigs fresh Italian parsley *or* 1½ teaspoons dried parsley flakes

4 sprigs fresh thyme *or* ½ teaspoon dried thyme

1. Coat inside of **CROCK-POT**® slow cooker with nonstick cooking spray. Heat oil in large skillet over medium-high heat. Add parsnips, carrots, onions and celery; cook and stir 5 minutes or until vegetables are softened. Remove parsnip mixture to **CROCK-POT**® slow cooker. Add chicken, broth, parsley and thyme.

2. Cover; cook on LOW 6 to 7 hours. Remove chicken to large cutting board; let stand 10 minutes. Remove and discard skin and bones from chicken. Shred chicken using two forks. Stir shredded chicken into **CROCK-POT**® slow cooker.

Makes 10 servings

Simmered Split Pea Soup

3 cans (about 14 ounces *each*) chicken broth

1 package (16 ounces) dried split peas, rinsed and sorted

8 slices bacon, crisp-cooked, chopped and divided

1 onion, chopped

2 carrots, chopped

1 teaspoon black pepper

½ teaspoon dried thyme

1 whole bay leaf

Combine broth, peas, half of bacon, onion, carrots, pepper, thyme and bay leaf in **CROCK-POT**® slow cooker. Cover; cook on LOW 6 to 8 hours. Remove and discard bay leaf. Garnish with remaining half of bacon.

Makes 6 servings

Country Sausage and Bean Soup

2 cans (about 14 ounces *each*) chicken broth

1½ cups hot water

1 cup dried black beans, rinsed and sorted

1 cup chopped onion

2 whole bay leaves

1 teaspoon sugar

⅛ teaspoon ground red pepper

Nonstick cooking spray

6 ounces country pork sausage

1 cup chopped tomato

1 tablespoon chili powder

1 tablespoon Worcestershire sauce

2 teaspoons extra virgin olive oil

1½ teaspoons ground cumin

½ teaspoon salt

¼ cup chopped fresh cilantro

1. Combine broth, water, beans, onion, bay leaves, sugar and ground red pepper in **CROCK-POT**® slow cooker. Cover; cook on LOW 8 hours or on HIGH 4 hours.

2. Spray large skillet with cooking spray; heat over medium-high heat. Add sausage and cook until beginning to brown, stirring to break up meat.

3. Add sausage and remaining ingredients except cilantro to **CROCK-POT**® slow cooker. Cover; cook on HIGH 15 minutes to blend flavors. To serve, sprinkle with cilantro.

Makes 9 servings

Broccoli Cheddar Soup

3 tablespoons butter

1 medium onion, chopped

3 tablespoons all-purpose flour

¼ teaspoon ground nutmeg

¼ teaspoon black pepper

4 cups vegetable broth

1 large bunch broccoli, chopped

1 medium red potato, peeled and chopped

1 teaspoon salt

1 whole bay leaf

1½ cups (6 ounces) shredded Cheddar cheese, plus additional for garnish

½ cup whipping cream

1. Melt butter in medium saucepan over medium heat. Add onion; cook and stir 6 minutes or until softened. Add flour, nutmeg and pepper; cook and stir 1 minute. Remove to **CROCK-POT**® slow cooker. Stir in broth, broccoli, potato, salt and bay leaf.

2. Cover; cook on HIGH 3 hours. Remove and discard bay leaf. Add soup in batches to food processor or blender; purée until desired consistency or use an immersion blender. Pour soup back into **CROCK-POT**® slow cooker. Stir in 1½ cups cheese and cream until cheese is melted. Garnish with additional cheese.

Makes 6 servings

Hearty Sausage and Tortellini Soup

3 hot Italian sausages, casings removed

3 sweet Italian sausages, casings removed

5 cups chicken broth

1 can (about 14 ounces) diced tomatoes with garlic and oregano

1 can (about 8 ounces) tomato sauce

1 large onion, chopped

2 medium carrots, chopped

1 teaspoon seasoned salt

½ teaspoon Italian seasoning

¼ teaspoon black pepper

1 package (9 ounces) refrigerated cheese tortellini

1 medium zucchini, chopped

2 cups broccoli, chopped

1. Cook sausages in large skillet over medium-high heat 8 to 10 minutes. Drain fat. Add sausages, broth, diced tomatoes, tomato sauce, onion, carrots, seasoned salt, Italian seasoning and pepper to **CROCK-POT®** slow cooker. Cover; cook on LOW 6 to 8 hours or on HIGH 3 to 4 hours.

2. Meanwhile, cook tortellini according to package directions. Add tortellini, zucchini and broccoli to **CROCK-POT®** slow cooker during last 15 to 20 minutes of cooking.

Makes 6 to 8 servings

Chicken Orzo Soup

1 tablespoon vegetable oil

1 onion, diced

1 fennel bulb, quartered, cored, thinly sliced, tops removed and fronds reserved for garnish

2 teaspoons minced garlic

8 cups chicken broth

2 boneless, skinless chicken breasts (8 ounces *each*)

2 carrots, peeled and thinly sliced

2 sprigs fresh thyme

1 whole bay leaf

Salt and black pepper

½ cup uncooked orzo

1. Heat oil in large skillet over medium heat. Add onion and fennel; cook 8 minutes or until tender. Add garlic; cook and stir 1 minute. Remove to **CROCK-POT**® slow cooker. Add broth, chicken, carrots, thyme and bay leaf. Season with salt and pepper. Cover; cook on HIGH 2 to 3 hours.

2. Remove chicken to large cutting board; shred with two forks. Add orzo to **CROCK-POT**® slow cooker. Cover; cook on HIGH 30 minutes. Stir shredded chicken into **CROCK-POT**® slow cooker. Remove and discard thyme sprigs and bay leaf. Garnish each serving with fennel fronds.

Makes 6 to 8 servings

Savory Pea Soup with Sausage

8 ounces smoked sausage links, casings removed and cut lengthwise into halves, then cut into ½-inch pieces

2 cans (about 14 ounces *each*) chicken broth

1 package (16 ounces) dried split peas, rinsed and sorted

3 medium carrots, sliced

2 stalks celery, sliced

1 medium onion, chopped

¾ teaspoon dried marjoram

1 whole bay leaf

1. Heat medium skillet over medium heat. Add sausage; cook 5 to 8 minutes or until browned. Drain fat. Combine sausage, broth, peas, carrots, celery, onion, marjoram and bay leaf in **CROCK-POT®** slow cooker.

2. Cover; cook on LOW 4 to 5 hours. Remove and discard bay leaf. Turn off heat. Cover; let stand 15 minutes to thicken.

Makes 6 servings

Vegetable Soup with Beans

4 cups vegetable broth

1 can (about 15 ounces) cannellini beans, rinsed and drained

1 can (about 14 ounces) diced tomatoes

16 baby carrots

1 medium onion, chopped

1 ounce dried oyster mushrooms, chopped

3 tablespoons tomato paste

2 teaspoons garlic powder

1 teaspoon dried basil

1 teaspoon dried oregano

½ teaspoon dried rosemary

½ teaspoon dried marjoram

½ teaspoon dried sage

½ teaspoon dried thyme

¼ teaspoon black pepper

French bread slices, toasted (optional)

Combine broth, beans, tomatoes, carrots, onion, mushrooms, tomato paste, garlic powder, basil, oregano, rosemary, marjoram, sage, thyme and pepper in **CROCK-POT®** slow cooker; stir to blend. Cover; cook on LOW 8 hours or on HIGH 4 to 5 hours. Serve with bread, if desired.

Makes 4 servings

Italian Wedding Soup
with Three-Cheese Tortellini

6 cups chicken broth

1 package (16 ounces) frozen Italian-style meatballs

2½ cups kale, stemmed and chopped

1 package (9 ounces) refrigerated three-cheese tortellini

1 cup celery, chopped

1 small onion, thinly sliced

1 teaspoon dried basil

Juice of 1 lemon

1 tablespoon minced garlic

⅛ teaspoon salt

⅛ teaspoon sugar

Salt and black pepper

Combine broth, meatballs, kale, tortellini, celery, onion, basil, lemon juice, garlic, salt, sugar and pepper in **CROCK-POT**® slow cooker. Cover; cook on LOW 3 to 4 hours, stirring once halfway through cooking time.

Makes 8 servings

Chicken Miso Soup with Shiitake Mushrooms

16 bone-in skin on chicken thighs (about 5 pounds)

3 to 4 cups chicken broth

3 tablespoons canola oil

2 large onions, coarsely chopped

1 pound shiitake mushrooms, stems discarded, large caps quartered

3 tablespoons finely chopped peeled ginger

3 tablespoons finely chopped garlic

1 cup mirin (Japanese sweet rice wine)

1 cup white miso paste

½ cup soy sauce

4 cups water

1 pound (about 16 cups) mustard greens, tough stems and ribs discarded and leaves coarsely chopped

Cooked rice (optional)

Thinly sliced green onions (optional)

1. Preheat oven to 500°F with rack in middle. Pat chicken dry, then roast, skin side up, in one layer on 17×12-inch rimmed sheet pan or jelly-roll pan with sides 35 to 40 minutes or until skin is golden brown.

2. Remove roasted chicken and pan liquids to large measure and spoon off any fat that rises to surface. Add enough broth to bring liquid to 4 cups total.

3. Heat oil in skillet over medium heat. Add onions; cook 5 to 7 minutes until softened and beginning to brown. Add mushrooms, ginger and garlic; cook and stir 3 to 5 minutes or until garlic is golden.

4. Add mirin to skillet; bring to a boil, stirring and scraping up any brown bits for 1 minute. Pour into **CROCK-POT**® slow cooker. Stir in miso paste and soy sauce, then add chicken, broth mixture and water. Cover; cook on LOW 8 to 9 hours or on HIGH 4 to 5 hours or until chicken is tender.

5. Stir in mustard greens and continue to cook, covered, 5 minutes or until greens are wilted. Taste and adjust seasonings as desired. Serve in shallow bowls with cooked rice, if desired. Garnish with green onions.

Makes 6 to 8 servings

Beef Barley Soup

1½ pounds cubed beef stew meat

1 teaspoon salt

½ teaspoon black pepper

5 cups beef broth

2 medium carrots, quartered lengthwise and cut into ½-inch pieces

1 cup chopped onion

1 package (8 ounces) sliced mushrooms

1 leek (white and pale green parts), halved and thinly sliced

2 tablespoons Worcestershire sauce

1 teaspoon soy sauce

1 whole bay leaf

1 cup frozen mixed vegetables, thawed

¾ cup uncooked barley

1. Season beef with salt and pepper. Place beef in **CROCK-POT**® slow cooker. Add broth, carrots, onion, mushrooms, leek, Worcestershire sauce, soy sauce and bay leaf. Cover; cook on LOW 6 hours.

2. Stir in mixed vegetables and barley. Cover; cook on LOW 1 to 2 hours or until barley is cooked through. Remove and discard bay leaf.

Makes 8 servings

Winter's Best Bean Soup

10 cups chicken broth

3 cans (about 15 ounces *each*) cannellini beans, rinsed and drained

1 can (about 14 ounces) diced tomatoes

1 onion, chopped

1 package (10 ounces) frozen sliced or diced carrots

6 ounces bacon, crisp-cooked and crumbled

2 teaspoons minced garlic

1 fresh rosemary sprig *or* 1 teaspoon dried rosemary

1 teaspoon black pepper

Add broth, beans, tomatoes, onion, carrots, bacon, garlic, rosemary sprig and pepper to **CROCK-POT**® slow cooker; stir to blend. Cover; cook on LOW 8 hours. Remove rosemary sprig; mince leaves. Stir into soup.

Makes 8 to 10 servings

Serving Suggestion: Place slices of toasted Italian bread in bottom of individual soup bowls. Drizzle with olive oil. Pour soup over bread and serve.

Hearty Vegetable and Potato Chowder

2 cups vegetable broth

1 can (10¾ ounces) condensed cream of mushroom soup

1 package (10 ounces) frozen mixed vegetables (corn, carrots, peas and green beans)

2 medium russet potatoes (about 1 pound), cut into ½-inch cubes

2 to 3 teaspoons minced garlic

1½ teaspoons dried thyme

½ cup (2 ounces) shredded Colby-Jack or Cheddar cheese

½ teaspoon black pepper

1. Coat inside of **CROCK-POT**® slow cooker with nonstick cooking spray. Add broth, soup, mixed vegetables, potatoes, garlic and thyme to **CROCK-POT**® slow cooker; stir to blend.

2. Cover; cook on LOW 7 to 8 hours or on HIGH 3 to 4 hours. Stir to blend. Top with cheese and pepper.

Makes 6 servings

Leek and Potato Soup

6 slices bacon, crisp-cooked, chopped and divided

5 cups shredded frozen hash brown potatoes

3 leeks (white and light green parts), cut into ¾-inch pieces

1 can (about 14 ounces) vegetable broth

1 can (10¾ ounces) condensed cream of potato soup, undiluted

2 stalks celery, sliced

1 can (5 ounces) evaporated milk

½ cup sour cream

Set aside 2 tablespoons bacon. Combine remaining bacon, potatoes, leeks, broth, soup, celery and evaporated milk in **CROCK-POT®** slow cooker. Cover; cook on LOW 6 to 7 hours. Stir in sour cream. Sprinkle each serving with reserved bacon.

Makes 4 to 6 servings

Parsnip and Carrot Soup

Nonstick cooking spray

1 medium leek, thinly sliced

4 medium parsnips, chopped

4 medium carrots, chopped

4 cups chicken broth

1 whole bay leaf

½ teaspoon salt

½ teaspoon black pepper

½ cup small pasta, cooked and drained

1 tablespoon chopped fresh Italian parsley

1 cup croutons

1. Spray small skillet with cooking spray; heat over medium heat. Add leek; cook and stir 3 to 5 minutes or until golden. Remove to **CROCK-POT®** slow cooker.

2. Add parsnips, carrots, broth, bay leaf, salt and pepper. Cover; cook on LOW 6 to 9 hours or on HIGH 2 to 4 hours or until vegetables are tender. Add pasta during last hour of cooking.

3. Remove and discard bay leaf. Sprinkle each serving evenly with parsley and croutons.

Makes 4 servings

Black Bean Chipotle Soup

1 pound dried black beans, rinsed and sorted

6 cups chicken or vegetable broth

1 large onion, chopped

1 cup crushed tomatoes

2 stalks celery, diced

2 carrots, diced

1 can (4 ounces) diced mild green chiles, drained

2 canned chipotle peppers in adobo sauce, chopped

2 teaspoons ground cumin

Salt and black pepper

Optional toppings: sour cream, salsa and/or chopped fresh cilantro

1. Place beans in large bowl; cover completely with water. Soak 6 to 8 hours or overnight.* Drain beans; discard water.

2. Place beans in **CROCK-POT**® slow cooker. Add broth, onion, tomatoes, celery, carrots, chiles, chipotle peppers and cumin; stir to blend.

3. Cover; cook on LOW 7 to 8 hours or on HIGH 4½ to 5 hours. Season with salt and black pepper. Place mixture in batches in food processor or blender; process to desired consistency. Top as desired.

*To quick soak beans, place beans in large saucepan. Cover with water; bring to a boil over high heat. Boil 2 minutes. Remove from heat; let soak, covered, 1 hour.

Makes 4 to 6 servings

Variation: For an even heartier soup, add 1 cup diced browned spicy sausage, such as linguiça or chourico.

Hearty Chicken Tequila Soup

1 small onion, cut into 8 wedges

1 cup frozen corn

1 can (about 14 ounces) diced tomatoes with mild green chiles

2 cloves garlic, minced

2 tablespoons chopped fresh cilantro, plus additional for garnish

1 whole fryer chicken (about 3½ pounds)

2 cups chicken broth

3 tablespoons tequila

¼ cup sour cream

1. Spread onion wedges on bottom of **CROCK-POT®** slow cooker. Add corn, tomatoes, garlic and 2 tablespoons cilantro. Mix well to combine. Place chicken on top of tomato mixture.

2. Combine broth and tequila in medium bowl. Pour over chicken and tomato mixture. Cover; cook on LOW 8 to 10 hours.

3. Remove chicken to cutting board; discard skin and bones. Shred chicken with two forks. Stir shredded chicken into **CROCK-POT®** slow cooker.

4. Serve with dollop of sour cream and garnish with cilantro.

Makes 2 to 4 servings

Fresh Lime and Black Bean Soup

2 cans (about 15 ounces *each*) black beans, undrained

1 can (about 14 ounces) vegetable broth

1½ cups chopped onions

1½ teaspoons chili powder

¾ teaspoon ground cumin

¼ teaspoon garlic powder

⅛ to ¼ teaspoon red pepper flakes

½ cup sour cream

2 tablespoons extra virgin olive oil

2 tablespoons chopped fresh cilantro

1 medium lime, cut into wedges

1. Coat inside of **CROCK-POT**® slow cooker with nonstick cooking spray. Add beans, broth, onions, chili powder, cumin, garlic powder and red pepper flakes. Cover; cook on LOW 7 hours or on HIGH 3½ hours or until onions are very soft.

2. Process 1 cup soup mixture in blender until smooth and return to **CROCK-POT**® slow cooker. Stir, check consistency and repeat with additional 1 cup soup mixture as desired. Turn off heat. Let stand 15 to 20 minutes before serving.

3. Ladle soup into bowls. Divide sour cream, oil and cilantro evenly among servings. Squeeze juice from lime wedges over each.

Makes 4 servings

Tip: Brighten the flavor of dishes cooked in the **CROCK-POT**® slow cooker by adding fresh herbs or fresh lemon or lime juice before serving.

Italian Hillside Garden Soup

1 tablespoon olive oil

1 cup chopped green bell pepper

1 cup chopped onion

½ cup sliced celery

1 can (about 14 ounces) diced tomatoes with basil, garlic and oregano

1 can (about 15 ounces) navy beans, rinsed and drained

1 medium zucchini, chopped

1 cup frozen cut green beans

2 cans (about 14 ounces *each*) chicken broth

¼ teaspoon garlic powder

1 package (9 ounces) refrigerated sausage- or cheese-filled tortellini pasta

3 tablespoons chopped fresh basil

Grated Asiago or Parmesan cheese (optional)

1. Heat oil in large skillet over medium-high heat. Add bell pepper, onion and celery; cook and stir 4 minutes or until onion is translucent. Remove to **CROCK-POT®** slow cooker.

2. Add tomatoes, navy beans, zucchini, green beans, broth and garlic powder. Cover; cook on LOW 7 hours or on HIGH 3½ hours.

3. Add tortellini. Cover; cook on HIGH 20 to 25 minutes or until pasta is tender. Stir in basil. Garnish with cheese.

Makes 6 servings

Tip: Cooking times are guidelines. **CROCK-POT®** slow cookers, just like ovens, cook differently depending on a variety of factors, including capacity and altitude.

Simmering Hot and Sour Soup

2 cans (about 14 ounces *each*) chicken broth

1 cup chopped cooked chicken or pork

4 ounces fresh shiitake mushroom caps, thinly sliced

½ cup thinly sliced bamboo shoots

3 tablespoons rice wine vinegar

2 tablespoons soy sauce

1½ teaspoons chili paste *or* 1 teaspoon hot chili oil

4 ounces firm tofu, drained and cut into ½-inch pieces

2 teaspoons sesame oil

2 tablespoons cold water

2 tablespoons cornstarch

Chopped fresh cilantro or sliced green onions

1. Combine broth, chicken, mushrooms, bamboo shoots, vinegar, soy sauce and chili paste in **CROCK-POT**® slow cooker. Cover; cook on LOW 3 to 4 hours or on HIGH 2 to 3 hours or until chicken is heated through.

2. Stir in tofu and sesame oil. Stir water into cornstarch in small bowl until smooth; whisk into soup. Cover; cook on HIGH 10 minutes or until soup is thickened. Garnish with cilantro.

Makes 6 servings

Roasted Tomato-Basil Soup

2 cans (28 ounces *each*) whole tomatoes,
   drained and 3 cups juice reserved

2½ tablespoons packed dark brown sugar

1 medium onion, finely chopped

3 cups vegetable broth

3 tablespoons tomato paste

¼ teaspoon ground allspice

1 can (5 ounces) evaporated milk

¼ cup chopped fresh basil

   Salt and black pepper (optional)

   Fresh basil leaves (optional)

1. Preheat oven to 450°F. Line baking sheet with foil; spray with nonstick cooking spray. Arrange tomatoes on foil in single layer. Top with brown sugar and onion. Bake 25 minutes or until tomatoes look dry and light brown. Let tomatoes cool slightly; finely chop.

2. Combine tomato mixture, 3 cups reserved juice, broth, tomato paste and allspice in **CROCK-POT®** slow cooker; stir to blend. Cover; cook on LOW 8 hours or on HIGH 4 hours.

3. Add evaporated milk and ¼ cup chopped basil; season with salt and pepper, if desired. Cover; cook on HIGH 30 minutes or until heated through. Garnish with basil leaves.

Makes 8 servings

Autumn Apple and Squash Soup

5 tablespoons butter

2½ pounds butternut squash, peeled, seeded and cut into ½-inch pieces (about 6 cups)

2 large red onions

3 to 4 large stalks celery

3 large green apples, peeled, cored and coarsely chopped

2 to 3 sprigs fresh thyme, stemmed

10 fresh sage leaves, minced

4 cups vegetable broth

Kosher salt and black pepper

½ cup pepitas*

1 tablespoon honey

1 tablespoon water

Crumbled blue cheese (optional)

Extra virgin olive oil (optional)

Pepitas, or shelled pumpkin seeds, are available at specialty and Latin food stores and make a great garnish to almost any soup or salad. They can be sweetened and spiced as desired and lightly toasted in a skillet on the stovetop.

1. Melt butter in large heavy saucepan over medium-high heat. Add squash, onions and celery; cook and stir 15 minutes or until slightly softened. Place vegetables in **CROCK-POT**® slow cooker. Mix in apples, thyme and sage. Add broth and cook on LOW 12 hours or on HIGH 8 hours.

2. Working in batches, purée soup in blender, pulsing to achieve coarser or smoother texture as desired. Return soup to **CROCK-POT**® slow cooker. Turn **CROCK-POT**® slow cooker to WARM. (If soup has cooled considerably, turn **CROCK-POT**® slow cooker to HIGH.)

3. Combine pepitas with honey and water in small skillet over medium heat. Toast lightly. Ladle soup into bowls. Top with honeyed pepitas and blue cheese. Drizzle with olive oil.

Makes 6 to 8 servings

Variations: Add lump crabmeat or serve with cinnamon and butter toasted croutons.

Kale, Olive Oil and Parmesan Soup

2 tablespoons olive oil

1 small Spanish onion, sliced

3 cloves garlic, minced
Kosher salt and black pepper

2 pounds kale, washed and chopped

8 cups chicken broth
Grated Parmesan cheese
Extra virgin olive oil (optional)

1. Heat olive oil in large heavy skillet over medium-high heat. Add onion and garlic; season with salt and pepper. Cook and stir 4 to 5 minutes or until onion begins to soften. Stir in kale; cook and stir 2 to 4 minutes or until kale becomes bright green and tender. Remove from heat and reserve in refrigerator until needed.

2. Add broth to **CROCK-POT®** slow cooker. Cover; cook on LOW 6 hours or on HIGH 3½ hours.

3. Add kale mixture. Cover; cook on HIGH 15 to 20 minutes or until heated through. Spoon into individual serving bowls. Sprinkle with cheese and drizzle with extra virgin olive oil just before serving.

Makes 6 servings

Potato Soup

8 slices smoked bacon, divided

1 large onion, chopped

2 stalks celery, chopped

2 carrots, chopped

3 cloves garlic, minced

1 teaspoon dried thyme

5 potatoes (about 3 pounds), cut into ½-inch cubes

4 cups chicken broth

1 cup half-and-half

¾ teaspoon salt

¼ teaspoon black pepper

1. Heat large skillet over medium heat. Add bacon; cook and stir until crisp. Remove to paper towel-lined plate using slotted spoon; crumble.

2. Pour off all but 2 tablespoons bacon fat from skillet and return to medium-high heat. Add onion, celery, carrots, garlic and thyme; cook and stir 5 to 6 minutes or until slightly softened.

3. Stir onion mixture, potatoes, half of bacon and broth into **CROCK-POT®** slow cooker. Cover; cook on LOW 7 to 8 hours or on HIGH 3 to 4 hours.

4. Mash potatoes with potato masher and stir in half-and-half, salt and pepper. Cover; cook on HIGH 15 minutes. Garnish each serving with remaining half of bacon.

Makes 8 servings

Plantation Peanut Soup

- 6 cups chicken broth
- 2 cups light cream
- 1 cup chunky peanut butter
- 1 cup chopped peanuts, divided
- ½ cup chopped onion
- ½ cup chopped celery
- 4 tablespoons (½ stick) butter
- ½ teaspoon salt
- ½ cup water
- ½ cup all-purpose flour

1. Combine broth, cream, peanut butter, ½ cup peanuts, onion, celery, butter and salt in **CROCK-POT®** slow cooker. Cover; cook on LOW 4 hours.

2. Turn **CROCK-POT®** slow cooker to HIGH. Stir water into flour in small bowl until smooth; whisk into soup. Cover, cook on HIGH 20 to 25 minutes or until thickened, stirring occasionally.

3. To serve, garnish with remaining ½ cup peanuts.

Makes 8 servings

Hearty Mushroom and Barley Soup

- 9 cups chicken broth
- 1 package (16 ounces) sliced mushrooms
- 1 onion, chopped
- 2 carrots, chopped
- 2 stalks celery, chopped
- ½ cup uncooked pearl barley
- ½ ounce dried porcini mushrooms
- 3 cloves garlic, minced
- 1 teaspoon salt
- ½ teaspoon dried thyme
- ½ teaspoon black pepper

Combine broth, sliced mushrooms, onion, carrots, celery, barley, dried mushrooms, garlic, salt, thyme and pepper in **CROCK-POT®** slow cooker; stir to blend. Cover; cook on LOW 4 to 6 hours.

Makes 8 to 10 servings

Variation: For added flavor, add a beef or ham bone to the **CROCK-POT®** slow cooker with the other ingredients.

Shrimp and Pepper Bisque

1 can (about 14 ounces) chicken broth

1 bag (12 ounces) frozen bell pepper stir-fry mix, thawed

½ pound frozen cauliflower florets, thawed

1 stalk celery, sliced

1 tablespoon seafood seasoning

½ teaspoon dried thyme

12 ounces medium raw shrimp, peeled and deveined

2 cups half-and-half

2 to 3 green onions, finely chopped

1. Combine broth, stir-fry mix, cauliflower, celery, seafood seasoning and thyme in **CROCK-POT®** slow cooker. Cover; cook on LOW 8 hours or on HIGH 4 hours.

2. Stir in shrimp. Cover; cook on HIGH 15 minutes or until shrimp are pink and opaque. Purée soup in batches in blender or food processor. Return to **CROCK-POT®** slow cooker. Stir in half-and-half. Ladle into bowls and sprinkle with green onions.

Makes 4 servings

Tip: For a creamier, smoother consistency, strain through several layers of damp cheesecloth.

AMAZING APPETIZERS

Bacon-Wrapped Dates

4 ounces goat cheese or blue cheese

1 package (8 ounces) dried pitted dates

1 pound thick-cut bacon (about 11 slices), halved

1. Fill **CROCK-POT®** slow cooker with about ½-inch water. Spoon goat cheese evenly into centers of dates; close. Wrap half slice of bacon around each date; secure with toothpicks.

2. Heat large skillet over medium heat. Add wrapped dates; cook and turn 5 to 10 minutes until browned. Remove to **CROCK-POT®** slow cooker.

3. Cover; cook on LOW 2 to 3 hours. Remove toothpicks before serving.

Makes 8 to 10 servings

Nacho Dip

1	tablespoon vegetable oil	1	can (about 15 ounces) refried beans
1	onion, chopped	1	can (about 15 ounces) cream-style corn
2	pounds ground beef	3	cloves garlic, minced
2	cans (about 15 ounces *each*) black beans, rinsed and drained	1	package (1¼ ounces) taco seasoning mix
1	can (28 ounces) diced tomatoes		Tortilla chips
			Queso blanco

1. Heat oil in large skillet over medium-high heat. Add onion; cook 2 to 3 minutes or until translucent. Add beef; brown 6 to 8 minutes, stirring to break up meat. Drain fat.

2. Stir beef mixture, black beans, tomatoes, refried beans, corn, garlic and taco seasoning into **CROCK-POT**® slow cooker. Cover; cook on LOW 5 to 6 hours or on HIGH 2½ to 3 hours. Serve on tortilla chips. Sprinkle with queso blanco.

Makes 10 cups

Parmesan Ranch Snack Mix

3	cups corn or rice cereal squares	1	cup pistachio nuts
2	cups oyster crackers	2	tablespoons grated Parmesan cheese
1	package (5 ounces) bagel chips, broken in half	¼	cup (½ stick) butter, melted
1½	cups mini pretzel twists	1	package (1 ounce) dry ranch salad dressing mix
		½	teaspoon garlic powder

1. Combine cereal, crackers, bagel chips, pretzels, nuts and cheese in **CROCK-POT**® slow cooker; mix gently.

2. Combine butter, salad dressing mix and garlic powder in small bowl. Pour over cereal mixture; toss lightly to coat. Cover; cook on LOW 3 hours.

3. Stir gently. Cook, uncovered, on LOW 30 minutes.

Makes about 9½ cups

Shrimp Fondue Dip

3 tablespoons butter, divided

8 ounces small raw shrimp, peeled and deveined

1 teaspoon seafood seasoning

¼ teaspoon ground red pepper

¼ teaspoon black pepper

1 tablespoon all-purpose flour

¾ cup half-and-half

¾ cup (3 ounces) shredded Gruyère cheese

¼ cup dry white wine

1 teaspoon Dijon mustard

Sliced French bread

1. Melt 2 tablespoons butter in medium saucepan over medium heat. Add shrimp; sprinkle with seafood seasoning, ground red pepper and black pepper. Cook 3 minutes or until shrimp are pink and opaque, stirring frequently. Remove to medium bowl.

2. Melt remaining 1 tablespoon butter in same saucepan over medium heat. Add flour; cook and stir 2 minutes. Gradually stir in half-and-half; cook and stir until mixture comes to a boil and thickens. Add cheese; cook and stir until cheese is melted. Stir in wine, mustard and cooked shrimp with any accumulated juices.

3. Coat inside of **CROCK-POT® LITTLE DIPPER®** slow cooker with nonstick cooking spray. Fill with warm dip. Serve with sliced French bread.

Makes 1¾ cups

Mini Swiss Steak Sandwiches

2 tablespoons all-purpose flour

¼ teaspoon salt

¼ teaspoon black pepper

1¾ pounds boneless beef chuck steak, about 1 inch thick

2 tablespoons vegetable oil

1 medium onion, sliced

1 green bell pepper, sliced

1 clove garlic, sliced

1 cup stewed tomatoes

¾ cup condensed beef broth, undiluted

2 teaspoons Worcestershire sauce

1 whole bay leaf

2 tablespoons cornstarch

2 packages (12 ounces *each*) sweet dinner rolls

1. Coat inside of **CROCK-POT**® slow cooker with nonstick cooking spray. Combine flour, salt and black pepper in large resealable food storage bag. Add steak. Seal bag; shake to coat.

2. Heat oil in large skillet over high heat. Brown steak on both sides. Remove to **CROCK-POT**® slow cooker.

3. Add onion and bell pepper to skillet; cook and stir over medium-high heat 3 minutes or until softened. Add garlic; cook and stir 30 seconds. Pour mixture over steak.

4. Add tomatoes, broth, Worcestershire sauce and bay leaf to **CROCK-POT**® slow cooker. Cover; cook on HIGH 3½ hours or until steak is tender. Remove steak to cutting board. Remove and discard bay leaf.

5. Stir 2 tablespoons cooking liquid into cornstarch in small bowl until smooth. Whisk into cooking liquid in **CROCK-POT**® slow cooker. Cover; cook on HIGH 10 minutes or until thickened.

6. Thinly slice steak against the grain to shred. Return steak to **CROCK-POT**® slow cooker; mix well. Serve steak mixture on rolls.

Makes 16 to 18 servings

Tip: Browning meat and poultry before cooking them in the **CROCK-POT**® slow cooker is not necessary but helps to enhance the flavor and appearance of the finished dish.

Creamy Cheesy Spinach Dip

2 packages (10 ounces *each*) frozen chopped spinach, thawed and undrained

2 cups chopped onions

1 teaspoon salt

½ teaspoon garlic powder

¼ teaspoon black pepper

12 ounces pasteurized process cheese spread with jalapeño peppers, cubed

Cherry tomatoes with pulp removed (optional)

Sliced cucumbers (optional)

Assorted crackers (optional)

1. Drain spinach and squeeze dry, reserving ¾ cup liquid. Place spinach, reserved liquid, onions, salt, garlic powder and black pepper in 1½-quart **CROCK-POT®** "No Dial" slow cooker; stir to blend. Cover; heat 1½ hours.

2. Stir in cheese spread. Cover; heat 30 minutes or until melted. Fill cherry tomato shells, spread on cucumber slices or serve with crackers, if desired.

Makes about 4 cups

Tip: To thaw spinach quickly, remove paper wrapper from spinach containers. Microwave on HIGH 3 to 4 minutes or just until thawed.

Spicy Sweet and Sour Cocktail Franks

2 packages (8 ounces *each*) cocktail franks

½ cup ketchup or chili sauce

½ cup apricot preserves

1 teaspoon hot pepper sauce

Combine cocktail franks, ketchup, preserves and hot pepper sauce in 1½-quart **CROCK-POT®** "No Dial" slow cooker; mix well. Cover; heat 2 to 3 hours.

Makes 10 to 12 servings

Creamy Artichoke-Parmesan Dip

1 teaspoon olive oil

2 tablespoons finely chopped onion

½ can (about 7 ounces) artichoke hearts, drained and chopped

½ cup half-and-half

½ cup (2 ounces) mozzarella cheese

⅓ cup grated Parmesan cheese

⅓ cup mayonnaise

⅛ teaspoon dried oregano

⅛ teaspoon garlic powder

4 pita bread rounds, toasted and cut into wedges

Fresh vegetables

1. Heat oil in medium saucepan over medium heat. Add onion; cook and stir 3 to 5 minutes or until tender. Add artichoke hearts, half-and-half, cheeses, mayonnaise, oregano and garlic powder; cook and stir 5 to 7 minutes or until mixture comes to a boil.

2. Coat inside of **CROCK-POT® LITTLE DIPPER®** slow cooker with nonstick cooking spray. Fill with warm dip. Serve with pita wedges and vegetables.

Makes 1½ cups

Lemon & Garlic Shrimp

1 pound large raw shrimp, peeled and deveined (with tails on)

½ cup (1 stick) unsalted butter, cubed

3 cloves garlic, crushed

2 tablespoons lemon juice

½ teaspoon paprika

Salt and black pepper

2 tablespoons finely chopped fresh Italian parsley

Crusty bread, sliced (optional)

1. Coat inside of **CROCK-POT**® slow cooker with nonstick cooking spray. Add shrimp, butter and garlic; mix well. Cover; cook on HIGH 1¼ hours.

2. Turn off heat. Stir in lemon juice, paprika, salt and pepper. Spoon shrimp and liquid into large serving bowl. Sprinkle with parsley. Serve with crusty bread for dipping. if desired.

Makes 6 to 8 servings

Salsa-Style Wings

2 tablespoons oil

1½ pounds chicken wings (about 18 wings)

2 cups salsa

¼ cup packed brown sugar

Sprigs fresh cilantro (optional)

1. Heat oil in large skillet over medium-high heat. Add wings in batches; cook 3 to 4 minutes or until browned on all sides. Remove to **CROCK-POT**® slow cooker.

2. Combine salsa and brown sugar in medium bowl; stir to blend. Pour over wings. Cover; cook on LOW 5 to 6 hours or on HIGH 2 to 3 hours. Serve with salsa mixture. Garnish with cilantro.

Makes 4 servings

Beans and Spinach Bruschetta

2 cans (about 15 ounces *each*) Great Northern
   or cannellini beans, rinsed and drained

3 cloves garlic, minced

   Salt and black pepper

3 tablespoons extra virgin olive oil, divided

6 cups spinach, loosely packed, finely chopped

1 tablespoon red wine vinegar

16 slices whole grain baguette

1. Combine beans, garlic, salt and black pepper in **CROCK-POT**® slow cooker. Cover; cook on LOW 3 hours or until beans are tender. Turn off heat. Mash beans with potato masher.

2. Heat 1 tablespoon oil in same skillet over medium heat. Add spinach; cook 2 to 3 minutes or until wilted. Stir in vinegar, salt and pepper. Remove from heat.

3. Preheat grill or broiler. Brush baguette slices with remaining 2 tablespoons oil. Grill 5 to 7 minutes or until bread is golden brown and crisp. Top with bean mixture and spinach. Serve immediately.

Makes 16 servings

Super Meatball Sliders

1 can (15 ounces) whole berry cranberry sauce	1 package (1 ounce) dry onion soup mix
1 can (about 15 ounces) tomato sauce	Nonstick cooking spray
⅛ teaspoon red pepper flakes (optional)	Baby arugula leaves (optional)
2 pounds ground beef or turkey	24 small potato rolls or dinner rolls
¾ cup dry seasoned bread crumbs	6 slices (1 ounce *each*) provolone cheese, cut into quarters
1 egg, lightly beaten	

1. Combine cranberry sauce, tomato sauce and red pepper flakes, if desired, in **CROCK-POT®** slow cooker; stir to blend. Cover; cook on LOW 3 to 4 hours.

2. Halfway through cooking time, prepare meatballs. Combine beef, bread crumbs, egg and soup mix in large bowl; mix well. Shape mixture into 24 meatballs (about 1¾ inches diameter). Spray large skillet with cooking spray; heat over medium heat. Add meatballs; cook 8 to 10 minutes or until browned on all sides. Remove to **CROCK-POT®** slow cooker.

3. Cover; cook on LOW 1 to 2 hours. Place arugula leaves on bottom of rolls, if desired. Top with meatballs, sauce, cheese and tops of rolls.

Makes 24 sliders

Hoisin Sriracha Chicken Wings

3 pounds chicken wings, tips removed and split at joints

½ cup hoisin sauce

¼ cup plus 1 tablespoon sriracha sauce, divided

2 tablespoons packed brown sugar

Green onions (optional)

1. Coat inside of **CROCK-POT®** slow cooker with nonstick cooking spray. Preheat broiler. Spray large baking sheet with nonstick cooking spray. Arrange wings on prepared baking sheet. Broil 6 to 8 minutes or until browned, turning once. Remove wings to **CROCK-POT®** slow cooker.

2. Combine hoisin sauce, ¼ cup sriracha sauce and brown sugar in medium bowl; stir to blend. Pour sauce mixture over wings in **CROCK-POT®** slow cooker; stir to coat. Cover; cook on LOW 3½ to 4 hours. Remove wings to large serving platter; cover with foil to keep warm.

3. Turn **CROCK-POT®** slow cooker to HIGH. Cook, uncovered, on HIGH 10 to 15 minutes or until sauce is thickened. Stir in remaining 1 tablespoon sriracha sauce. Spoon sauce over wings to serve.

Makes 5 to 6 servings

Reuben Dip

1 jar or bag (about 32 ounces) sauerkraut, drained

2 cups (8 ounces) shredded Swiss cheese

3 packages (2½ ounces *each*) corned beef, shredded

½ cup (1 stick) butter, melted

1 egg, beaten

Cocktail rye bread

Combine sauerkraut, cheese, corned beef, butter and egg in **CROCK-POT®** slow cooker. Cover; cook on HIGH 2 hours. Serve with bread.

Makes 12 servings

Note: Sauerkraut, a popular German food, is chopped or shredded cabbage that is salted and fermented in its own juice. Sauerkraut is an essential ingredient in a Reuben sandwich.

Slow Cooker Cheese Dip

1 pound ground beef

1 pound bulk Italian sausage

1 package (16 ounces) pasteurized process
   cheese product, cubed

1 can (11 ounces) sliced jalapeño peppers,
   drained

1 onion, chopped

8 ounces Cheddar cheese, cubed

1 package (8 ounces) cream cheese, cubed

1 container (8 ounces) cottage cheese

1 container (8 ounces) sour cream

1 can (about 14 ounces) diced tomatoes

3 cloves garlic, minced

   Salt and black pepper

   Tortilla chips

1. Brown beef and sausage in large skillet over medium-high heat 6 to 8 minutes, stirring to break up meat. Remove to **CROCK-POT**® slow cooker using slotted spoon.

2. Add cheese product, jalapeño peppers, onion, Cheddar cheese, cream cheese, cottage cheese, sour cream, tomatoes and garlic to **CROCK-POT**® slow cooker; stir to blend. Cover; cook on HIGH 1½ to 2 hours. Season with salt and black pepper. Serve with chips.

Makes 16 to 18 servings

Maple-Glazed Meatballs

1½ cups ketchup

1 cup maple syrup

⅓ cup soy sauce

1 tablespoon quick-cooking tapioca

1½ teaspoons ground allspice

1 teaspoon dry mustard

2 packages (about 16 ounces *each*) frozen fully cooked meatballs, partially thawed and separated

1 can (20 ounces) pineapple chunks in juice, drained

1. Combine ketchup, syrup, soy sauce, tapioca, allspice and dry mustard in **CROCK-POT®** slow cooker. Carefully stir meatballs and pineapple chunks into ketchup mixture.

2. Cover; cook on LOW 5 to 6 hours. Stir before serving. Serve warm; insert cocktail picks, if desired.

Makes about 48 meatballs

Bacon-Wrapped Fingerling Potatoes

1 pound fingerling potatoes

2 tablespoons olive oil

1 tablespoon minced fresh thyme

½ teaspoon black pepper

¼ teaspoon paprika

½ pound bacon slices, cut crosswise into halves

¼ cup chicken broth

1. Toss potatoes with oil, thyme, pepper and paprika in large bowl. Wrap half slice of bacon tightly around each potato.

2. Heat large skillet over medium heat; add potatoes. Reduce heat to medium-low; cook until lightly browned and bacon has tightened around potatoes. Place potatoes in **CROCK-POT®** slow cooker. Add broth. Cover; cook on HIGH 3 hours.

Makes 4 to 6 servings

Juicy Reuben Sliders

1 corned beef brisket (about 1½ pounds), trimmed

2 cups sauerkraut, drained

½ cup beef broth

1 small onion, sliced

1 clove garlic, minced

4 to 6 whole white peppercorns

¼ teaspoon caraway seeds

48 slices pumpernickel or cocktail rye bread

12 slices deli Swiss cheese

Dijon mustard (optional)

1. Place corned beef in **CROCK-POT®** slow cooker. Add sauerkraut, broth, onion, garlic, peppercorns and caraway seeds. Cover; cook on LOW 7 to 9 hours.

2. Remove corned beef to cutting board. Cut across grain into 16 slices. Cut each slice into 3 pieces. Place 2 pieces corned beef on each of 24 slices of bread. Place 1 heaping tablespoon sauerkraut on each sandwich. Cut each slice of Swiss cheese into quarters; place 2 quarters on each sandwich. Spread remaining 24 slices of bread with mustard, if desired, and place on top of sandwiches.

Makes 24 sliders

Stewed Fig and Blue Cheese Dip

1 tablespoon olive oil

1 medium onion, chopped

½ cup dry port wine

1 package (6 ounces) dried Calimyrna figs, finely chopped, plus additional fig halves for garnish

½ cup orange juice

½ cup crumbled blue cheese, divided

1 tablespoon unsalted butter

Assorted crackers and grapes

1. Heat oil in small skillet over medium-high heat. Add onion; cook and stir 7 to 8 minutes or until light golden. Stir in port. Bring to a boil; cook 1 minute. Remove to 1½-quart **CROCK-POT®** "No Dial" slow cooker; stir in 1 package figs and orange juice.

2. Cover; heat 1 to 1½ hours or until figs are plump and tender. Stir in ¼ cup blue cheese and butter. Sprinkle with remaining blue cheese. Garnish with additional fig halves. Serve with crackers and grapes.

Makes 6 to 8 servings

Channa Chat (Indian-Spiced Snack Mix)

2 teaspoons canola oil

1 medium onion, finely chopped and divided

2 cloves garlic, minced

2 cans (about 15 ounces *each*) chickpeas, rinsed and drained

¼ cup vegetable broth or water

2 teaspoons tomato paste

¼ teaspoon ground cinnamon

¼ teaspoon ground cumin

¼ teaspoon black pepper

1 whole bay leaf

½ cup balsamic vinegar

1 tablespoon packed brown sugar

1 plum tomato, chopped

½ jalapeño pepper, seeded and minced *or* ¼ teaspoon ground red pepper (optional)*

½ cup crisp rice cereal

3 tablespoons chopped fresh cilantro (optional)

Jalapeño peppers can sting and irritate the skin, so wear rubber gloves when handling peppers and do not touch your eyes.

1. Heat oil in small skillet over medium-high heat. Add half of onion and garlic. Reduce heat to medium; cook and stir 2 minutes or until soft. Remove to **CROCK-POT®** slow cooker. Stir in chickpeas, broth, tomato paste, cinnamon, cumin, black pepper and bay leaf. Cover; cook on LOW 6 hours or on HIGH 3 hours. Remove and discard bay leaf.

2. Remove chickpeas with slotted spoon to large bowl. Cool 15 minutes. Meanwhile, combine vinegar and brown sugar in small saucepan; cook over medium-low heat until vinegar is reduced by half and mixture becomes syrupy, stirring frequently.

3. Add tomato, remaining onion and jalapeño pepper, if desired, to chickpeas; toss to combine. Gently fold in cereal. Drizzle with balsamic syrup and garnish with cilantro.

Makes 6 to 8 servings

Pizza Fondue

½ pound bulk Italian sausage

1 cup chopped onion

2 jars (26 ounces *each*) meatless pasta sauce

4 ounces thinly sliced ham, finely chopped

1 package (3 ounces) sliced pepperoni, finely chopped

¼ teaspoon red pepper flakes

1 pound mozzarella cheese, cut into ¾-inch cubes

1 loaf Italian or French bread, cut into 1-inch cubes

1. Brown sausage and onion in large skillet over medium-high heat 6 to 8 minutes, stirring to break up meat. Remove to **CROCK-POT**® slow cooker using slotted spoon.

2. Stir in pasta sauce, ham, pepperoni and red pepper flakes. Cover; cook on LOW 3 to 4 hours. Serve with cheese and bread cubes.

Makes 20 to 25 servings

Spiced Beer Fondue

2 tablespoons butter

2 tablespoons all-purpose flour

1 can (8 ounces) light-colored beer, such as ale or lager

½ cup half-and-half

1 cup (4 ounces) shredded smoked gouda cheese

2 teaspoons coarse grain mustard

1 teaspoon Worcestershire sauce

⅛ teaspoon salt

⅛ teaspoon ground red pepper

Dash ground nutmeg (optional)

Apple slices and cooked potato wedges

1. Melt butter in medium saucepan over medium heat. Sprinkle with flour; whisk until smooth. Stir in beer and half-and-half; bring to a boil. Cook and stir 2 minutes. Stir in cheese, mustard, Worcestershire sauce, salt and ground red pepper; cook and stir until cheese is melted.

2. Coat inside of **CROCK-POT® LITTLE DIPPER®** slow cooker with nonstick cooking spray. Fill with warm fondue. Sprinkle with nutmeg, if desired, and serve with apples and potatoes.

Makes 1½ cups

Caramelized Onion Dip

1 tablespoon olive oil

1½ cups chopped sweet onion

1 teaspoon sugar

⅛ teaspoon dried thyme

¼ teaspoon salt

2 ounces cream cheese, cubed

½ cup sour cream

⅓ cup mayonnaise

⅓ cup (about 1 ounce) shredded Swiss cheese

¼ teaspoon beef soup base or beef bouillon granules

Potato chips

Carrot sticks

Pretzels

1. Heat oil in medium skillet over medium heat. Add onion, sugar and thyme; cook 12 minutes or until golden, stirring occasionally. Stir in salt.

2. Grease **CROCK-POT® LITTLE DIPPER®** slow cooker. Add onion mixture, cream cheese, sour cream, mayonnaise, Swiss cheese and beef base; mix well. Cover; heat 1 hour or until warm; mix well. Serve with potato chips, carrot sticks and pretzels.

Makes 12 servings

Barley "Caviar"

4½ cups water

¾ cup uncooked pearl barley

1 teaspoon salt, divided

½ cup sliced pimiento-stuffed olives

½ cup finely chopped red bell pepper

1 stalk celery, chopped

1 large shallot, finely chopped

1 jalapeño pepper,* minced, or ¼ teaspoon red pepper flakes

2 tablespoons plus 1 teaspoon olive oil

4 teaspoons white wine vinegar

¼ teaspoon ground cumin

⅛ teaspoon black pepper

8 leaves endive or Bibb lettuce

Jalapeño peppers can sting and irritate the skin, so wear rubber gloves when handling peppers and do not touch your eyes.

1. Add water, barley and ½ teaspoon salt to **CROCK-POT®** slow cooker. Cover; cook on LOW 4 to 5 hours or on HIGH 2½ to 3 hours or until barley is tender and liquid is absorbed.

2. Turn off heat. Stir in olives, bell pepper, celery, shallot and jalapeño pepper. Combine oil, vinegar, remaining ½ teaspoon salt, cumin and black pepper in small bowl; stir well. Pour over barley mixture in **CROCK-POT®** slow cooker; stir gently to coat. Let stand 10 minutes. To serve, spoon barley mixture evenly into endive leaves.

Makes 8 servings

Raspberry BBQ Chicken Wings

3 pounds (10 to 12) chicken drummettes and wings, tips removed and split at joints

¾ cup seedless raspberry jam

½ cup sweet and tangy prepared barbecue sauce

1 tablespoon raspberry red wine vinegar

1 teaspoon chili powder

1. Coat inside of **CROCK-POT**® slow cooker with nonstick cooking spray. Preheat broiler. Spray large baking sheet with nonstick cooking spray. Arrange wings on prepared sheet. Broil 6 to 8 minutes until browned, turning once. Remove to **CROCK-POT**® slow cooker.

2. Combine jam, barbecue sauce, vinegar and chili powder in medium bowl; stir to blend. Pour sauce over wings in **CROCK-POT**® slow cooker; stir to coat. Cover; cook on LOW 3½ to 4 hours. Remove wings to large serving platter; cover to keep warm.

3. Turn **CROCK-POT**® slow cooker to HIGH. Cook, uncovered, on HIGH 10 to 15 minutes or until sauce is thickened. Spoon sauce over wings to serve.

Makes 5 to 6 servings

Pulled Pork Sliders with Cola Barbecue Sauce

1 teaspoon vegetable oil

3 pounds boneless pork shoulder roast, cut evenly into 4 pieces

1 cup cola

¼ cup tomato paste

2 tablespoons packed brown sugar

2 teaspoons Worcestershire sauce

2 teaspoons spicy brown mustard

Hot pepper sauce

Salt

16 dinner rolls or potato rolls

Sliced pickles (optional)

1. Heat oil in large skillet over medium-high heat. Brown pork on all sides. Remove to **CROCK-POT®** slow cooker. Pour cola over pork. Cover; cook on LOW 7½ to 8 hours or on HIGH 3½ to 4 hours.

2. Turn off heat. Remove pork to large cutting board; shred with two forks. Let cooking liquid stand 5 minutes. Skim off and discard fat. Whisk tomato paste, brown sugar, Worcestershire sauce and mustard into cooking liquid. Cover; cook on HIGH 15 minutes or until thickened.

3. Stir shredded pork into **CROCK-POT®** slow cooker. Season with hot pepper sauce and salt. Serve on rolls. Top with pickles, if desired.

Makes 16 sliders

BEEF-PACKED FAVORITES

Brisket with Sweet Onions

2 large sweet onions, cut into 10 (½-inch) slices*

1 flat-cut boneless beef brisket (about 3½ pounds)

Salt and black pepper (optional)

2 cans (about 14 ounces *each*) beef broth

1 teaspoon cracked black peppercorns

¾ cup crumbled blue cheese (optional)

Preferably Maui, Vidalia or Walla Walla onions.

1. Coat inside of **CROCK-POT**® slow cooker with nonstick cooking spray. Line bottom with onion slices.

2. Season brisket with salt and black pepper, if desired. Heat large skillet over medium-high heat. Add brisket; cook 10 to 12 minutes or until browned on all sides. Remove to **CROCK-POT**® slow cooker.

3. Pour broth into **CROCK-POT**® slow cooker. Sprinkle brisket with peppercorns. Cover; cook on HIGH 5 to 7 hours.

4. Remove brisket to cutting board. Cover loosely with foil; let stand 10 to 15 minutes. Slice evenly against the grain into ten slices. To serve, arrange onions on serving platter and spread slices of brisket on top. Sprinkle with blue cheese, if desired. Serve with cooking liquid.

Makes 10 servings

Tip: Use freshly ground pepper as a quick and simple flavor enhancer for **CROCK-POT**® slow cooker dishes.

Slow Cooker Braised Short Ribs with Aromatic Spices

1 tablespoon olive oil

3 pounds bone-in beef short ribs, trimmed

1 teaspoon ground cumin, divided

1 teaspoon salt, divided

½ teaspoon black pepper, divided

2 medium onions, halved and thinly sliced

10 cloves garlic, thinly sliced

2 tablespoons balsamic vinegar

2 tablespoons honey

1 cinnamon stick

2 whole star anise pods

2 large sweet potatoes, peeled and cut into ¾-inch cubes

1 cup beef broth

1. Heat oil in large skillet over medium-high heat. Season ribs with ½ teaspoon cumin, ¾ teaspoon salt and ¼ teaspoon pepper. Add to skillet; cook 8 minutes or until browned, turning occasionally. Remove ribs to large plate.

2. Heat skillet over medium heat. Add onions and garlic; cook 12 to 14 minutes or until onions are lightly browned. Stir in vinegar; cook 1 minute. Add remaining ½ teaspoon cumin, honey, cinnamon stick and star anise; cook and stir 30 seconds. Remove mixture to **CROCK-POT®** slow cooker. Stir in potatoes; top with ribs. Pour in broth.

3. Cover; cook on LOW 8 to 9 hours or until meat is falling off the bones. Remove and discard bones from ribs. Skim fat from surface of sauce. Stir remaining ¼ teaspoon salt and black pepper into sauce. Serve meat with sauce and vegetables.

Makes 4 servings

Steak San Marino

¼ cup all-purpose flour

1 teaspoon salt

½ teaspoon black pepper

1 boneless beef round steak (about 1½ pounds), cut into 4 pieces *or* 2 beef top round steaks, cut in half

1 can (8 ounces) tomato sauce

2 carrots, chopped

½ onion, chopped

1 stalk celery, chopped

1 teaspoon Italian seasoning

½ teaspoon Worcestershire sauce

1 whole bay leaf

Hot cooked rice

1. Combine flour, salt and pepper in small bowl. Dredge each steak in flour mixture; place in **CROCK-POT**® slow cooker. Combine tomato sauce, carrots, onion, celery, Italian seasoning, Worcestershire sauce and bay leaf in small bowl; pour into **CROCK-POT**® slow cooker.

2. Cover; cook on LOW 8 to 10 hours or on HIGH 4 to 5 hours. Remove and discard bay leaf. Serve steaks and sauce over rice.

Makes 4 servings

Tex-Mex Beef Wraps

1 tablespoon chili powder

2 teaspoons ground cumin

1 teaspoon salt

¼ teaspoon ground red pepper

1 boneless beef chuck roast (2½ to 3 pounds), cut into 4 pieces

1 onion, chopped

3 cloves garlic, minced

1 cup salsa, divided

12 (6- to 7-inch) flour or corn tortillas, warmed

1 cup (4 ounces) shredded Cheddar or Monterey Jack cheese

1 cup chopped tomato

1 ripe avocado, diced

¼ cup chopped fresh cilantro

1. Combine chili powder, cumin, salt and ground red pepper in small bowl. Rub spice mixture all over beef. Place onion and garlic in bottom of **CROCK-POT**® slow cooker; top with beef. Spoon ½ cup salsa over beef. Cover; cook on LOW 8 to 9 hours or on HIGH 3½ to 4½ hours.

2. Remove beef to cutting board; shred with two forks. Skim off fat from cooking liquid. Stir beef into cooking liquid in **CROCK-POT**® slow cooker. Serve beef on tortillas with cheese, tomato, avocado, cilantro and remaining salsa.

Makes 6 servings

Garlic and Mushroom Roast with Savory Gravy

1 boneless beef roast (3 to 4 pounds)
  Salt and black pepper
¼ cup all-purpose flour
1 to 2 tablespoons vegetable oil
1 to 2 jars (12 ounces *each*) beef gravy
1 to 2 cans (4 ounces *each*) mushrooms, drained

1 medium onion, thinly sliced
3 large cloves garlic, sliced
  Hot cooked rice or couscous
  Chopped fresh Italian parsley (optional)

*Unless you have a 5-, 6- or 7-quart CROCK-POT® slow cooker, cut any roast larger than 2½ pounds in half so it cooks completely.

1. Season roast with salt and black pepper; coat with flour. Heat oil in large skillet over medium-high heat. Brown roast 5 minutes on each side.

2. Place roast, gravy, mushrooms, onion and garlic in **CROCK-POT®** slow cooker. Cover; cook on LOW 8 to 10 hours. Serve over rice. Garnish with parsley.

Makes 8 to 10 servings

Tavern Burger

2 pounds ground beef
½ cup ketchup
¼ cup packed brown sugar
¼ cup yellow mustard
8 hamburger buns

1. Brown beef in large skillet over medium-high heat 6 to 8 minutes, stirring to break up meat. Remove beef to **CROCK-POT®** slow cooker using slotted spoon.

2. Add ketchup, brown sugar and mustard to **CROCK-POT®** slow cooker; stir to blend. Cover; cook on LOW 4 to 6 hours. Serve on buns.

Makes 8 servings

Variation: For additional flavor, add a can of pork and beans when adding the other ingredients.

Beef and Quinoa Stuffed Cabbage Rolls

8 large green cabbage leaves, veins trimmed at bottom of each leaf

1 pound ground beef

1½ cups cooked quinoa

1 medium onion, chopped

1 cup tomato juice, divided

Salt and black pepper

1. Heat salted water in large saucepan over high heat; bring to a boil. Add cabbage leaves; return to boil. Cook 2 minutes. Drain and let cool.

2. Combine beef, quinoa, onion, ¼ cup tomato juice, salt and pepper in large bowl; mix well. Place cabbage leaf on large work surface; top center with 2 to 3 tablespoons beef mixture. Starting at stem end, roll up jelly-roll style, folding sides in as you go. Repeat with remaining cabbage rolls and beef mixture.

3. Place cabbage rolls seam side down and side by side in single layer in **CROCK-POT®** slow cooker. Pour in remaining ¾ cup tomato juice. Cover; cook on LOW 5 to 6 hours.

Makes 4 servings

Slow Cooker Pizza Casserole

1½ pounds ground beef

1 pound bulk pork sausage

4 jars (14 ounces *each*) pizza sauce

2 cups (8 ounces) shredded mozzarella cheese

2 cups grated Parmesan cheese

2 cans (4 ounces *each*) mushroom stems and pieces, drained

2 packages (3 ounces *each*) sliced pepperoni

½ cup finely chopped onion

½ cup finely chopped green bell pepper

1 clove garlic, minced

1 pound corkscrew pasta, cooked and drained

1. Brown beef and sausage in large nonstick skillet over medium-high heat 6 to 8 minutes, stirring to break up meat. Drain fat. Remove beef mixture to **CROCK-POT®** slow cooker.

2. Add pizza sauce, cheeses, mushrooms, pepperoni, onion, bell pepper and garlic; stir to blend. Cover; cook on LOW 3½ hours or on HIGH 2 hours. Stir in pasta. Cover; cook on HIGH 15 to 20 minutes or until pasta is heated through.

Makes 6 servings

Asian Short Ribs

½ cup beef broth

¼ cup dry sherry

¼ cup soy sauce

1 tablespoon minced fresh ginger*

1 tablespoon honey

2 teaspoons minced garlic

3 pounds boneless beef short ribs

1 teaspoon salt

½ teaspoon black pepper

½ cup chopped green onions (optional)

Hot cooked rice

To mince ginger quickly, cut a small chunk, remove the skin and put through a garlic press. Store remaining unpeeled ginger in a plastic food storage bag in the refrigerator for up to 3 weeks.

1. Stir broth, sherry, soy sauce, ginger, honey and garlic into **CROCK-POT®** slow cooker.

2. Season short ribs with salt and pepper. Place in **CROCK-POT®** slow cooker, turning to coat all sides with sauce. Cover; cook on LOW 7 to 8 hours or until beef is fork-tender.

3. Remove beef and place on serving dish. Garnish with green onions. Serve with rice.

Makes 4 to 6 servings

Korean Barbecue Beef

2 pounds beef short ribs

¼ cup chopped green onions

¼ cup soy sauce

¼ cup water

1 tablespoon packed brown sugar

2 teaspoons minced fresh ginger

2 teaspoons minced garlic

½ teaspoon black pepper

Dark sesame oil (optional)

Hot cooked rice or linguine (optional)

2 teaspoons sesame seeds, toasted (optional)*

To toast sesame seeds, place in small skillet. Shake skillet over medium heat 2 minutes or until seeds begin to pop and turn golden brown.

1. Place ribs in **CROCK-POT®** slow cooker. Combine green onions, soy sauce, water, brown sugar, ginger, garlic and pepper in medium bowl; mix well. Pour over ribs. Cover; cook on LOW 7 to 8 hours or until ribs are fork-tender.

2. Turn off heat. Remove ribs to large cutting board; cut rib meat into 1-inch pieces. Discard bones and fat. Let cooking liquid stand 5 minutes. Skim off and discard fat. Turn **CROCK-POT®** slow cooker to HIGH. Stir oil into cooking liquid, if desired. Return beef to **CROCK-POT®** slow cooker. Cover; cook on HIGH 15 to 30 minutes or until heated through. Serve over rice, if desired. Garnished with sesame seeds.

Makes 8 servings

Tip: Three pounds of boneless short ribs can be substituted for the beef short ribs.

Tomato and Red Wine Brisket

1 beef brisket (3 to 3½ pounds), trimmed

¾ teaspoon salt, divided

¼ teaspoon black pepper

1 tablespoon olive oil

1 large red onion, sliced

½ cup dry red wine

1 can (28 ounces) diced tomatoes with basil, oregano and garlic

1. Coat inside of **CROCK-POT®** slow cooker with nonstick cooking spray. Season beef with ½ teaspoon salt and pepper. Heat oil in large skillet over medium-high heat. Add beef; cook 5 minutes per side until browned. Remove to **CROCK-POT®** slow cooker.

2. Return skillet to medium-high heat. Add onion; cook and stir 5 minutes or until softened. Pour in wine. Bring mixture to a boil, scraping up any browned bits from bottom of pan. Cook 3 to 4 minutes until mixture nearly evaporates. Stir in tomatoes. Bring to a boil; cook 6 to 7 minutes or until slightly thickened. Stir in remaining ¼ teaspoon salt. Pour mixture over beef in **CROCK-POT®** slow cooker.

3. Cover; cook on LOW 7 to 8 hours. Remove beef to large cutting board; let stand 15 minutes before slicing. Turn **CROCK-POT®** slow cooker to HIGH. Cook, uncovered, on HIGH 10 minutes or until sauce is thickened. Serve sauce over brisket.

Makes 8 servings

Pot Roast with Bacon and Mushrooms

6 slices bacon

1 boneless beef chuck roast (2½ to 3 pounds), trimmed*

¾ teaspoon salt, divided

¼ teaspoon black pepper

¾ cup chopped shallots

8 ounces sliced white mushrooms

¼ ounce dried porcini mushrooms (optional)

4 cloves garlic, minced

1 teaspoon dried oregano

1 cup chicken broth

2 tablespoons tomato paste

Unless you have a 5-, 6- or 7-quart CROCK-POT® slow cooker, cut any roast larger than 2½ pounds in half so it cooks completely.

1. Heat large skillet over medium heat. Add bacon; cook and stir until crisp. Remove to large paper towel-lined plate using slotted spoon. Crumble when cool enough to handle.

2. Pour off all but 2 tablespoons fat from skillet. Season roast with ½ teaspoon salt and pepper. Heat skillet over medium-high heat. Add roast; cook 8 minutes or until well browned. Remove to large plate. Add shallots, white mushrooms, porcini mushrooms, if desired, garlic, oregano and remaining ¼ teaspoon salt; cook 3 to 4 minutes. Remove shallot mixture to **CROCK-POT®** slow cooker.

3. Stir bacon into **CROCK-POT®** slow cooker. Place roast on top of vegetables. Combine broth and tomato paste in small bowl; stir to blend. Pour broth mixture over roast. Cover; cook on LOW 8 hours. Remove roast to large cutting board. Let stand 10 minutes before slicing. Top with vegetables and cooking liquid.

Makes 6 to 8 servings

Roasted Cauliflower:
Preheat oven to 375°F. Break cauliflower into florets; coat with olive oil. Roast 20 minutes. Turn; roast 15 minutes. Makes 6 servings.

Beefy Tostada Pie

2 teaspoons olive oil

1½ cups chopped onion

2 pounds ground beef

1 teaspoon chili powder

1 teaspoon ground cumin

1 teaspoon salt

2 cloves garlic, minced

1 can (15 ounces) tomato sauce

1 cup sliced black olives

8 (6-inch) flour tortillas

3½ cups (14 ounces) shredded Cheddar cheese

Optional toppings: sour cream, salsa and chopped green onion

1. Heat oil in large skillet over medium heat. Add onion; cook and stir 3 to 5 minutes or until tender. Add beef, chili powder, cumin, salt and garlic; cook and stir 6 to 8 minutes or until beef is browned. Drain fat. Stir in tomato sauce; cook until heated through. Stir in olives.

2. Make foil handles using three 18×2-inch strips of heavy-duty foil or use regular foil folded to double thickness. Crisscross foil in spoke design; place across bottom and up side of **CROCK-POT®** slow cooker. Lay 1 tortilla on foil strips. Spread with meat sauce and ½ cup cheese. Top with another tortilla, meat sauce and cheese. Repeat layers five times, ending with tortilla. Cover; cook on HIGH 1½ hours.

3. To serve, lift out of **CROCK-POT®** slow cooker using foil handles and remove to large serving platter. Discard foil. Cut into wedges. Serve with sour cream, salsa and green onion, if desired.

Makes 4 to 6 servings

Easy Salisbury Steak

1½ pounds ground beef

1 egg

½ cup plain dry bread crumbs

1 package (about 1 ounce) onion soup mix*

1 can (10½ ounces) golden mushroom soup, undiluted

*You may pulse onion soup mix in a small food processor or coffee grinder for a finer grind, if desired.

1. Coat inside of **CROCK-POT**® slow cooker with nonstick cooking spray. Combine beef, egg, bread crumbs and dry onion soup mix in large bowl. Form mixture evenly into four 1-inch thick patties.

2. Heat large skillet over medium-high heat. Add patties; cook 2 minutes per side until lightly browned. Remove to **CROCK-POT**® slow cooker, in single layer. Spread mushroom soup evenly over patties. Cover; cook on LOW 3 to 3½ hours.

Makes 4 servings

Italian Meatball Hoagies

½ pound ground beef

½ pound Italian sausage, casings removed

¼ cup seasoned dry bread crumbs

¼ cup grated Parmesan cheese

1 egg

1 tablespoon olive oil

1 cup pasta sauce

2 tablespoons tomato paste

¼ teaspoon red pepper flakes (optional)

4 (6-inch) hoagie rolls, split and lightly toasted

1 cup (4 ounces) shredded mozzarella cheese

1. Coat inside of **CROCK-POT**® slow cooker with nonstick cooking spray. Combine beef, sausage, bread crumbs, Parmesan cheese and egg in large bowl; mix well. Shape to form 16 (1½-inch) meatballs.

2. Heat oil in large skillet over medium heat. Add meatballs; cook 6 to 8 minutes or until browned on all sides, turning occasionally. Remove meatballs to **CROCK-POT**® slow cooker using slotted spoon.

3. Combine pasta sauce, tomato paste and red pepper flakes, if desired, in medium bowl; stir to blend. Spoon over meatballs; gently toss.

4. Cover; cook on LOW 5 to 7 hours or on HIGH 2½ to 3 hours. Place meatballs in rolls. Spoon sauce over meatballs; top with mozzarella cheese.

Makes 4 servings

Shredded Beef Wraps

1 beef flank steak or beef skirt steak (1 to 1½ pounds)

1 cup beef broth

½ cup sun-dried tomatoes (not packed in oil), chopped

3 to 4 cloves garlic, minced

¼ teaspoon ground cumin

4 (8-inch) flour tortillas

Shredded lettuce, diced tomatoes and shredded Monterey Jack cheese (optional)

1. Cut steak into quarters. Place steak, broth, sun-dried tomatoes, garlic and cumin in **CROCK-POT®** slow cooker. Cover; cook on LOW 7 to 8 hours or until steak shreds easily.

2. Remove steak to cutting board; shred with two forks or cut into thin strips. Place remaining juices from **CROCK-POT®** slow cooker in blender or food processor; blend until sauce is smooth.

3. Spoon steak onto tortillas with small amount of sauce. Garnish with lettuce, diced tomatoes and cheese.

Makes 4 servings

Beef and Veal Meatloaf

1 tablespoon olive oil

1 small onion, chopped

½ red bell pepper, chopped

3 cloves garlic, minced

1 teaspoon dried oregano

1 pound ground beef

1 pound ground veal

1 egg

3 tablespoons tomato paste

1 teaspoon salt

½ teaspoon black pepper

1. Coat inside of **CROCK-POT®** slow cooker with nonstick cooking spray. Heat oil in large skillet over medium-high heat. Add onion, bell pepper, garlic and oregano; cook and stir 5 minutes until vegetables are softened. Remove onion mixture to large bowl; cool 6 minutes.

2. Add beef, veal, egg, tomato paste, salt and black pepper; mix well. Form into 9×5-inch loaf; place in **CROCK-POT®** slow cooker. Cover; cook on LOW 5 to 6 hours. Remove meatloaf to large cutting board; let stand 10 minutes before slicing.

Makes 6 servings

Herbed Pot Roast with Fingerling Potatoes

1 boneless beef chuck roast (3 pounds)	1 teaspoon dried oregano
¼ cup all-purpose flour	½ teaspoon dried rosemary
2 tablespoons olive oil	½ teaspoon dried marjoram
16 baby carrots	½ teaspoon dried sage
8 fingerling potatoes, halved crosswise	½ teaspoon dried thyme
1 medium onion, chopped	¼ teaspoon black pepper
2 teaspoons garlic powder	1½ cups beef broth
1 teaspoon dried basil	

1. Combine beef and flour in large bowl; toss to coat. Heat oil in large skillet over medium-high heat. Remove beef from flour, reserving flour. Add beef to skillet; cook 6 to 8 minutes or until browned.

2. Meanwhile, add carrots, potatoes, onion, garlic powder, basil, oregano, rosemary, marjoram, sage, thyme and pepper to **CROCK-POT®** slow cooker. Combine reserved flour with broth in small bowl; add to **CROCK-POT®** slow cooker. Top with beef.

3. Cover; cook on LOW 10 to 12 hours or on HIGH 5 to 6 hours. Remove beef to cutting board. Cover loosely with foil; let stand 10 to 15 minutes before evenly slicing into eight pieces. Serve with gravy and vegetables.

Makes 8 servings

Sicilian Steak Pinwheels

¾ pound mild or hot Italian sausage, casings removed

1¼ cups fresh bread crumbs

¾ cup grated Parmesan cheese

2 eggs

3 tablespoons minced fresh Italian parsley, plus additional for garnish

1½ to 2 pounds beef round steak

1 cup frozen peas

   Kitchen string, cut into 15-inch lengths

1 cup pasta sauce

1 cup beef broth

1. Coat inside of **CROCK-POT**® slow cooker with nonstick cooking spray. Combine sausage, bread crumbs, cheese, eggs and 3 tablespoons parsley in large bowl until well blended; mix well.

2. Place round steak between two large sheets of plastic wrap. Using tenderizer mallet or back of skillet, pound steak until meat is about ⅜ inch thick. Remove top layer of plastic wrap. Spread sausage mixture over steak. Press frozen peas into sausage mixture. Lift edge of plastic wrap at short end; roll up steak completely. Tie at 2-inch intervals with kitchen string. Remove to **CROCK-POT**® slow cooker.

3. Combine pasta sauce and broth in medium bowl. Pour over steak. Cover; cook on LOW 6 hours.

4. Turn off heat. Remove steak to large serving platter. Cover loosely with foil 10 to 15 minutes before removing string and slicing. Let cooking liquid stand 5 minutes. Skim off fat and discard. Serve steak with cooking liquid.

Makes 4 to 6 servings

Corned Beef and Cabbage

2 onions, thickly sliced

1 corned beef brisket (about 3 pounds) with seasoning packet

1 package (8 to 10 ounces) baby carrots

6 medium potatoes, cut into wedges

1 cup water

3 to 5 slices bacon

1 head green cabbage, cut into wedges

1. Place onions in bottom of **CROCK-POT**® slow cooker. Add corned beef with seasoning packet, carrots and potato wedges. Pour 1 cup water over top. Cover; cook on LOW 10 hours.

2. With 30 minutes left in cooking time, heat large saucepan over medium heat. Add bacon; cook and stir until crisp. Remove to paper towel-lined plate using slotted spoon. Reserve drippings in pan. Crumble bacon when cool enough to handle.

3. Place cabbage in saucepan with bacon drippings, cover with water. Bring to a boil; cook 20 to 30 minutes or until cabbage in tender. Drain. Serve corned beef with vegetables; topped with bacon.

Makes 6 servings

Shredded Beef Fajitas

1 beef flank steak (about 1½ pounds), cut into 6 pieces

1 can (about 14 ounces) diced tomatoes with mild green chiles

1 cup chopped onion

1 medium green bell pepper, chopped

2 cloves garlic, minced *or* ¼ teaspoon garlic powder

1 package (about 1½ ounces) fajita seasoning mix

12 (8-inch) flour tortillas

Optional toppings: chopped fresh cilantro, guacamole, shredded Cheddar cheese and/ or salsa

1. Place beef in **CROCK-POT®** slow cooker. Combine tomatoes, onion, bell pepper, garlic and fajita seasoning mix in medium bowl; pour over steak. Cover; cook on LOW 8 to 10 hours or on HIGH 4 to 5 hours.

2. Remove beef to cutting board; shred with two forks. Stir shredded beef back into **CROCK-POT®** slow cooker. Divide beef evenly among tortillas. Top as desired.

Makes 12 servings

Nana's Beef Brisket

1 large onion, thinly sliced

1 beef brisket (2 to 2½ pounds), trimmed

Salt and black pepper

⅔ cup chili sauce, divided

1½ tablespoons packed brown sugar

¼ teaspoon ground cinnamon

2 large sweet potatoes, cut into 1-inch pieces

1 cup (5 ounces) pitted prunes

2 tablespoons cold water

2 tablespoons cornstarch

1. Place onion in **CROCK-POT®** slow cooker; top with brisket. Sprinkle with salt and pepper; top with ⅓ cup chili sauce. Cover; cook on HIGH 3½ hours.

2. Combine remaining ⅓ cup chili sauce, brown sugar and cinnamon in large bowl. Add potatoes and prunes; toss to coat. Spoon mixture over brisket. Cover; cook on HIGH 1¼ to 1½ hours.

3. Remove brisket to large cutting board. Cover loosely with foil; let stand 10 to 15 minutes before slicing. Remove sweet potato mixture to large serving platter using slotted spoon. Keep warm.

4. Stir water into cornstarch in small bowl until smooth; whisk into cooking liquid. Cover; cook on HIGH 10 to 15 minutes or until sauce is thickened. Serve brisket with sweet potato mixture and sauce.

Makes 8 servings

Delicious Pepper Steak

2 tablespoons toasted sesame oil

2 pounds beef round steak, cut into strips

½ medium red bell pepper, sliced

½ medium green bell pepper, sliced

½ medium yellow bell pepper, sliced

1 medium onion, sliced

14 grape tomatoes

⅓ cup hoisin sauce

¼ cup water

3 tablespoons all-purpose flour

3 tablespoons soy sauce

2 teaspoons garlic powder

1 teaspoon ground cumin

1 teaspoon dried oregano

1 teaspoon paprika

⅛ teaspoon ground red pepper

Hot cooked rice (optional)

1. Heat oil in large skillet over medium-high heat. Add beef in batches; cook 4 to 5 minutes or until browned. Remove to large paper towel-lined plate.

2. Add bell peppers, onion and tomatoes to **CROCK-POT**® slow cooker. Combine hoisin sauce, water, flour, soy sauce, garlic powder, cumin, oregano, paprika and ground red pepper in medium bowl; stir to blend. Add to **CROCK-POT**® slow cooker. Top with beef. Cover; cook on LOW 8 to 9 hours or on HIGH 4 to 4½ hours. Serve with rice, if desired.

Makes 6 servings

Southwest-Style Meat Loaf

1½ pounds ground beef

2 eggs

1 small onion, chopped (about ½ cup)

½ medium green bell pepper, chopped (about ½ cup)

½ cup plain dry bread crumbs

¾ cup chunky salsa, divided

1½ teaspoons ground cumin

¾ cup (3 ounces) shredded Mexican cheese blend

¾ teaspoon salt

¼ teaspoon black pepper

1. Combine beef, eggs, onion, bell pepper, bread crumbs, ¼ cup salsa, cumin, cheese, salt and black pepper in large bowl; mix well. Form mixture into 9×5-inch loaf.

2. Fold two long pieces of foil in half lengthwise. (Each should be about 24 inches long.) Crisscross pieces on work surface, coat with nonstick cooking spray and set meat loaf on top. Use ends of foil as handles to gently lower meat loaf into **CROCK-POT®** slow cooker, letting ends hang over the top. Top meat loaf with remaining ½ cup salsa.

3. Cover; cook on LOW 7 to 8 hours or on HIGH 3 to 4 hours or until meat loaf is firm and cooked through. Remove meat loaf to cutting board; let stand 5 minutes before slicing.

Makes 6 servings

Best-Ever Roast

1 can (10¾ ounces) condensed cream of mushroom soup, undiluted

1 package (about 1 ounce) onion soup mix

1 boneless beef chuck shoulder roast (3 to 5 pounds)*

4 to 5 medium potatoes, unpeeled and quartered

4 cups baby carrots

Unless you have a 5-, 6- or 7-quart CROCK-POT® slow cooker, cut any roast larger than 2½ pounds in half so it cooks completely.

1. Combine mushroom soup and dry soup mix in **CROCK-POT®** slow cooker; stir to blend. Place roast in **CROCK-POT®** slow cooker. Cover; cook on LOW 4 hours.

2. Stir in potatoes and carrots. Cover; cook on LOW 2 hours.

Makes 6 to 8 servings

Meatballs and Spaghetti Sauce

2 pounds ground beef

1 cup plain dry bread crumbs

1 medium yellow onion, chopped

2 eggs, beaten

¼ cup minced fresh Italian parsley

3 cloves garlic, minced and divided

½ teaspoon dry mustard

½ teaspoon black pepper

3 tablespoons olive oil, divided

1 can (about 28 ounces) whole tomatoes

½ cup chopped fresh basil, plus additional for garnish

1 teaspoon sugar

Hot cooked spaghetti (optional)

1. Combine beef, bread crumbs, onion, eggs, parsley, 1 clove garlic, dry mustard and pepper in large bowl. Form into walnut-sized meatballs. Heat 1 tablespoon oil in large skillet over medium heat. Add meatballs; cook 6 to 8 minutes or until browned on all sides. Remove to **CROCK-POT**® slow cooker.

2. Combine tomatoes, ½ cup basil, remaining 2 tablespoons oil, remaining 2 cloves garlic and sugar in medium bowl. Pour over meatballs, stirring to coat. Cover; cook on LOW 3 to 5 hours or on HIGH 2 to 4 hours. Serve over spaghetti, if desired. Garnish with additional basil.

Makes 8 servings

Deep Dark Black Coffee'd Beef

2 cups sliced mushrooms

1 cup chopped onions

2 teaspoons instant coffee granules

1½ teaspoons chili powder

½ teaspoon black pepper

1 lean boneless beef chuck roast (about 2 pounds)

1 tablespoon vegetable oil

½ cup water

1 tablespoon Worcestershire sauce

1 teaspoon beef bouillon granules *or* 1 cube beef bouillon

½ teaspoon garlic powder

Hot cooked asparagus (optional)

1. Coat inside of **CROCK-POT**® slow cooker with nonstick cooking spray. Add mushrooms and onions.

2. Combine coffee granules, chili powder and pepper in small bowl; stir to blend. Rub evenly onto beef. Heat oil in large skillet over medium-high heat. Add beef; cook 3 minutes per side or until browned. Place beef on vegetables in **CROCK-POT**® slow cooker.

3. Add water, Worcestershire sauce, bouillon granules and garlic powder. Cover; cook on LOW 8 hours or HIGH 4 hours.

4. Turn off heat. Remove beef to large serving platter. Pour cooking liquid through fine-mesh sieve to drain well, reserving liquid and vegetables. Place vegetables over beef. Allow cooking liquid to stand 2 to 3 minutes. Skim and discard excess fat. Serve with remaining liquid and asparagus, if desired.

Makes 6 servings

Tip: "Au jus" means "with juice," and usually refers to the cooking liquid in which meats have cooked. If you prefer a thicker sauce, blend 1 tablespoon cornstarch and 2 tablespoons water. Whisk into the cooking liquid and continue cooking until it thickens.

Beef with Green Chiles

¼ cup plus 1 tablespoon all-purpose flour, divided

¼ teaspoon black pepper

1 pound cubed beef stew meat

1 tablespoon vegetable oil

2 cloves garlic, minced

1 cup beef broth

1 can (7 ounces) diced mild green chiles, drained

½ teaspoon dried oregano

2 tablespoons water

1½ cups hot cooked rice

½ cup diced tomato

1. Combine ¼ cup flour and pepper in large bowl; stir to blend. Add beef; toss to coat. Heat oil in large skillet over medium-high heat. Add beef and garlic; cook and stir 6 to 8 minutes or until beef is browned on all sides. Remove beef mixture to **CROCK-POT**® slow cooker using slotted spoon. Add broth to skillet, stirring to scrape up any browned bits. Pour broth mixture into **CROCK-POT**® slow cooker. Add chiles and oregano.

2. Cover; cook on LOW 7 to 8 hours. Turn **CROCK-POT**® slow cooker to HIGH. Stir water into remaining 1 tablespoon flour in small bowl until smooth. Whisk into **CROCK-POT**® slow cooker. Cover; cook on HIGH 15 minutes or until thickened. Serve over rice and top with tomato.

Makes 6 servings

Tip: Use 2 cans of chiles for a slightly hotter flavor.

Cheeseburger Sloppy Joes

1½ pounds ground beef

3 cloves garlic, minced

1 small onion, chopped

½ cup ketchup

¼ cup water

1 tablespoon packed brown sugar

1 teaspoon Worcestershire sauce

2 cups (8 ounces) shredded sharp Cheddar cheese

6 to 8 hamburger rolls

Carrot and celery sticks (optional)

1. Coat inside of **CROCK-POT**® slow cooker with nonstick cooking spray. Brown beef in large skillet over medium-high heat 6 to 8 minutes, stirring to break up meat. Drain fat. Remove beef to **CROCK-POT**® slow cooker using slotted spoon. Return skillet to heat. Stir in garlic and onion; cook and stir 3 to 4 minutes.

2. Add garlic mixture, ketchup, water, brown sugar and Worcestershire sauce to **CROCK-POT**® slow cooker; stir to blend. Cover; cook on LOW 4 to 5 hours or on HIGH 2 to 2½ hours. Stir in cheese until melted. Serve on rolls with carrot and celery sticks, if desired.

Makes 6 to 8 servings

Shepherd's Pie

1 pound ground beef

1 pound ground lamb

1 package (12 ounces) frozen chopped onions

2 teaspoons minced garlic

1 package (16 ounces) frozen peas and carrots

1 can (about 14 ounces) diced tomatoes, drained

3 tablespoons quick-cooking tapioca

2 teaspoons dried oregano

1 teaspoon salt

½ teaspoon black pepper

2 packages (24 ounces *each*) prepared mashed potatoes

1. Brown beef and lamb in large nonstick skillet over medium-high heat 6 to 8 minutes, stirring to break up meat. Drain fat. Remove to **CROCK-POT®** slow cooker using slotted spoon. Return skillet to heat. Add onions and garlic; cook and stir until onions are tender. Remove to **CROCK-POT®** slow cooker.

2. Stir peas and carrots, tomatoes, tapioca, oregano, salt and pepper into **CROCK-POT®** slow cooker. Cover; cook on LOW 7 to 8 hours.

3. Top with prepared mashed potatoes. Cover; cook on LOW 30 minutes or until potatoes are heated through.

Makes 6 servings

Beefy Tortellini

½ pound ground beef or turkey

1 jar (24 to 26 ounces) roasted tomato and garlic pasta sauce

1 package (12 ounces) uncooked three-cheese tortellini

8 ounces sliced button or exotic mushrooms, such as oyster, shiitake and cremini

½ cup water

½ teaspoon red pepper flakes (optional)

¾ cup grated Asiago or Romano cheese

Chopped fresh Italian parsley (optional)

1. Coat inside of **CROCK-POT**® slow cooker with nonstick cooking spray. Brown beef in large skillet over medium-high heat 6 to 8 minutes, stirring to break up meat. Remove to **CROCK-POT**® slow cooker using slotted spoon.

2. Stir pasta sauce, tortellini, mushrooms, water and red pepper flakes, if desired, into **CROCK-POT**® slow cooker. Cover; cook on LOW 2 hours or on HIGH 1 hour. Stir.

3. Cover; cook on LOW 2 to 2½ hours or on HIGH ½ to 1 hour. Serve in shallow bowls topped with cheese and parsley, if desired.

Makes 6 servings

Carne Rellenos

1 can (4 ounces) whole mild green chiles, drained

4 ounces cream cheese, softened

1 flank steak (about 2 pounds)

1½ cups salsa verde

Hot cooked rice (optional)

1. Slit green chiles open on one side with sharp knife; stuff with cream cheese.

2. Open steak flat on sheet of waxed paper. Score steak; turn over. Lay stuffed chiles across unscored side of steak. Roll up; tie with kitchen string.

3. Place steak in **CROCK-POT**® slow cooker; pour in salsa. Cover; cook on LOW 6 to 8 hours or on HIGH 3 to 4 hours or until cooked through. Remove steak to cutting board. Let stand 10 to 15 minutes before slicing. Serve over rice with sauce, if desired.

Makes 6 servings

Easy Beef Sandwiches

1 large onion, sliced

1 boneless beef bottom round roast (about 3 to 5 pounds)*

1 cup water

1 package (about 1 ounce) au jus gravy mix

French rolls, sliced lengthwise

Provolone cheese

Unless you have a 5-, 6- or 7-quart CROCK-POT® slow cooker, cut any roast larger than 2½ pounds in half so it cooks completely.

1. Place onion slices in bottom of **CROCK-POT**® slow cooker; top with roast. Combine water and dry gravy mix in small bowl; pour over roast. Cover; cook on LOW 7 to 9 hours.

2. Remove roast to cutting board; shred with two forks. Serve on rolls; top with cheese. Serve cooking liquid on the side for dipping.

Makes 6 to 8 servings

Barbecued Beef Sandwiches

2 cups ketchup

1 onion, chopped

¼ cup cider vinegar

¼ cup dark molasses

2 tablespoons Worcestershire sauce

2 cloves garlic, minced

½ teaspoon salt

½ teaspoon ground mustard

½ teaspoon black pepper

¼ teaspoon garlic powder

¼ teaspoon red pepper flakes

1 boneless beef chuck shoulder roast (about 3 pounds), trimmed*

Sesame seed buns

Unless you have a 5-, 6- or 7-quart CROCK-POT® slow cooker, cut any roast larger than 2½ pounds in half so it cooks completely.

1. Combine ketchup, onion, vinegar, molasses, Worcestershire sauce, garlic, salt, mustard, black pepper, garlic powder and red pepper flakes in **CROCK-POT**® slow cooker; stir to blend. Place beef in **CROCK-POT**® slow cooker. Cover; cook on LOW 8 to 10 hours or on HIGH 4 to 5 hours.

2. Turn off heat. Remove beef to large cutting board; shred with two forks. Let cooking liquid stand 5 minutes. Skim off fat and discard.

3. Turn **CROCK-POT**® slow cooker to HIGH. Add shredded beef; stir to coat. Cover; cook on HIGH 15 to 30 minutes or until heated through. Spoon filling into buns; top with additional sauce, if desired.

Makes 12 servings

Sauerbraten

1 boneless beef rump roast (1¼ pounds)

3 cups baby carrots

1½ cups fresh or frozen pearl onions

¼ cup raisins

½ cup water

½ cup red wine vinegar

1 tablespoon honey

½ teaspoon salt

½ teaspoon dry mustard

½ teaspoon garlic-pepper seasoning

¼ teaspoon ground cloves

¼ cup crushed crisp gingersnap cookies (5 cookies)

1. Heat large nonstick skillet over medium-high heat. Brown roast on all sides, turning as it browns. Place roast, carrots, onions and raisins in **CROCK-POT**® slow cooker.

2. Combine water, vinegar, honey, salt, mustard, garlic-pepper seasoning and cloves in large bowl; mix well. Pour mixture over meat and vegetables in **CROCK-POT**® slow cooker. Cover; cook on LOW 4 to 6 hours.

3. Remove roast to cutting board. Cover loosely with foil; let stand 10 to 15 minutes before slicing. Remove vegetables from **CROCK-POT**® slow cooker to bowl using slotted spoon; cover to keep warm.

4. Stir crushed cookies into sauce mixture in **CROCK-POT**® slow cooker. Turn **CROCK-POT**® slow cooker to HIGH. Cover; cook on HIGH 10 to 15 minutes or until sauce thickens. Serve meat and vegetables with sauce.

Makes 5 servings

Hearty Beef Short Ribs

1½ pounds flanken-style beef short ribs, bone-in	1 large yellow onion, diced
1 tablespoon black pepper	3 cloves garlic, minced
2¼ teaspoons coarse salt	3 whole bay leaves
1 tablespoon olive oil	⅓ cup canned crushed tomatoes
2 carrots, diced	⅓ cup dry red wine
2 stalks celery, diced	⅓ cup balsamic vinegar

1. Season ribs with black pepper and salt. Heat oil in large skillet. Add ribs; cook 2 to 3 minutes on each side or just until browned. Remove to **CROCK-POT®** slow cooker. Add carrots, celery, onion, garlic and bay leaves.

2. Combine tomatoes, wine and vinegar in small bowl. Pour mixture into **CROCK-POT®** slow cooker. Cover; cook on LOW 8 to 9 hours or on HIGH 5½ to 6 hours, turning once or twice, until meat is tender and falling off the bone.

3. Remove ribs to large serving platter. Remove and discard bay leaves. Pour sauce into food processor or blender; process to desired consistency. To serve, pour sauce evenly over ribs.

Makes 8 servings

Tip: For a change of pace from ordinary short rib recipes, ask your butcher for flanken-style beef short ribs. Flanken-style ribs are cut across the bones into wide, flat portions. They provide all the meaty flavor of the more common English-style short ribs with smaller, more manageable bones.

Texas-Style Barbecued Brisket

3	tablespoons Worcestershire sauce	2	cloves garlic, minced
1	tablespoon chili powder	1	beef brisket (3 to 4 pounds), trimmed
1	teaspoon celery salt	2	whole bay leaves
1	teaspoon black pepper	1¾	cups barbecue sauce, plus additional for serving
1	teaspoon liquid smoke		

1. Combine Worcestershire sauce, chili powder, celery salt, pepper, liquid smoke and garlic in small bowl. Spread mixture on all sides of beef. Place beef in large resealable food storage bag; seal bag. Refrigerate 24 hours.

2. Place beef, marinade and bay leaves in **CROCK-POT®** slow cooker, cutting meat in half to fit, if necessary. Cover; cook on LOW 7 hours.

3. Remove beef to large cutting board. Pour cooking liquid into 2-cup measure; let stand 5 minutes. Skim off and discard fat. Remove and discard bay leaves. Stir 1 cup juice into 1¾ cups barbecue sauce in medium bowl. Discard any remaining juice.

4. Return beef and barbecue sauce mixture to **CROCK-POT®** slow cooker. Cover; cook on LOW 1 hour or until meat is fork-tender. Remove beef to cutting board. Cut across grain into ¼-inch-thick slices. Serve with additional barbecue sauce.

Makes 10 to 12 servings

Asian Ginger Beef over Bok Choy

2 tablespoons peanut oil

1½ pounds boneless beef chuck roast, cut into 1-inch pieces

3 green onions, cut into ½-inch slices

6 cloves garlic

1 cup chicken broth

½ cup water

¼ cup soy sauce

2 teaspoons ground ginger

1 teaspoon Asian chili paste

9 ounces fresh udon noodles or vermicelli, cooked and drained

9 ounces bok choy, trimmed, washed and cut into 1-inch pieces

½ cup minced fresh cilantro (optional)

1. Heat oil in large skillet over medium-high heat. Add beef in batches with green onions and garlic; cook and stir 6 to 8 minutes or until beef is browned on all sides. Remove to **CROCK-POT**® slow cooker. Add broth, water, soy sauce, ginger and chili paste; stir to blend. Cover; cook on LOW 7 to 8 hours or on HIGH 3 to 4 hours.

2. Stir in noodles and bok choy. Cover; cook on HIGH 15 minutes or until bok choy is tender-crisp. Garnish with cilantro.

Makes 8 servings

HEARTY CHILIES

Three-Bean Chili with Chorizo

2 Mexican chorizo sausages (about 6 ounces *each*), casings removed

1 tablespoon vegetable oil

1 large onion, chopped

1 tablespoon salt

1 tablespoon tomato paste

1 tablespoon minced garlic

1 tablespoon chili powder

1 tablespoon ancho chili powder

2 to 3 teaspoons chipotle chili powder

2 teaspoons ground cumin

1 teaspoon ground coriander

3 cups water

2 cans (about 14 ounces *each*) crushed tomatoes

½ cup dried pinto beans, rinsed and sorted

½ cup dried kidney beans, rinsed and sorted

½ cup dried black beans, rinsed and sorted

Optional toppings: sour cream, green onions and/or chopped fresh cilantro

1. Heat large nonstick skillet over medium-high heat. Add sausages; cook 3 to 4 minutes, stirring to break up meat. Remove to **CROCK-POT**® slow cooker using slotted spoon.

2. Wipe out skillet. Heat oil in same skillet over medium heat. Add onion; cook and stir 6 minutes or until softened. Add salt, tomato paste, garlic, chili powders, cumin and coriander; cook and stir 1 minute. Remove to **CROCK-POT**® slow cooker. Stir in water, tomatoes and beans.

3. Cover; cook on LOW 10 hours. Serve with desired toppings.

Makes 6 to 8 servings

Note: For spicier chili, use 1 tablespoon chipotle chili powder.

Hearty Pork and Bacon Chili

2½ pounds pork shoulder, cut into 1-inch pieces

3½ teaspoons salt, divided

1¼ teaspoons black pepper, divided

1 tablespoon vegetable oil

4 slices thick-cut bacon, diced

2 medium onions, chopped

1 red bell pepper, chopped

¼ cup chili powder

2 tablespoons tomato paste

1 tablespoon minced garlic

1 tablespoon ground cumin

1 tablespoon smoked paprika

1 bottle (12 ounces) pale ale

2 cans (about 14 ounces *each*) diced tomatoes

2 cups water

¾ cup dried kidney beans, rinsed and sorted

¾ cup dried black beans, rinsed and sorted

3 tablespoons cornmeal

Chopped fresh cilantro and feta cheese (optional)

1. Season pork with 1 teaspoon salt and 1 teaspoon black pepper. Heat oil in large skillet over medium-high heat. Cook pork in batches 6 minutes or until browned on all sides. Remove to **CROCK-POT®** slow cooker using slotted spoon.

2. Heat same skillet over medium heat. Add bacon; cook and stir until crisp. Remove to **CROCK-POT®** slow cooker using slotted spoon.

3. Pour off all but 2 tablespoons fat from skillet. Return skillet to medium heat. Add onions and bell pepper; cook and stir 6 minutes or just until softened. Stir in chili powder, tomato paste, garlic, cumin, paprika, remaining 2½ teaspoons salt and remaining ¼ teaspoon black pepper; cook and stir 1 minute. Stir in ale. Bring to a simmer, scraping up any browned bits from the bottom of skillet. Pour over pork in **CROCK-POT®** slow cooker. Stir in tomatoes, water, beans and cornmeal.

4. Cover; cook on LOW 10 hours. Turn off heat. Let stand 10 minutes. Skim fat from surface. Garnish each serving with cilantro and cheese.

Makes 8 to 10 servings

Black Bean Mushroom Chili

1   tablespoon vegetable oil

2   cups (8 ounces) sliced baby bella or button
    mushrooms

1   cup chopped onion

4   cloves garlic, minced

1   can (about 15 ounces) black beans, rinsed
    and drained

1   can (about 14 ounces) fire-roasted diced
    tomatoes

1   cup salsa

1   yellow or green bell pepper, finely diced

2   teaspoons chili powder or ground cumin
    Sour cream (optional)

1. Coat inside of **CROCK-POT**® slow cooker with nonstick cooking spray. Heat oil in large skillet over medium heat. Add mushrooms, onion and garlic; cook 8 minutes or until mushrooms have released their liquid and liquid has thickened slightly.

2. Combine mushroom mixture, beans, tomatoes, salsa, bell pepper and chili powder in **CROCK-POT**® slow cooker; mix well. Cover; cook on LOW 5 to 6 hours or on HIGH 2½ to 3 hours. Ladle into shallow bowls. Top with sour cream, if desired.

Makes 4 servings

Pork Tenderloin Chili

1½ to 2 pounds pork tenderloin, cooked and cut into 2-inch pieces

2 cans (about 15 ounces *each*) pinto beans, rinsed and drained

2 cans (about 15 ounces *each*) black beans, rinsed and drained

2 cans (about 14 ounces *each*) whole tomatoes

2 cans (4 ounces *each*) diced mild green chiles

1 package (1¼ ounces) taco seasoning mix

Optional toppings: diced avocado, shredded cheese, chopped onion, cilantro and/or tortilla chips

Combine pork, beans, tomatoes, chiles and taco seasoning mix in **CROCK-POT®** slow cooker. Cover; cook on LOW 4 hours. Top as desired.

Makes 8 servings

Cincinnati Chili

1 tablespoon vegetable oil	2½ teaspoons ground cinnamon
2 onions, chopped	2 teaspoons salt
2 pounds ground beef	1½ teaspoons ground cumin
1 can (28 ounces) diced tomatoes	1½ teaspoons Worcestershire sauce
1 cup tomato sauce	1¼ teaspoons ground allspice
½ cup water	¾ teaspoon ground red pepper
3 cloves garlic, minced	12 ounces cooked spaghetti
1 tablespoon unsweetened cocoa powder	Optional toppings: chopped onions, shredded Cheddar cheese, kidney beans and/or oyster crackers
1 tablespoon chili powder	

1. Heat oil in large skillet over medium-high heat. Add onions; cook about 2 to 3 minutes or until translucent. Add beef; cook until beef is browned, stirring to break up meat. Drain fat. Remove beef mixture to **CROCK-POT**® slow cooker with slotted spoon.

2. Stir tomatoes, tomato sauce, water, garlic, cocoa, chili powder, cinnamon, salt, cumin, Worcestershire sauce, allspice and ground red pepper into **CROCK-POT**® slow cooker. Cover; cook on LOW 7 to 8 hours or on HIGH 3½ to 4 hours. Spoon chili over spaghetti. Top as desired.

Makes 6 servings

Slow-Cooked Southwest Chipotle Chili

3 links chorizo sausage (1 pound total), casings removed

1 pound ground beef

3 cans (about 14 ounces *each*) diced tomatoes

1 can (about 15 ounces) dark red kidney beans, rinsed and drained

1 can (about 15 ounces) black beans, rinsed and drained

1 can (about 14 ounces) stewed tomatoes, plus 1 can water

1 can (about 14 ounces) tomato sauce

2 medium bell peppers, chopped

3 canned chipotle peppers in adobo sauce, chopped, plus 1 tablespoon adobo sauce reserved*

2 to 3 small serrano peppers, chopped*

1 poblano pepper, chopped*

1 medium onion, chopped

2 tablespoons ground red pepper

2 tablespoons chili powder

2 tablespoons hot pepper sauce

1 tablespoon sugar

Salt and black pepper

Chipotle, serrano and poblano peppers can sting and irritate the skin. Wear rubber gloves when handling peppers and do not touch your eyes.

1. Brown chorizo and ground beef in large skillet over medium-high heat 6 to 8 minutes, stirring to break up meat. Drain fat.

2. Combine chorizo and beef, diced tomatoes, beans, stewed tomatoes, tomato sauce, bell peppers, chipotle peppers with reserved sauce, serrano peppers, poblano pepper, onion, ground red pepper, chili powder, hot pepper sauce, sugar, salt and black pepper in **CROCK-POT®** slow cooker. Cover; cook on LOW 5 to 6 hours or on HIGH 2 to 3 hours.

Makes 12 servings

Turkey Chili

2 tablespoons olive oil, divided

1½ pounds ground turkey

2 medium onions, chopped

1 medium red bell pepper, chopped

1 medium green bell pepper, chopped

5 cloves garlic, minced

1 jalapeño pepper, finely chopped*

2 cans (about 14 ounces *each*) fire-roasted diced tomatoes

4 teaspoons chili powder

1 teaspoon ground cumin

1 teaspoon dried oregano

½ teaspoon salt

Jalapeño peppers can sting and irritate the skin. Wear rubber gloves when handling peppers and do not touch your eyes.

1. Heat 1 tablespoon oil in large skillet over medium-high heat. Add turkey; cook 7 to 8 minutes, stirring to break up meat. Remove to **CROCK-POT®** slow cooker using slotted spoon.

2. Heat remaining 1 tablespoon oil in same skillet over medium-high heat. Add onions, bell peppers, garlic and jalapeño pepper; cook and stir 4 to 5 minutes or until softened. Stir in tomatoes, chili powder, cumin, oregano and salt; cook 1 minute. Remove onion mixture to **CROCK-POT®** slow cooker. Cover; cook on LOW 6 hours.

Makes 6 servings

Texas Chili

3½ to 4 pounds cubed beef stew meat
  Salt and black pepper
  4 tablespoons vegetable oil, divided
  1 large onion, diced
  1 tablespoon minced garlic
  ¼ cup chili powder
  1 teaspoon dried oregano

  1 tablespoon ground cumin
  2 teaspoons ground coriander
  1 tablespoon tomato paste
  3 tablespoons cornmeal or masa harina
  1 tablespoon packed light brown sugar
  3 cans (about 14 ounces *each*) diced tomatoes

1. Season beef with salt and pepper. Heat 3 tablespoons oil in large skillet over medium-high heat. Cook beef in batches 8 minutes or until browned on all sides. Remove to **CROCK-POT®** slow cooker using slotted spoon.

2. Heat remaining 1 tablespoon oil in same skillet. Add onion; cook and stir 6 minutes or until softened. Stir in garlic, chili powder, oregano, cumin, coriander, tomato paste and additional salt and pepper as desired; cook and stir 1 minute. Stir in brown sugar, cornmeal and tomatoes; bring to a simmer. Remove to **CROCK-POT®** slow cooker. Cover; cook on LOW 7 to 8 hours.

Makes 8 servings

Variation: Add ¼ teaspoon ground red pepper if a spicier chili is desired.

Corn and Two Bean Chili

1 can (about 15 ounces) pinto or kidney beans, rinsed and drained

1 can (about 15 ounces) black beans, rinsed and drained

1 can (about 14 ounces) fire-roasted diced tomatoes

1 cup salsa

1 cup frozen corn

½ cup minced onion

1 teaspoon chili powder

1 teaspoon ground cumin

½ cup sour cream (optional)

1 cup (4 ounces) shredded Cheddar cheese (optional)

1. Coat inside of **CROCK-POT®** slow cooker with nonstick cooking spray. Combine beans, tomatoes, salsa, corn, onion, chili powder and cumin in **CROCK-POT®** slow cooker; stir to blend.

2. Cover; cook on LOW 5 to 6 hours or on HIGH 2½ to 3 hours. Top each serving with sour cream and cheese, if desired.

Makes 4 servings

Mediterranean Chili

2 cans (about 28 ounces *each*) chickpeas, rinsed and drained

1 can (28 ounces) diced tomatoes

1 can (about 14 ounces) vegetable broth

2 onions, chopped

10 kalamata olives, chopped

4 cloves garlic, chopped

2 teaspoons ground cumin

¼ teaspoon ground red pepper

½ cup chopped fresh mint

1 teaspoon dried oregano

½ teaspoon grated lemon peel

1 cup crumbled feta cheese

Sprigs fresh mint (optional)

1. Combine chickpeas, tomatoes, broth, onions, olives, garlic, cumin and ground red pepper in **CROCK-POT** slow cooker. Cover; cook on LOW 7 to 8 hours or on HIGH 3½ hours.

2. Stir in chopped mint, oregano and lemon peel; top each serving with feta. Garnish with mint sprigs.

Makes 6 servings

Vegetarian Chili

1 tablespoon vegetable oil

1 cup chopped onion

1 cup chopped red bell pepper

2 tablespoons minced jalapeño pepper*

1 clove garlic, minced

1 can (about 28 ounces) stewed tomatoes

1 can (about 15 ounces) black beans, rinsed and drained

1 can (about 15 ounces) chickpeas, rinsed and drained

½ cup frozen corn

¼ cup tomato paste

1 teaspoon sugar

1 teaspoon ground cumin

1 teaspoon dried basil

1 teaspoon chili powder

¼ teaspoon black pepper

Sour cream and shredded Cheddar cheese (optional)

*Jalapeño peppers can sting and irritate the skin, so wear rubber gloves when handling peppers and do not touch your eyes.

1. Heat oil in large skillet over medium-high heat. Add onion, bell pepper, jalapeño pepper and garlic; cook and stir 5 minutes. Remove onion mixture to **CROCK-POT**® slow cooker using slotted spoon. Add tomatoes, beans, chickpeas, corn, tomato paste, sugar, cumin, basil, chili powder and black pepper; stir to blend.

2. Cover; cook on LOW 4 to 5 hours. Serve with sour cream and cheese, if desired.

Makes 4 servings

Chipotle Vegetable Chili with Chocolate

2 tablespoons olive oil

1 medium onion, chopped

1 medium green bell pepper, chopped

1 medium red bell pepper, chopped

1 cup frozen corn

1 can (28 ounces) diced tomatoes

1 can (about 15 ounces) black beans, rinsed and drained

1 can (about 15 ounces) pinto beans, rinsed and drained

1 tablespoon chili powder

1 teaspoon ground cumin

½ teaspoon chipotle chili powder

1 ounce semisweet chocolate, chopped

1. Heat oil in large skillet over medium-high heat. Add onion and bell peppers; cook and stir 4 minutes or until softened. Stir in corn; cook 3 minutes. Remove to **CROCK-POT**® slow cooker.

2. Stir tomatoes, beans, chili powder, cumin and chipotle chili powder into **CROCK-POT**® slow cooker. Cover; cook on LOW 6 to 7 hours. Stir chocolate into **CROCK-POT**® slow cooker until melted.

Makes 6 servings

Easy Chili

1 teaspoon vegetable oil

1 pound ground beef

1 medium onion, chopped

2 cans (10¾ ounces *each*) condensed tomato soup, undiluted

1 cup water

Salt and black pepper

Chili powder

Shredded Cheddar cheese

Italian or French bread (optional)

1. Heat oil in large skillet over medium-high heat. Brown beef and onion 6 to 8 minutes, stirring to break up meat. Remove beef mixture to **CROCK-POT**® slow cooker using slotted spoon.

2. Add soup and water to **CROCK-POT**® slow cooker; stir to blend. Season with salt, pepper and chili powder. Cover; cook on LOW 6 to 8 hours. Top with cheese and serve with bread, if desired.

Makes 4 servings

Black and White Chili

Nonstick cooking spray

1 pound boneless, skinless chicken breasts, cut into ¾-inch pieces

1 cup chopped onion

1 can (about 15 ounces) Great Northern beans, rinsed and drained

1 can (about 15 ounces) black beans, rinsed and drained

1 can (about 14 ounces) stewed tomatoes

2 tablespoons Texas-style chili seasoning mix

1. Spray large skillet with cooking spray; heat over medium heat. Add chicken and onion; cook and stir 5 minutes or until chicken is browned.

2. Combine chicken mixture, beans, tomatoes and chili seasoning in **CROCK-POT®** slow cooker. Cover; cook on LOW 4 to 4½ hours.

Makes 6 servings

Serving Suggestion: For a change of pace, this delicious chili is excellent served over cooked rice or pasta.

Three-Bean Turkey Chili

1 pound ground turkey

1 small onion, chopped

1 can (28 ounces) diced tomatoes

1 can (about 15 ounces) chickpeas, rinsed and drained

1 can (about 15 ounces) kidney beans, rinsed and drained

1 can (about 15 ounces) black beans, rinsed and drained

1 can (8 ounces) tomato sauce

1 can (4 ounces) diced mild green chiles

1 to 2 tablespoons chili powder

1. Place turkey and onion in medium skillet over medium-high heat; cook and stir until turkey is browned. Drain fat. Remove to **CROCK-POT®** slow cooker using slotted spoon.

2. Add tomatoes, chickpeas, beans, tomato sauce, chiles and chili powder to **CROCK-POT®** slow cooker; mix well. Cover; cook on HIGH 6 to 8 hours.

Makes 6 to 8 servings

Savory Chicken and Oregano Chili

3 cans (about 15 ounces *each*) Great Northern or cannellini beans, rinsed and drained

3½ cups chicken broth

2 cups chopped cooked chicken

2 red bell peppers, chopped

1 onion, chopped

1 can (4 ounces) diced mild green chiles, drained

3 cloves garlic, minced

2 teaspoons ground cumin

1 teaspoon salt

1 tablespoon minced fresh oregano

1. Place beans, broth, chicken, bell peppers, onion, chiles, garlic, cumin and salt in **CROCK-POT®** slow cooker; mix well. Cover; cook on LOW 8 to 10 hours or on HIGH 4 to 5 hours.

2. Stir in oregano just before serving.

Makes 8 servings

White Chicken Chili

8 ounces dried navy beans, rinsed and sorted

1 tablespoon vegetable oil

2 pounds boneless, skinless chicken breasts (about 4)

2 onions, chopped

1 tablespoon minced garlic

2 teaspoons ground cumin

2 teaspoons salt

1 teaspoon dried oregano

¼ teaspoon black pepper

¼ teaspoon ground red pepper (optional)

4 cups chicken broth

1 can (4 ounces) fire-roasted diced mild green chiles, rinsed and drained

¼ cup chopped fresh cilantro

Tortilla chips (optional)

Lime wedges (optional)

1. Place beans on bottom of **CROCK-POT**® slow cooker. Heat oil in large skillet over medium-high heat. Add chicken; cook 8 minutes or until browned on all sides. Remove to **CROCK-POT**® slow cooker.

2. Heat same skillet over medium heat. Add onions; cook 6 minutes or until softened and lightly browned. Add garlic, cumin, salt, oregano, black pepper and ground red pepper, if desired; cook and stir 1 minute. Add broth and chiles; bring to a simmer, stirring to scrape up any browned bits from bottom of skillet. Remove onion mixture to **CROCK-POT**® slow cooker.

3. Cover; cook on LOW 5 hours. Remove chicken to large cutting board; shred with two forks. Return chicken to **CROCK-POT**® slow cooker. Stir in cilantro. Serve with tortilla chips and lime wedges, if desired.

Makes 6 to 8 servings

Simple Beef Chili

3 pounds ground beef

2 cans (about 14 ounces *each*) unsalted diced tomatoes

2 cans (about 15 ounces *each*) kidney beans, rinsed and drained

2 cups chopped onions

1 package (10 ounces) frozen corn

1 cup chopped green bell pepper

1 can (8 ounces) tomato sauce

3 tablespoons chili powder

1 teaspoon garlic powder

½ teaspoon ground cumin

½ teaspoon dried oregano

Prepared cornbread (optional)

1. Brown beef in large skillet over medium-high heat 6 to 8 minutes, stirring to break up meat. Remove to **CROCK-POT®** slow cooker using slotted spoon.

2. Add tomatoes, beans, onions, corn, bell pepper, tomato sauce, chili powder, garlic powder, cumin and oregano to **CROCK-POT®** slow cooker. Cover; cook on LOW 4 hours. Serve with cornbread, if desired.

Makes 8 servings

Tip: The flavor and aroma of crushed or ground herbs and spices may lessen during a longer cooking time. So, when slow cooking in your **CROCK-POT®** slow cooker, be sure to taste and adjust seasonings, if necessary, before serving.

Kick'n Chili

2 pounds ground beef

2 cloves garlic, minced

1 tablespoon *each* salt, ground cumin, chili powder, paprika, dried oregano and black pepper

2 teaspoons red pepper flakes

¼ teaspoon ground red pepper

1 tablespoon vegetable oil

3 cans (about 14 ounces *each*) diced tomatoes with mild green chiles

1 jar (16 ounces) salsa

1 onion, chopped

1. Combine beef, garlic, salt, cumin, chili powder, paprika, oregano, black pepper, red pepper flakes and ground red pepper in large bowl.

2. Heat oil in large skillet over medium-high heat. Brown beef 6 to 8 minutes, stirring to break up meat. Drain fat. Add tomatoes, salsa and onion; mix well. Remove to **CROCK-POT**® slow cooker. Cover; cook on LOW 4 to 6 hours.

Makes 6 servings

Tip: This chunky chili is perfect for the spicy food lover in your family. Reduce the red pepper flakes for a milder flavor.

Dynamite Chili

½ pound ground beef

Salt and black pepper

2 cans (about 14 ounces *each*) Italian-style stewed tomatoes

1 can (about 15 ounces) light red kidney beans, rinsed and drained

1 can (about 15 ounces) dark red kidney beans, rinsed and drained

1½ cups water

1 large onion, thinly sliced

½ cup chopped red bell pepper

½ cup chopped yellow bell pepper

2 cloves garlic, minced

2 tablespoons ground chili powder

1 tablespoon dried parsley flakes

1 tablespoon ground coriander

1 tablespoon ground cumin

1 teaspoon red pepper flakes

Optional toppings: diced green onions, sour cream and shredded Cheddar cheese

1. Season beef with salt and black pepper. Brown beef in large skillet over medium-high heat 6 to 8 minutes, stirring to break up meat. Drain fat.

2. Add beef, tomatoes, beans, water, onion, bell peppers, garlic, chili powder, parsley flakes, coriander, cumin and red pepper flakes to **CROCK-POT**® slow cooker. Cover; cook on LOW 4 to 6 hours or on HIGH 2 to 3 hours.

Makes 6 servings

Chili with Turkey and Beans

2 cans (about 15 ounces *each*) red kidney beans, rinsed and drained

2 cans (about 14 ounces *each*) whole tomatoes, drained

1 pound cooked ground turkey

1 can (about 15 ounces) black beans, rinsed and drained

1 can (12 ounces) tomato sauce

1 cup finely chopped onion

1 cup finely chopped celery

1 cup finely chopped carrot

½ cup amaretto (optional)

3 tablespoons chili powder

1 tablespoon Worcestershire sauce

4 teaspoons ground cumin

2 teaspoons ground red pepper

1 teaspoon salt

    Shredded Cheddar cheese (optional)

Combine kidney beans, whole tomatoes, turkey, black beans, tomato sauce, onion, celery, carrot, amaretto, if desired, chili powder, Worcestershire sauce, cumin, ground red pepper and salt in **CROCK-POT**® slow cooker. Cover; cook on HIGH 7 hours. Top with cheese, if desired.

Makes 4 servings

PLEASING PORK

German Kraut and Sausage

5 medium potatoes, cut into ½-inch pieces

1 large yellow onion, cut into ¼-inch slices

½ green bell pepper, chopped

1 can (16 ounces) sauerkraut

1 pound smoked sausage, cut into 1-inch pieces

¼ cup packed brown sugar

1 teaspoon garlic powder

½ teaspoon black pepper

1. Layer potatoes, onion, bell pepper and sauerkraut in **CROCK-POT**® slow cooker. Brown sausage in large skillet over medium-high heat. Remove to **CROCK-POT**® slow cooker using slotted spoon.

2. Combine brown sugar, garlic powder and black pepper in small bowl; stir to combine. Sprinkle evenly over sausage. Cover; cook on LOW 8 hours.

Makes 8 servings

Mexican Carnitas

2 pounds boneless pork shoulder roast

1 tablespoon garlic salt

1 tablespoon black pepper

1½ teaspoons adobo seasoning

1 medium onion, chopped

1 can (16 ounces) green salsa

½ cup water

¼ cup chopped fresh cilantro

Juice of 2 medium limes

3 cloves garlic, minced

4 (6-inch) flour tortillas, warmed

Optional toppings: chopped green bell pepper, tomatoes and red onion

1. Coat inside of **CROCK-POT®** slow cooker with nonstick cooking spray. Season pork with garlic salt, black pepper and adobo seasoning.

2. Place pork, onion, salsa, water, cilantro, lime juice and garlic in **CROCK-POT®** slow cooker. Cover; cook on LOW 4 to 5 hours. Serve in tortillas with desired toppings.

Makes 4 servings

Couscous Stuffed Bell Peppers

4 medium assorted color bell peppers

1¼ cups water, divided

½ teaspoon salt

⅔ cup uncooked couscous

8 ounces Mexican chorizo sausage, casings removed, cooked and crumbled

1 cup shredded sharp Cheddar cheese, plus additional for garnish

1 cup prepared corn and black bean salsa, divided

1. Cut top ¼ off each bell pepper. Remove and discard seeds. Finely dice tops of each pepper. Add diced peppers, ¾ cup water and salt to small saucepan; bring to a boil over high heat. Add couscous; cover and remove from heat. Let stand 5 minutes.

2. Remove couscous to large bowl. Add chorizo, 1 cup cheese and ½ cup salsa; mix well. Divide couscous mixture evenly among peppers.

3. Place ½ cup water in **CROCK-POT®** slow cooker. Place filled peppers in bottom, filling side up. Cover; cook on LOW 4 to 5 hours until filling is cooked and peppers are tender. Serve peppers topped with remaining ½ cup salsa and additional cheese.

Makes 4 servings

Pork Tenderloin with Cabbage

3 cups shredded red cabbage

¼ cup chopped onion

¼ cup chicken broth

1 clove garlic, minced

1½ pounds pork tenderloin

¾ cup apple juice concentrate

3 tablespoons honey mustard

1½ tablespoons Worcestershire sauce

1. Add cabbage, onion, broth and garlic to **CROCK-POT®** slow cooker. Place pork over cabbage mixture. Combine apple juice concentrate, mustard and Worcestershire sauce in small bowl; stir to blend. Pour over pork. Cover; cook on LOW 6 to 8 hours or on HIGH 3 to 4 hours.

2. Remove pork to cutting board; cover loosely with foil. Let stand 10 to 15 minutes before slicing. Serve pork with cabbage and cooking liquid.

Makes 6 servings

Maple-Dry Rubbed Ribs

2 teaspoons chili powder, divided	3 tablespoons maple syrup, divided
1 teaspoon ground coriander	1 can (about 8 ounces) tomato sauce
1 teaspoon garlic powder, divided	¼ teaspoon ground cinnamon
½ teaspoon salt	¼ teaspoon ground ginger
¼ teaspoon black pepper	
3 to 3½ pounds pork baby back ribs, trimmed and cut in half	

1. Coat inside of **CROCK-POT®** slow cooker with nonstick cooking spray. Combine 1 teaspoon chili powder, coriander, ½ teaspoon garlic powder, salt and pepper in small bowl; stir to blend. Brush ribs with 1 tablespoon syrup; rub with spice mixture. Remove ribs to **CROCK-POT®** slow cooker.

2. Combine tomato sauce, remaining 1 teaspoon chili powder, remaining ½ teaspoon garlic powder, remaining 2 tablespoons syrup, cinnamon and ginger in medium bowl; stir to blend. Pour tomato sauce mixture over ribs in **CROCK-POT®** slow cooker. Cover; cook on LOW 8 to 9 hours.

3. Remove ribs to large serving platter; cover with foil to keep warm. If desired, remove sauce from **CROCK-POT®** slow cooker to large skillet. Bring to a boil over medium-high heat. Cook 8 to 9 minutes or until sauce is thickened. Brush ribs with sauce and serve any remaining sauce on the side.

Makes 4 servings

Pork Loin with Sherry and Red Onions

2½ **pounds boneless pork loin, tied**

½ **teaspoon salt**

½ **teaspoon black pepper**

2 **tablespoons unsalted butter**

3 **large red onions, thinly sliced**

1 **cup pearl onions, blanched and peeled**

½ **cup dry sherry**

2 **tablespoons chopped fresh Italian parsley**

2 **tablespoons water**

1½ **tablespoons cornstarch**

1. Rub pork with salt and pepper. Place pork in **CROCK-POT**® slow cooker. Melt butter in medium skillet over medium heat. Add red and pearl onions; cook and stir 5 to 7 minutes or until softened.

2. Add onion mixture, sherry and parsley to **CROCK-POT**® slow cooker over pork. Cover; cook on LOW 8 to 10 hours or on HIGH 4 to 5 hours.

3. Remove pork to cutting board; cover loosely with foil. Let stand 10 to 15 minutes before slicing.

4. Stir water into cornstarch in small bowl until smooth; whisk into cooking liquid. Cover; cook on HIGH 15 minutes or until thickened. Serve pork with onions and sherry sauce.

Makes 8 servings

Note: The mild flavor of pork is awakened by this rich, delectable sauce.

Tip: Double all ingredients except for the sherry, cornstarch and water if using a 5-, 6- or 7-quart **CROCK-POT**® slow cooker.

Pineapple and Pork Teriyaki

Nonstick cooking spray

2 (1¼ pounds *each*) pork tenderloins

1 (8-ounce) can pineapple chunks

½ cup teriyaki sauce

3 tablespoons honey

1 tablespoon minced fresh ginger

1. Spray large skillet with nonstick cooking spray; heat over medium-high heat. Add pork; cook 8 minutes or until browned on all sides. Remove to oval-shaped **CROCK-POT®** slow cooker.

2. Combine pineapple, teriyaki sauce, honey and ginger in large bowl; stir to blend. Pour over pork. Cover; cook on LOW 6 to 7 hours or on HIGH 3 to 4 hours. Remove to large cutting board. Let stand 15 minutes before slicing.

3. Cover; cook on HIGH 10 to 15 minutes or until sauce is thickened. Serve sliced pork with pineapple and cooking liquid.

Makes 6 to 8 servings

Ham and Potato Hash

1½ pounds red potatoes, sliced

8 ounces thinly sliced ham

2 poblano peppers, cut into thin strips

2 tablespoons olive oil

1 tablespoon dried oregano

¼ teaspoon salt

1 cup (4 ounces) shredded Monterey Jack or pepper jack cheese

2 tablespoons finely chopped fresh cilantro

1. Combine potatoes, ham, poblano peppers, oil and oregano in **CROCK-POT®** slow cooker; stir to blend. Cover; cook on LOW 7 hours or on HIGH 4 hours.

2. Remove mixture to large serving platter; sprinkle with cheese and cilantro. Let stand 3 minutes or until cheese is melted.

Makes 6 to 7 servings

Sausage and Peppers over Polenta

1 to 1½ pounds Italian sausage

2 bell peppers, sliced

1 medium onion, sliced

1 can (about 14 ounces) diced tomatoes with basil, oregano and garlic

1 tube (18 ounces) prepared polenta, cut into ½-inch-thick slices

Salt (optional)

1. Heat large skillet over medium heat. Add sausage; cook 8 minutes or until browned. Cut sausage into 1-inch pieces; add to **CROCK-POT®** slow cooker. Stir in peppers, onion and tomatoes. Cover; cook on LOW 5½ to 6 hours until vegetables are tender.

2. Preheat broiler. Spray large baking sheet with nonstick cooking spray.

3. Place polenta on prepared baking sheet. Broil 2 to 3 minutes on each side or until heated through and lightly browned. Serve polenta topped with sausage mixture.

Makes 4 servings

Holiday Ham

1 bone-in cooked ham (about 5 to 7 pounds), trimmed

16 whole cloves

1 cup water

1½ teaspoons vegetable oil

1 shallot, chopped

1 jar (12 ounces) cherry preserves or currant jelly

¾ cup dried orange-flavored cranberries or raisins

½ cup packed brown sugar

½ cup orange juice

½ teaspoon dry mustard

1. Score ham. Place 1 clove in center of each diamond. Pour water into **CROCK-POT**® slow cooker; add ham. Cover; cook on LOW 5 to 6 hours or on HIGH 2½ to 3 hours or until ham is heated through.

2. Heat oil in small saucepan over medium-high heat. Add shallot; cook and stir 2 to 3 minutes or until translucent. Stir in preserves, cranberries, brown sugar, orange juice and dry mustard. Reduce heat to medium; cook until sugar is dissolved.

3. Remove ham from **CROCK-POT**® slow cooker; drain liquid. Place ham back into **CROCK-POT**® slow cooker; pour preserve mixture over ham. Cover; cook on HIGH 10 to 20 minutes or until fruit plumps.

Makes 12 to 14 servings

Pulled Pork with Honey-Chipotle Barbecue Sauce

1 tablespoon chili powder, divided

1 teaspoon ground chipotle chili, divided

1 teaspoon ground cumin, divided

1 teaspoon garlic powder, divided

1 teaspoon salt

1 bone-in pork shoulder roast (3½ pounds), trimmed*

1 can (15 ounces) tomato sauce

5 tablespoons honey, divided

Unless you have a 5-, 6- or 7-quart CROCK-POT® slow cooker, cut any roast larger than 2½ pounds in half so it cooks completely.

1. Coat inside of **CROCK-POT®** slow cooker with nonstick cooking spray. Combine 1 teaspoon chili powder, ½ teaspoon chipotle chili, ½ teaspoon cumin, ½ teaspoon garlic powder and salt in small bowl. Rub pork with chili powder mixture. Place pork in **CROCK-POT®** slow cooker.

2. Combine tomato sauce, 4 tablespoons honey, remaining 2 teaspoons chili powder, ½ teaspoon chipotle chili, ½ teaspoon cumin and ½ teaspoon garlic powder in large bowl. Pour tomato mixture over pork in **CROCK-POT®** slow cooker. Cover; cook on LOW 8 hours.

3. Remove pork to large bowl. Turn **CROCK-POT®** slow cooker to HIGH. Cover; cook on HIGH 30 minutes or until thickened. Stir in remaining 1 tablespoon honey.

4. Remove bone from pork and discard. Shred pork using two forks. Stir shredded pork back into **CROCK-POT®** slow cooker to coat well with sauce.

Makes 8 servings

Pork Roast with Fruit Medley

1 cup water

½ cup salt

2 tablespoons sugar

1 teaspoon dried thyme

2 whole bay leaves

1 boneless pork roast (about 4 pounds), trimmed*

Olive oil

2 cups green grapes

1 cup dried apricots

1 cup dried prunes

1 cup dry red wine

2 cloves garlic, minced

Juice of ½ lemon

*Unless you have a 5-, 6- or 7-quart CROCK-POT® slow cooker, cut any roast larger than 2½ pounds in half so it cooks completely.

1. Combine water, salt, sugar, thyme and bay leaves in large resealable food storage bag; add roast. Marinate overnight or up to 2 days in refrigerator, turning occasionally.

2. Remove roast from marinade; lightly pat dry. Heat oil in large skillet over medium heat. Add roast; cook 5 to 10 minutes or until browned on all sides. Remove to **CROCK-POT®** slow cooker.

3. Add grapes, apricots, prunes, wine, garlic and lemon juice; stir to blend. Cover; cook on LOW 7 to 9 hours or on HIGH 3 to 5 hours.

Makes 6 to 8 servings

Chinese Barbecue Pork Ribs

2½ pounds pork baby back ribs, cut in half

½ cup orange marmalade

½ cup barbecue sauce

¼ cup soy sauce

1 teaspoon prepared horseradish

1 tablespoon Dijon mustard

1 teaspoon minced garlic

½ teaspoon salt

1 tablespoon water

1 tablespoon cornstarch

1. Coat inside of **CROCK-POT®** slow cooker with nonstick cooking spray. Place ribs, marmalade, barbecue sauce, soy sauce, horseradish, mustard, garlic and salt in **CROCK-POT®** slow cooker. Cover; cook on LOW 6 hours.

2. Remove ribs to serving platter; keep warm. Turn **CROCK-POT®** slow cooker to HIGH. Stir water into cornstarch in small bowl until smooth. Whisk into **CROCK-POT®** slow cooker. Cover; cook on HIGH 15 minutes or until thickened. Serve ribs with sauce.

Makes 4 servings

Knockwurst and Cabbage

Olive oil

8 to 10 knockwurst sausage links

1 head red cabbage, cut into ¼-inch slices

½ cup thinly sliced white onion

2 teaspoons caraway seeds

1 teaspoon salt

4 cups chicken broth

Chopped fresh Italian parsley (optional)

1. Heat oil in large skillet over medium heat. Cook sausages 5 to 7 minutes until browned on all sides. Remove to **CROCK-POT®** slow cooker.

2. Add cabbage and onion to **CROCK-POT®** slow cooker. Sprinkle with caraway seeds and salt. Add broth. Cover; cook on LOW 4 hours or on HIGH 2 hours. Garnish with parsley.

Makes 8 servings

Gingered Sherry Pork Roast

2 tablespoons extra virgin olive oil

1 clove garlic, chopped

1 boneless pork loin roast (about 2½ pounds)

12 baby red potatoes

12 baby carrots

6 petite onions

1 cup dry sherry

3 tablespoons hoisin sauce

1 tablespoon soy sauce

2 teaspoons grated fresh ginger

¼ teaspoon black pepper

2 tablespoons chopped fresh chives

1. Heat oil in large skillet over medium-high heat. Add garlic; cook and stir 30 seconds. Remove garlic with slotted spoon. Add pork roast; brown about 3 to 4 minutes per side. Remove roast; set aside.

2. Place potatoes, carrots and onions in **CROCK-POT®** slow cooker. Place roast on top of vegetables. Combine sherry, hoisin sauce, soy sauce, ginger and pepper in small bowl. Pour over roast in **CROCK-POT®** slow cooker. Cover; cook on LOW 6 to 8 hours or on HIGH 4 to 5 hours. Baste occasionally with sherry sauce.

3. Remove roast to cutting board. Cover loosely with foil; let stand 10 to 15 minutes. Slice and return roast to **CROCK-POT®** slow cooker. Serve pork with vegetables and sauce. Garnish with chives.

Makes 4 servings

Simply Delicious Pork Roast

1½ pounds boneless pork loin, cut into 6 pieces *or* 6 boneless pork loin chops

4 medium Golden Delicious apples, cored and sliced

3 tablespoons packed light brown sugar

1 teaspoon ground cinnamon

½ teaspoon salt

1. Place pork in **CROCK-POT®** slow cooker; cover with apples.

2. Combine brown sugar, cinnamon and salt in small bowl; sprinkle over apples. Cover; cook on LOW 6 to 8 hours.

Makes 6 servings

Andouille and Cabbage Crock

Nonstick cooking spray

1 pound andouille sausage, cut evenly into
   3- to 4-inch pieces

1 small head cabbage, cut evenly into 8 wedges

1 medium onion, cut into ½-inch wedges

3 medium carrots, quartered lengthwise and
   cut into 3-inch pieces

8 new potatoes, cut in half

½ cup apple juice

1 can (about 14 ounces) chicken broth

   Honey mustard (optional)

   Crusty rolls (optional)

1. Coat inside of **CROCK-POT®** slow cooker with cooking spray. Spray large skillet with cooking spray; heat over medium-high heat. Add sausage; cook and stir 6 to 8 minutes or until browned. Remove from heat.

2. Add cabbage, onion, carrots, potatoes, apple juice and broth to **CROCK-POT®** slow cooker; top with sausage. Cover; cook on HIGH 4 hours. Remove with slotted spoon to large serving bowl. Serve with honey mustard and crusty rolls, if desired.

Makes 8 servings

Tip: Andouille is a spicy, smoked pork sausage. Feel free to substitute your favorite smoked sausage or kielbasa.

Vegetable-Stuffed Pork Chops

4 bone-in pork chops	½ cup Italian-style seasoned dry bread crumbs
Salt and black pepper	1 small onion, chopped
1 cup frozen corn	½ cup uncooked converted long grain rice
1 medium green bell pepper, chopped	1 can (8 ounces) tomato sauce

1. Cut pocket into each pork chop, cutting from edge to bone. Lightly season pockets with salt and pepper. Combine corn, bell pepper, bread crumbs, onion and rice in large bowl; stir to blend. Stuff pork chops with rice mixture. Secure open side with toothpicks.

2. Place any remaining rice mixture in **CROCK-POT**® slow cooker. Add stuffed pork chops to **CROCK-POT**® slow cooker. Pour tomato sauce over pork chops. Cover; cook on LOW 8 to 10 hours.

3. Remove pork chops to large serving platter. Remove and discard toothpicks. Serve with extra rice mixture.

Makes 4 servings

Tip: Your butcher can cut a pocket in the pork chops to save you time and to ensure even cooking.

Mango Ginger Pork Roast

1 pork shoulder roast (about 4 pounds)*

½ to 1 teaspoon ground ginger

Salt and black pepper

2 cups mango salsa

2 tablespoons honey

¼ cup apricot preserves

Hot cooked rice

*Unless you have a 5-, 6- or 7-quart CROCK-POT® slow cooker, cut any roast larger than 2½ pounds in half so it cooks completely.

1. Season roast with ginger, salt and pepper. Remove to **CROCK-POT®** slow cooker.

2. Combine salsa, honey and preserves in medium bowl. Pour over roast. Cover; cook on LOW 6 to 8 hours. Turn **CROCK-POT®** slow cooker to HIGH. Cover; cook on HIGH 3 to 4 hours or until roast is tender. Serve with rice.

Makes 4 to 6 servings

Kielbasa and Cabbage

2 pounds kielbasa, cut into ¾-inch-thick pieces

2 pounds small red potatoes, quartered

1 pound cabbage, shredded

1 large onion, coarsely chopped

¼ cup chicken broth

4 cloves garlic, minced

2 teaspoons fennel seed

1 teaspoon caraway seeds

¼ teaspoon black pepper

Place kielbasa, potatoes, cabbage, onion, broth, garlic, fennel seed, caraway seeds and pepper in **CROCK-POT®** slow cooker. Cover; cook on HIGH 4 to 5 hours or until potatoes are fork-tender and cabbage is crisp-tender.

Makes 6 servings

Saucy Pork Loin and Potatoes

1 tablespoon olive oil

1 pork tenderloin (2 pounds)

½ cup chicken broth

3 tablespoons cornstarch

½ cup packed brown sugar

⅓ cup soy sauce

¼ cup lemon juice

¼ cup dry white wine

2 cloves garlic, minced

1 tablespoon mustard

1 tablespoon Worcestershire sauce

3 cups potatoes, cut into wedges

Chopped fresh Italian parsley (optional)

1. Heat oil in large skillet over medium-high heat. Brown pork tenderloin 4 to 6 minutes on each side. Stir broth into cornstarch in small bowl until smooth. Place pork, broth mixture, brown sugar, soy sauce, lemon juice, wine, garlic, mustard and Worcestershire sauce in **CROCK-POT**® slow cooker. Cover; cook on LOW 4 hours.

2. Stir potatoes into **CROCK-POT**® slow cooker; turn tenderloin. Cover; cook on LOW 2 hours. Garnish with parsley.

Makes 6 servings

Pork Roast Landaise

1 boneless center-cut pork loin roast (2½ pounds)

Salt and black pepper (optional)

2 tablespoons olive oil

1 medium yellow onion, diced

2 cloves garlic, minced

2 teaspoons dried thyme

2 parsnips, cut into ¾-inch slices

¼ cup red wine vinegar

¼ cup sugar

2 cups chicken broth, divided

2 tablespoons cornstarch

3 pears, cored and sliced ¾ inch thick

1 cup pitted prunes

1. Season pork with salt and pepper, if desired. Heat oil in large skillet over medium-high heat. Add pork; cook 5 to 7 minutes on each side until browned. Remove to **CROCK-POT®** slow cooker using slotted spoon.

2. Add onion and garlic to skillet; cook and stir 2 to 3 minutes. Stir in thyme. Remove to **CROCK-POT®** slow cooker. Add parsnips; stir well.

3. Combine vinegar and sugar in same skillet; cook and stir 5 to 7 minutes or until thickened. Add 1¾ cups broth. Stir remaining ¼ cup of broth into cornstarch in small bowl until smooth. Whisk cornstarch mixture into skillet; cook until slightly thickened. Pour into **CROCK-POT®** slow cooker.

4. Cover; cook on LOW 8 hours or on HIGH 4 hours. Add pears and prunes during last 30 minutes of cooking. Remove roast to cutting board. Cut roast evenly into eight pieces.

Makes 8 servings

Simple Shredded Pork Tacos

1 boneless pork roast (2 pounds)

1 cup salsa

1 can (4 ounces) chopped mild green chiles

½ teaspoon garlic salt

½ teaspoon black pepper

Flour or corn tortillas

Optional toppings: salsa, sour cream, diced tomatoes, shredded cheese, shredded lettuce

1. Place roast, 1 cup salsa, chiles, garlic salt and pepper in **CROCK-POT®** slow cooker. Cover; cook on LOW 8 hours or until meat is tender.

2. Remove pork to large cutting board; shred with two forks. Serve on tortillas with sauce and desired toppings.

Makes 6 servings

Tip: Cut the pork roast to fit in the bottom of your **CROCK-POT®** slow cooker in one or two layers.

Polska Kielbasa with Beer & Onions

1 can (18 ounces) brown
   ale or beer

2 kielbasa sausages
   (16 ounces *each*), cut
   into 4-inch pieces

2 onions, quartered

⅓ cup packed dark brown
   sugar

⅓ cup honey mustard

Combine ale, sausages,
onions, brown sugar
and honey mustard in
CROCK-POT® slow cooker;
stir to blend. Cover; cook on
LOW 4 to 5 hours.

Makes 6 to 8 servings

Harvest Ham Supper

6 carrots, cut into 2-inch pieces

3 medium sweet potatoes, quartered

1 to 1½ pounds boneless ham

1 cup maple syrup

1. Arrange carrots and sweet potatoes in bottom of **CROCK-POT**® slow cooker.

2. Place ham on top of vegetables. Pour syrup over ham and vegetables. Cover; cook on LOW 6 to 8 hours.

Makes 6 servings

Big Al's Hot and Sweet Sausage Sandwiches

4 to 5 pounds hot Italian sausage links

1 jar (26 ounces) pasta sauce

1 large Vidalia onion (or other sweet onion), sliced

1 green bell pepper, sliced

1 red bell pepper, sliced

¼ cup packed dark brown sugar

Italian rolls, cut in half

Provolone cheese, sliced (optional)

1. Combine sausages, pasta sauce, onion, bell peppers and brown sugar in **CROCK-POT®** slow cooker. Cover; cook on LOW 8 to 10 hours or on HIGH 4 to 6 hours.

2. Place sausages on rolls. Top with vegetable mixture. Add provolone cheese, if desired.

Makes 8 to 10 servings

Cuban Pork Sandwiches

1 pork loin roast (about 2 pounds)
½ cup orange juice
2 tablespoons lime juice
1 tablespoon minced garlic
1½ teaspoons salt
½ teaspoon red pepper flakes

2 tablespoons yellow mustard
8 crusty bread rolls, split in half (6 inches *each*)
8 slices Swiss cheese
8 thin ham slices
4 small dill pickles, thinly sliced lengthwise
  Nonstick cooking spray

1. Coat inside of **CROCK-POT**® slow cooker with nonstick cooking spray. Add pork loin.

2. Combine orange juice, lime juice, garlic, salt and red pepper flakes in small bowl. Pour over pork. Cover; cook on LOW 7 to 8 hours or on HIGH 3½ to 4 hours. Remove pork to cutting board. Cover loosely with foil; let stand 10 to 15 minutes before slicing.

3. To serve, spread mustard on both sides of rolls. Divide pork slices among roll bottoms. Top with Swiss cheese slice, ham slice and pickle slices; cover with top of roll.

4. Coat large skillet with nonstick cooking spray; heat over medium heat. Working in batches, arrange sandwiches in skillet. Cover with foil and top with dinner plate to press down sandwiches. (If necessary, weigh down with 2 to 3 cans to compress sandwiches lightly.) Heat about 8 minutes or until cheese is slightly melted.*

Or use table top grill to compress and heat sandwiches.

Makes 8 servings

Shredded Apricot Pork Sandwiches

2 onions, thinly sliced

1 cup apricot preserves

½ cup packed dark brown sugar

½ cup barbecue sauce

¼ cup cider vinegar

2 tablespoons Worcestershire sauce

½ teaspoon red pepper flakes

1 boneless pork top loin roast (4 pounds)*

¼ cup water

2 tablespoons cornstarch

1 tablespoon grated fresh ginger

1 teaspoon salt

1 teaspoon black pepper

10 to 12 sesame or onion rolls, toasted

Unless you have a 5-, 6-, or 7-quart CROCK-POT® slow cooker, cut any roast larger than 2½ pounds in half so it cooks completely.

1. Combine onions, preserves, brown sugar, barbecue sauce, vinegar, Worcestershire sauce and red pepper flakes in large bowl. Place pork in **CROCK-POT®** slow cooker. Pour apricot mixture over top. Cover; cook on LOW 8 to 9 hours.

2. Remove pork to cutting board; cool slightly. Shred pork with two forks. Skim fat from sauce in **CROCK-POT®** slow cooker.

3. Stir water into cornstarch in small bowl until smooth. Stir in ginger, salt and black pepper. Whisk cornstarch mixture into sauce. Turn **CROCK-POT®** slow cooker to HIGH. Cook, uncovered, on HIGH 15 to 30 minutes or until thickened. Return pork to **CROCK-POT®** slow cooker; mix well. Serve on rolls.

Makes 10 to 12 sandwiches

Sauerkraut Pork Ribs

1 **tablespoon vegetable oil**	¼ **to ½ teaspoon black pepper**
3 **to 4 pounds pork country-style ribs**	¾ **cup water**
1 **large onion, thinly sliced**	2 **jars (about 28 ounces *each*) sauerkraut**
1 **teaspoon caraway seeds**	12 **medium red potatoes, quartered**
½ **teaspoon garlic powder**	

1. Heat oil in large skillet over medium-low heat. Brown ribs on all sides. Remove to **CROCK-POT®** slow cooker using slotted spoon.

2. Add onion to skillet; cook until tender. Add caraway seeds, garlic powder and pepper; cook 15 minutes. Remove onion mixture to **CROCK-POT®** slow cooker.

3. Add water to skillet, stirring to scrape up brown bits. Pour pan juices into **CROCK-POT®** slow cooker. Partially drain sauerkraut, leaving some liquid; pour over meat. Top with potatoes. Cover; cook on LOW 6 to 8 hours or until potatoes are tender, stirring once during cooking.

Makes 12 servings

Scalloped Potatoes and Ham

6 large russet potatoes, sliced into ¼-inch rounds

1 ham steak (about 1½ pounds), cut into cubes

1 can (10½ ounces) condensed cream of mushroom soup, undiluted

1 soup can water

1 cup (4 ounces) shredded Cheddar cheese

1. Coat inside of **CROCK-POT**® slow cooker with nonstick cooking spray. Arrange potatoes and ham in layers in **CROCK-POT**® slow cooker.

2. Combine soup, water and cheese in medium bowl; pour over potatoes and ham. Cover; cook on HIGH 3½ hours or until potatoes are tender. Turn **CROCK-POT**® slow cooker to LOW. Cover; cook on LOW 1 hour.

Makes 5 to 6 servings

Sweet and Spicy Pork Picadillo

1 tablespoon olive oil

1 yellow onion, cut into ¼-inch pieces

2 cloves garlic, minced

1 pound boneless pork country-style ribs, trimmed and cut into 1-inch cubes

1 can (about 14 ounces) diced tomatoes

3 tablespoons cider vinegar

2 canned chipotle peppers in adobo sauce, chopped*

½ cup raisins, chopped

½ teaspoon ground cumin

½ teaspoon ground cinnamon

Hot cooked rice (optional)

Black beans (optional)

You may substitute dried chipotles, soaked in warm water about 20 minutes to soften before chopping.

1. Heat oil in large skillet over medium-low heat. Add onion and garlic; cook and stir 4 minutes. Add pork; cook and stir 5 to 7 minutes or until browned. Remove to **CROCK-POT**® slow cooker.

2. Combine tomatoes, vinegar, chipotle peppers, raisins, cumin and cinnamon in medium bowl. Pour over pork in **CROCK-POT**® slow cooker. Cover; cook on LOW 5 hours or on HIGH 3 hours. Remove pork to cutting board; shred with two forks. Serve with rice and beans, if desired.

Makes 4 servings

Honey Ribs

1 can (about 14 ounces) beef broth

½ cup water

3 tablespoons soy sauce

2 tablespoons honey

2 tablespoons maple syrup

2 tablespoons barbecue sauce

½ teaspoon dry mustard

2 pounds pork baby back ribs, trimmed and cut into 3- to 4-rib portions

Hot cooked corn (optional)

1. Combine broth, water, soy sauce, honey, syrup, barbecue sauce and dry mustard in **CROCK-POT®** slow cooker; stir to blend. Add ribs.

2. Cover; cook on LOW 6 to 8 hours or on HIGH 4 to 6 hours. Serve with sauce and corn, if desired.

Makes 4 servings

Pizza-Style Mostaccioli

1 jar (24 to 26 ounces) marinara sauce or tomato basil pasta sauce

½ cup water

2 cups (6 ounces) uncooked mostaccioli pasta

1 package (8 ounces) sliced mushrooms

1 small yellow or green bell pepper, finely diced

½ cup (1 ounce) sliced pepperoni, halved

1 teaspoon dried oregano

¼ teaspoon red pepper flakes

1 cup (4 ounces) shredded pizza cheese blend or Italian cheese blend

Chopped fresh oregano (optional)

Garlic bread (optional)

1. Coat inside of **CROCK-POT®** slow cooker with nonstick cooking spray. Combine marinara sauce and water in **CROCK-POT®** slow cooker. Stir in pasta, mushrooms, bell pepper, pepperoni, dried oregano and red pepper flakes; mix well. Cover; cook on LOW 2 hours or on HIGH 1 hour.

2. Stir well. Cover; cook on LOW 1½ to 2 hours or on HIGH 45 minutes to 1 hour or until pasta and vegetables are tender. Spoon into shallow bowls. Top with cheese and garnish with fresh oregano. Serve with bread, if desired.

Makes 4 servings

Tip: To prevent the pasta from becoming overcooked on the bottom of the **CROCK-POT®** slow cooker, stir it halfway through cooking time.

Southern Smothered Pork Chops

8 pounds pork chops
Salt and black pepper
2 tablespoons vegetable oil
3 cups water
1 can (10½ ounces) cream of mushroom soup
1 large onion, chopped

5 cloves garlic, chopped
2 tablespoons Italian seasoning
1 package (about ½ ounce) pork gravy mix
1 package (about 1 ounce) mushroom and onion soup mix
Corn on the cob (optional)

1. Season pork with salt and pepper. Heat oil in large skillet over medium-high heat. Add pork; brown 3 to 4 minutes on each side.

2. Place pork, water, soup, onion, garlic, Italian seasoning, gravy mix and dry soup mix in **CROCK-POT**® slow cooker. Cover; cook on LOW 5 hours. Serve with corn, if desired.

Makes 6 to 8 servings

Fall-Apart Pork Roast with Mole

⅔ cup whole almonds

⅔ cup raisins

3 tablespoons vegetable oil, divided

½ cup chopped onion

4 cloves garlic, chopped

1 boneless pork shoulder roast (2¾ pounds), well trimmed*

1 can (about 14 ounces) diced fire-roasted tomatoes or diced tomatoes

1 cup cubed bread, any variety

½ cup chicken broth

2 ounces Mexican chocolate, chopped

2 tablespoons canned chipotle peppers in adobo sauce, chopped

1 teaspoon salt

Chopped fresh cilantro (optional)

*Unless you have a 5-, 6- or 7-quart CROCK-POT® slow cooker, cut any roast larger than 2½ pounds in half so it cooks completely.

1. Heat large skillet over medium-high heat. Add almonds; cook and stir 3 to 4 minutes until fragrant. Add raisins; cook and stir 1 to 2 minutes or until raisins begin to plump. Place half of almond mixture in large bowl. Reserve remaining half for garnish.

2. Heat 1 tablespoon oil in same skillet. Add onion and garlic; cook and stir 2 minutes or until softened. Add to almond mixture; set aside.

3. Heat remaining 2 tablespoons oil in same skillet. Add pork; cook 5 to 7 minutes or until browned on all sides. Remove to **CROCK-POT®** slow cooker.

4. Add tomatoes, bread, broth, chocolate, chipotle peppers and salt to almond mixture. Add tomato mixture in batches to food processor or blender; process until smooth. Pour purée mixture over pork in **CROCK-POT®** slow cooker. Cover; cook on LOW 7 to 8 hours or on HIGH 3 to 4 hours.

5. Remove pork to large serving platter. Whisk sauce until smooth before spooning over pork. Garnish with reserved almond mixture and chopped cilantro.

Makes 6 servings

Heavenly Harvest Pork Roast

¼ cup pomegranate juice

¼ cup sugar

1 teaspoon salt

1 tablespoon garlic salt

1 tablespoon steak seasoning

1 teaspoon black pepper

1 lean pork loin roast (2¾ pounds)*

2 pears, cored, peeled and sliced thick

2 oranges with peel, sliced thick

Unless you have a 5-, 6-, or 7-quart CROCK-POT® slow cooker, cut any roast larger than 2½ pounds in half so it cooks completely.

1. Combine pomegranate juice and sugar in small saucepan; cook and stir about 2 minutes or until sugar dissolves. Pour into **CROCK-POT®** slow cooker.

2. Blend salt, garlic salt, steak seasoning and pepper in small bowl. Rub mixture over roast. Place roast in **CROCK-POT®** slow cooker. Turn roast to cover with juice mixture.

3. Top roast with pear and orange slices. Cover; cook on HIGH 6 to 8 hours or until tender. Serve with juice and fruit slices.

Makes 10 servings

Crock and Go Ham with Pineapple Glaze

1 ham (3 to 5 pounds)

10 to 12 whole cloves

1 can (8 ounces) sliced pineapple, juice reserved and divided

2 tablespoons packed brown sugar

1 jar (4 ounces) maraschino cherries plus 1 tablespoon juice, reserved and divided

1. Stud ham with cloves. Place ham in **CROCK-POT**® slow cooker.

2. Combine reserved pineapple juice, brown sugar and reserved 1 tablespoon cherry juice in medium bowl; stir until glaze forms. Pour glaze over ham in **CROCK-POT**® slow cooker. Arrange sliced pineapple and cherries over ham. Cover; cook on LOW 6 to 8 hours. Remove cloves before serving.

Makes 6 to 8 servings

Asian Noodles with Pork and Vegetables

¾ cup soy sauce

¾ cup honey

4 cloves garlic, chopped

1 tablespoon ground ginger

2½ pounds boneless pork shoulder roast, trimmed

¾ cup Asian sweet chili sauce

¼ cup water

3 tablespoons cornstarch

2 packages (16 ounces *each*) frozen mixed Asian vegetables

1 tablespoon toasted sesame oil

Hot cooked soba noodles, rice or spaghetti

1. Mix soy sauce, honey, garlic and ginger in **CROCK-POT®** slow cooker. Add pork. Cover; cook on LOW 8 to 10 hours or on HIGH 5 to 6 hours or until pork is fork-tender. Remove pork to cutting board.

2. Stir chili sauce into **CROCK-POT®** slow cooker; bring to a boil. Stir water into cornstarch in small bowl until smooth. Whisk cornstarch mixture into **CROCK-POT®** slow cooker until thickened. Meanwhile, shred pork.

3. Add vegetables and shredded pork to **CROCK-POT®** slow cooker. Cover; cook on HIGH 10 to 20 minutes. Stir in oil. Serve over soba noodles.

Makes 6 servings

SATISFYING STEWS

Chinese Chicken Stew

1 pound boneless, skinless chicken thighs, cut into 1-inch pieces

1 teaspoon Chinese five-spice powder*

½ to ¾ teaspoon red pepper flakes

1 tablespoon peanut or vegetable oil

1 large onion, coarsely chopped

1 package (8 ounces) mushrooms, sliced

2 cloves garlic, minced

1 can (about 14 ounces) chicken broth, divided

1 tablespoon cornstarch

1 large red bell pepper, cut into ¾-inch pieces

2 tablespoons soy sauce

2 large green onions, cut into ½-inch pieces

1 tablespoon sesame oil

3 cups hot cooked rice (optional)

¼ cup coarsely chopped fresh cilantro (optional)

Chinese five-spice powder is a blend of cinnamon, cloves, fennel seed, anise and Szechuan peppercorns. It is available in most supermarkets and Asian grocery stores.

1. Toss chicken with five-spice powder and red pepper flakes in large bowl. Heat peanut oil in large skillet. Add chicken and onion; cook and stir about 5 minutes or until chicken is browned. Add mushrooms and garlic; cook and stir until chicken is no longer pink.

2. Stir ¼ cup broth into cornstarch in small bowl until smooth; set aside. Place chicken mixture, remaining broth, bell pepper and soy sauce in **CROCK-POT®** slow cooker. Cover; cook on LOW 3½ hours or until peppers are tender.

3. Whisk cornstarch mixture, green onions and sesame oil into **CROCK-POT®** slow cooker. Cover; cook on LOW 30 to 45 minutes or until thickened. Ladle into soup bowls. Scoop ½ cup rice into each bowl. Sprinkle with cilantro.

Makes 6 servings

Chicken Stew with Herb Dumplings

2	cups sliced carrots	6	ounces mushrooms, halved
1	cup chopped onion	¾	cup frozen peas
1	green bell pepper, sliced	1¼	teaspoons dried basil, divided
½	cup sliced celery	1	teaspoon dried rosemary, divided
2	cans (about 14 ounces *each*) chicken broth, divided	½	teaspoon dried tarragon, divided
⅔	cup all-purpose flour	¼	cup whipping cream
1	pound boneless, skinless chicken breasts, cut into 1-inch pieces	¾	to 1 teaspoon salt
		¼	teaspoon black pepper
1	large red potato, unpeeled and cut into 1-inch pieces	1	cup biscuit baking mix
		⅓	cup milk

1. Combine carrots, onion, bell pepper, celery and all but 1 cup broth in **CROCK-POT®** slow cooker. Cover; cook on LOW 2 hours.

2. Stir remaining 1 cup broth into flour in small bowl until smooth. Stir into vegetable mixture. Add chicken, potato, mushrooms, peas, 1 teaspoon basil, ¾ teaspoon rosemary and ¼ teaspoon tarragon. Cover; cook on LOW 4 hours or until vegetables and chicken are tender. Stir in cream, salt and black pepper.

3. Combine baking mix, remaining ¼ teaspoon basil, ¼ teaspoon rosemary and ¼ teaspoon tarragon in small bowl. Stir in milk until soft dough forms. Add dumpling mixture to top of stew in four large spoonfuls. Cook on LOW, uncovered, 30 minutes. Cover; cook on LOW 30 to 45 minutes or until dumplings are firm and toothpick inserted into center comes out clean. Serve in shallow bowls.

Makes 4 servings

Hearty Meatball Stew

3 pounds ground beef or ground turkey

1 cup seasoned dry bread crumbs

4 eggs

½ cup milk

¼ cup grated Romano cheese

2 teaspoons salt

2 teaspoons garlic salt

2 teaspoons black pepper

2 tablespoons olive oil

2 cups water

2 cups beef broth

1 can (about 14 ounces) stewed tomatoes, undrained

1 can (12 ounces) tomato paste

1 cup chopped carrots

1 cup chopped onions

¼ cup chopped celery

1 tablespoon Italian seasoning

1. Combine beef, bread crumbs, eggs, milk, cheese, salt, garlic salt and pepper in large bowl. Shape into 2-inch-round meatballs. Heat oil in skillet over medium-high heat. Brown meatballs on all sides. Remove to **CROCK-POT**® slow cooker.

2. Add remaining ingredients; stir well to combine. Cover; cook on LOW 4 to 6 hours or on HIGH 2 to 4 hours.

Makes 6 to 8 servings

Hearty Lentil Stew

1 cup dried lentils, rinsed and sorted	2 teaspoons ground cumin
1 package (16 ounces) frozen green beans	¾ teaspoon ground ginger
2 cups cauliflower florets	1 can (15 ounces) chunky tomato sauce with garlic and herbs
1 cup chopped onion	½ cup dry-roasted peanuts
1 cup baby carrots, cut into halves crosswise	
3 cups vegetable broth	

1. Layer lentils, green beans, cauliflower, onion and carrots in **CROCK-POT®** slow cooker. Combine broth, cumin and ginger in large bowl; stir to blend. Pour over vegetables in **CROCK-POT®** slow cooker.

2. Cover; cook on LOW 9 to 11 hours. Stir in tomato sauce. Cover; cook on LOW 10 minutes or until heated through. Sprinkle each serving evenly with peanuts.

Makes 6 servings

Caribbean Sweet Potato and Bean Stew

2 medium sweet potatoes (about 1 pound),
   cut into 1-inch cubes

2 cups frozen cut green beans

1 can (about 15 ounces) black beans, rinsed
   and drained

1 can (about 14 ounces) vegetable broth

1 small onion, sliced

2 teaspoons Caribbean jerk seasoning

½ teaspoon dried thyme

¼ teaspoon salt

¼ teaspoon ground cinnamon

⅓ cup slivered almonds, toasted*

*To toast almonds, spread in single layer in heavy skillet.
Cook and stir over medium heat 1 to 2 minutes or until
nuts are lightly browned.

Combine sweet potatoes, beans, broth, onion, jerk seasoning, thyme, salt and cinnamon in **CROCK-POT®** slow cooker. Cover; cook on LOW 5 to 6 hours. Sprinkle each serving evenly with almonds.

Makes 4 servings

Summer Vegetable Stew

1 cup vegetable broth

1 can (about 15 ounces) chickpeas, rinsed and drained

1 medium zucchini, cut into ½-inch pieces

1 summer squash, cut into ½-inch pieces

4 large plum tomatoes, cut into ½-inch pieces

1 cup frozen corn

½ to 1 teaspoon dried rosemary

¼ cup grated Asiago or Parmesan cheese

1 tablespoon chopped fresh Italian parsley

Combine broth, chickpeas, zucchini, squash, tomatoes, corn and rosemary in **CROCK-POT**® slow cooker; stir to blend. Cover; cook on LOW 8 hours or on HIGH 5 hours. Top each serving evenly with cheese and parsley.

Makes 4 servings

Tip: Layer the ingredients in the order given to ensure they are all cooked properly.

Easy Beef Stew

1½ to 2 pounds cubed beef stew meat

  4 medium potatoes, cubed

  4 carrots, cut into 1½-inch pieces *or*
     4 cups baby carrots

  1 medium onion, cut into 8 pieces

  2 cans (8 ounces *each*) tomato sauce

  1 teaspoon salt

  ½ teaspoon black pepper

Combine beef, potatoes, carrots, onion, tomato sauce, salt and pepper in **CROCK-POT**® slow cooker. Cover; cook on LOW 8 to 10 hours or until vegetables are tender.

Makes 6 to 8 servings

Favorite Beef Stew

  3 carrots, halved and cut into 1-inch pieces

  3 stalks celery, cut into 1-inch pieces

  2 large potatoes, cut into ½-inch pieces

1½ cups chopped onions

  3 cloves garlic, chopped

4½ teaspoons Worcestershire sauce

  ¾ teaspoon dried thyme

  ¾ teaspoon dried basil

  ½ teaspoon black pepper

  1 whole bay leaf

  2 pounds cubed beef stew meat

  1 can (about 14 ounces) diced tomatoes

  1 can (about 14 ounces) beef broth

  ½ cup cold water

  ¼ cup all-purpose flour

1. Layer carrots, celery, potatoes, onions, garlic, Worcestershire sauce, thyme, basil, pepper, bay leaf, beef, tomatoes and broth in **CROCK-POT**® slow cooker. Cover; cook on LOW 8 to 9 hours.

2. Remove beef and vegetables to large serving bowl using slotted spoon. Turn **CROCK-POT**® slow cooker to HIGH. Remove and discard bay leaf. Cover and keep warm.

3. Stir water into flour in small bowl until smooth. Add ½ cup cooking liquid; mix well. Whisk flour mixture into **CROCK-POT**® slow cooker. Cover; cook on HIGH 15 minutes or until thickened. Pour sauce over beef and vegetables. Serve immediately.

Makes 8 servings

Butternut Squash, Chickpea and Lentil Stew

2 cups peeled and diced butternut squash
(½-inch pieces)

2 cups vegetable broth

1 can (about 15 ounces) chickpeas, rinsed and drained

1 can (about 14 ounces) fire-roasted diced tomatoes

1 cup chopped sweet onion

¾ cup dried brown lentils, rinsed and sorted

2 teaspoons ground cumin or coriander *or* 1 teaspoon *each*)

¾ teaspoon salt

Olive oil (optional)

Sprigs fresh thyme (optional)

Coat inside of **CROCK-POT®** slow cooker with nonstick cooking spray. Combine squash, broth, chickpeas, tomatoes, onion, lentils, cumin and salt in **CROCK-POT®** slow cooker. Cover; cook on LOW 8 to 9 hours or on HIGH 4 to 4½ hours or until squash and lentils are tender. Ladle into shallow bowls. Drizzle with oil, if desired. Garnish with thyme.

Makes 6 servings

Cajun Pork Sausage and Shrimp Stew

1 can (28 ounces) diced tomatoes

1 package (16 ounces) frozen mixed vegetables (potatoes, carrots, celery and onions)

1 package (14 to 16 ounces) kielbasa or smoked sausage, cut diagonally into ¾-inch slices

2 teaspoons Cajun seasoning

¾ pound large raw shrimp, peeled and deveined (with tails on)

2 cups (8 ounces) frozen sliced okra, thawed

Hot cooked rice

1. Coat inside of **CROCK-POT®** slow cooker with nonstick cooking spray. Combine tomatoes, vegetables, sausage and Cajun seasoning in **CROCK-POT®** slow cooker. Cover; cook on LOW 5 to 6 hours or on HIGH 2 to 2½ hours.

2. Stir shrimp and okra into **CROCK-POT®** slow cooker. Cover; cook on HIGH 30 to 35 minutes or until shrimp are opaque. Serve over rice.

Makes 6 servings

Serving Suggestion: Can also be served over hot cooked grits.

Classic Beef Stew

2½ pounds cubed beef stew meat

¼ cup all-purpose flour

2 tablespoons olive oil

3 cups beef broth

16 baby carrots

8 fingerling potatoes, halved crosswise

1 medium onion, chopped

1 ounce dried oyster mushrooms, chopped

2 teaspoons garlic powder

1 teaspoon dried basil

1 teaspoon dried oregano

½ teaspoon dried rosemary

½ teaspoon dried marjoram

½ teaspoon dried sage

½ teaspoon dried thyme

Salt and black pepper (optional)

Fresh chopped Italian parsley (optional)

1. Combine beef and flour in large bowl; toss well to coat. Heat 1 tablespoon oil in large skillet over medium-high heat. Add half of beef; cook and stir 4 minutes or until browned. Remove to **CROCK-POT**® slow cooker. Repeat with remaining oil and beef.

2. Add broth, carrots, potatoes, onion, mushrooms, garlic powder, basil, oregano, rosemary, marjoram, sage and thyme to **CROCK-POT**® slow cooker; stir to blend. Cover; cook on LOW 10 to 12 hours or on HIGH 5 to 6 hours. Season with salt and pepper, if desired. Garnish with parsley.

Makes 8 servings

Jamaican Quinoa and Sweet Potato Stew

3 cups vegetable broth

1 large or 2 small sweet potatoes (12 ounces), cut into ¾-inch pieces

1 cup uncooked quinoa, rinsed and drained

1 large red bell pepper, cut into ¾-inch pieces

1 tablespoon Caribbean jerk seasoning

¼ cup chopped fresh cilantro

¼ cup sliced almonds, toasted*

Hot pepper sauce or Pickapeppa sauce (optional)

To toast almonds, spread in single layer in heavy skillet. Cook over medium heat 1 to 2 minutes or until nuts are lightly browned, stirring frequently.

1. Coat inside of **CROCK-POT®** slow cooker with nonstick cooking spray. Combine broth, sweet potatoes, quinoa, bell pepper and jerk seasoning in **CROCK-POT®** slow cooker. Cover; cook on LOW 5 to 6 hours or on HIGH 2 to 2½ hours or until vegetables are tender.

2. Ladle into shallow bowls; top with cilantro and almonds. Serve with hot pepper sauce.

Makes 4 servings

Wild Mushroom Beef Stew

1½ to 2 pounds cubed beef stew meat

2 tablespoons all-purpose flour

½ teaspoon salt

½ teaspoon black pepper

1½ cups beef broth

4 shiitake mushrooms, sliced

2 medium carrots, sliced

2 medium potatoes, diced

1 small white onion, chopped

1 stalk celery, sliced

1 teaspoon paprika

1 clove garlic, minced

1 teaspoon Worcestershire sauce

1 whole bay leaf

Place beef in **CROCK-POT**® slow cooker. Combine flour, salt and pepper in small bowl; stir to blend. Sprinkle flour mixture over meat; toss to coat. Add broth, mushrooms, carrots, potatoes, onion, celery, paprika, garlic, Worcestershire sauce and bay leaf; stir to blend. Cover; cook on LOW 10 to 12 hours or on HIGH 4 to 6 hours. Remove and discard bay leaf.

Makes 5 servings

Note: This classic beef stew is given a twist with the addition of flavorful shiitake mushrooms. If shiitake mushrooms are unavailable in your local grocery store, you can substitute other mushrooms of your choice. For extra punch, add a few dried porcini mushrooms.

Tip: You may double the amount of meat, mushrooms, carrots, potatoes, onion and celery for a 5-, 6- or 7-quart **CROCK-POT**® slow cooker.

Chicken and Sweet Potato Stew

4 boneless, skinless chicken breasts, cut into
   1-inch pieces

2 medium sweet potatoes, cubed

2 medium Yukon Gold potatoes, cubed

2 medium carrots, cut into ½-inch slices

1 can (28 ounces) whole stewed tomatoes

1 cup chicken broth

1 teaspoon salt

1 teaspoon paprika

1 teaspoon celery seeds

½ teaspoon black pepper

⅛ teaspoon ground cinnamon

⅛ teaspoon ground nutmeg

¼ cup fresh basil, chopped

Combine chicken, sweet potatoes, Yukon Gold potatoes, carrots, tomatoes, broth, salt, paprika, celery seeds, pepper, cinnamon and nutmeg in **CROCK-POT**® slow cooker. Cover; cook on LOW 6 to 8 hours or on HIGH 3 to 4 hours. Sprinkle with basil just before serving.

Makes 6 servings

Tip: Recipe can be doubled for a 5-, 6- or 7-quart **CROCK-POT**® slow cooker.

Caribbean Chicken Stew

2 boneless, skinless chicken breasts (½ pound total)

1¼ teaspoons salt, divided

1 teaspoon ground cumin, divided

1 teaspoon dried thyme, divided

1 teaspoon black pepper, divided

½ teaspoon allspice, divided

1 tablespoon extra virgin olive oil

1 can (13½ ounces) unsweetened canned coconut milk

1½ cups chicken broth

1 cup onion, chopped

1 jalapeño pepper, seeded and minced*

2 cloves garlic, minced

1 whole bay leaf

2 sweet potatoes, cubed

1 can (about 15 ounces) chickpeas, rinsed and drained

⅓ cup chopped fresh cilantro

Juice of 1 medium lime

Jalapeño peppers can sting and irritate the skin, so wear rubber gloves when handling peppers and do not touch your eyes.

1. Season chicken with ½ teaspoon salt, ½ teaspoon cumin, ½ teaspoon thyme, ½ teaspoon black pepper and ¼ teaspoon allspice. Heat oil in medium skillet over medium-high heat. Add chicken; brown 2 minutes on each side.

2. Add chicken, coconut milk, broth, onion, jalapeño pepper, garlic, remaining ¾ teaspoon salt, ½ teaspoon cumin, ½ teaspoon thyme, ½ teaspoon black pepper, ¼ teaspoon allspice and bay leaf to **CROCK-POT**® slow cooker. Cover; cook on LOW 7 hours or on HIGH 3 hours.

3. Turn off heat. Remove chicken to cutting board; shred with two forks. Let cooking liquid stand 5 minutes. Skim off and discard fat. Stir chicken, sweet potatoes and chickpeas into **CROCK-POT**® slow cooker. Cover; cook on LOW 1 hour or on HIGH 30 minutes. Remove and discard bay leaf. Add cilantro and lime juice just before serving.

Makes 4 servings

Fall Harvest Stew

2½ pounds cubed beef stew meat

¼ cup all-purpose flour

2 tablespoons olive oil

1 tablespoon butter

1 medium onion, chopped

1 head garlic, minced

2 whole bay leaves

1 tablespoon fresh rosemary, chopped

1½ teaspoons fresh thyme, chopped

½ cup beef broth, divided

1 pound carrots, cut into 2-inch pieces

4 turnips, cut into 1-inch pieces

1 butternut squash, cut into 2-inch pieces

1 can (12 ounces) stout, divided

⅛ teaspoon white pepper

   Dash apple pie spice

   Salt and black pepper

1. Place beef and flour in large bowl; toss to coat beef. Heat oil and butter in large skillet over medium-high heat. Add beef; brown on all sides. Place in **CROCK-POT®** slow cooker.

2. Return skillet to heat. Add onion, garlic, bay leaves, rosemary and thyme; cook until onion begins to soften. Add mixture to **CROCK-POT®** slow cooker.

3. Return skillet to heat. Add ¼ cup broth; deglaze pan. Add broth mixture, carrots, turnips, squash, stout, white pepper and apple pie spice to **CROCK-POT®** slow cooker. Season with salt and black pepper. Add remaining ¼ cup broth. Cover; cook on LOW 8 hours. Remove and discard bay leaves.

Makes 8 servings

Lamb Shank and Mushroom Stew

2 tablespoons olive oil, divided

2 large lamb shanks (about 2 pounds total)

2 tablespoons all-purpose flour

2 cups sliced mushrooms*

1 red onion, thinly sliced

1 clove garlic, minced

1¼ cups chicken broth

½ cup pitted sliced green olives

¼ teaspoon salt

⅛ teaspoon black pepper

⅛ teaspoon dried thyme

2 tablespoons capers, drained

4 cups hot cooked noodles

*Shiitake mushroom caps are preferred for this dish, but you may use other mushroom varieties, if necessary.

1. Heat 1 tablespoon oil in large skillet over medium-high heat. Dust lamb shanks with flour, reserving leftover flour. Brown lamb on all sides. Remove to **CROCK-POT®** slow cooker.

2. Heat remaining 1 tablespoon oil in same skillet over medium-high heat. Add mushrooms, onion and garlic; cook and stir 3 minutes or until vegetables are tender. Remove to **CROCK-POT®** slow cooker.

3. Sprinkle reserved flour into skillet. Pour broth into skillet, stirring to scrape up any browned bits. Cook and stir 2 minutes or until mixture is slightly thickened. Pour into **CROCK-POT®** slow cooker.

4. Stir in olives, salt, pepper and thyme. Cover; cook on LOW 7 to 8 hours or on HIGH 4 to 5 hours.

5. Turn off heat. Remove lamb to cutting board. Gently pull meat from bones with fork. Discard bones. Let cooking liquid stand 5 minutes. Skim off and discard excess fat. Return lamb to **CROCK-POT®** slow cooker. Stir in capers. Serve lamb and sauce over noodles.

Makes 4 servings

Tip: Recipes often provide a range of cooking times to account for variables, such as the altitude, the temperature of the ingredients before cooking or the quantity of food in your **CROCK-POT®** slow cooker. Check for doneness before serving the dish.

Chicken and Mushroom Stew

4 tablespoons vegetable oil, divided

2 medium leeks (white and light green parts only), halved lengthwise and thinly sliced crosswise

1 carrot, cut into 1-inch pieces

1 stalk celery, diced

6 boneless, skinless chicken thighs (about 2 pounds)

Salt and black pepper

12 ounces cremini mushrooms, quartered

1 ounce dried porcini mushrooms, rehydrated in 1½ cups hot water and chopped, soaking liquid strained and reserved

1 teaspoon minced garlic

1 sprig fresh thyme

1 whole bay leaf

¼ cup all-purpose flour

½ cup dry white wine

1 cup chicken broth

1. Heat 1 tablespoon oil in large skillet over medium heat. Add leeks; cook 8 minutes or until softened. Remove to **CROCK-POT®** slow cooker. Add carrot and celery.

2. Heat 1 tablespoon oil in same skillet over medium-high heat. Season chicken with salt and pepper. Add chicken in batches; cook 8 minutes or until browned on both sides. Remove to **CROCK-POT®** slow cooker.

3. Heat remaining 2 tablespoons oil in same skillet. Add cremini mushrooms; cook 7 minutes or until mushrooms have released their liquid and started to brown. Add porcini mushrooms, garlic, thyme, bay leaf and flour; cook and stir 1 minute. Add wine; cook and stir until evaporated, stirring to scrape any browned bits from bottom of skillet. Add reserved soaking liquid and broth; bring to a simmer. Pour mixture into **CROCK-POT®** slow cooker.

4. Cover; cook on HIGH 2 to 3 hours. Remove thyme sprig and bay leaf before serving.

Makes 6 servings

Curried Vegetable and Cashew Stew

1 medium potato, cut into ½-inch cubes

1 can (about 15 ounces) chickpeas, rinsed and drained

1 can (about 14 ounces) diced tomatoes

1 medium (about ½ pound) eggplant, cut into ½-inch cubes

1 medium onion, chopped

1 cup vegetable broth

2 tablespoons quick-cooking tapioca

2 teaspoons grated fresh ginger

2 teaspoons curry powder

½ teaspoon salt

¼ teaspoon black pepper

1 medium zucchini (about 8 ounces), cut into ½-inch cubes

2 tablespoons golden raisins

½ cup frozen peas

½ cup lightly salted cashew nuts

1. Combine potato, chickpeas, tomatoes, eggplant, onion, broth, tapioca, ginger, curry powder, salt and pepper in **CROCK-POT®** slow cooker. Cover; cook on LOW 8 to 9 hours.

2. Stir zucchini, raisins, peas and cashews into **CROCK-POT®** slow cooker. Turn **CROCK-POT®** slow cooker to HIGH. Cover; cook on HIGH 1 hour or until zucchini is tender.

Makes 8 servings

Lamb and Chickpea Stew

1	pound lamb stew meat	¼	teaspoon black pepper
2	teaspoons salt, divided	2	cups chicken broth
2	tablespoons vegetable oil, divided	1	cup diced canned tomatoes, drained
1	large onion, chopped	1	cup dried chickpeas, rinsed and sorted
1	tablespoon minced garlic	½	cup chopped dried apricots
1½	teaspoons ground cumin	¼	cup chopped fresh Italian parsley
1	teaspoon ground turmeric	2	tablespoons honey
1	teaspoon ground coriander	2	tablespoons lemon juice
1	teaspoon ground cinnamon		Hot cooked couscous

1. Season lamb with 1 teaspoon salt. Heat 1 tablespoon oil in large skillet over medium-high heat. Add lamb; cook and stir 8 minutes or until browned on all sides. Remove to **CROCK-POT**® slow cooker.

2. Heat remaining 1 tablespoon oil in same skillet over medium heat. Add onion; cook and stir 6 minutes or until softened. Add garlic, remaining 1 teaspoon salt, cumin, turmeric, coriander, cinnamon and pepper; cook and stir 1 minute. Add broth and tomatoes; cook and stir 5 minutes, scraping up any brown bits from bottom of skillet. Remove to **CROCK-POT**® slow cooker. Stir in chickpeas.

3. Cover; cook on LOW 7 hours. Stir in apricots. Cover; cook on LOW 1 hour. Turn off heat. Let stand 10 minutes. Skim off and discard fat from stew. Stir in parsley, honey and lemon juice. Serve over couscous.

Makes 6 servings

Harvest Beef Stew

1½ pounds cubed beef stew meat

1 quart (32 ounces) canned or stewed tomatoes, undrained

6 carrots, cut into 1-inch pieces

3 medium potatoes, cut into 1-inch pieces

3 stalks celery, chopped (about 1 cup)

1 medium onion, sliced

1 cup apple juice

2 tablespoons dried parsley flakes

1 tablespoon dried basil

2 teaspoons salt

1 clove garlic, minced

½ teaspoon black pepper

2 whole bay leaves

½ cup warm water

¼ cup all-purpose flour

1. Heat large skillet over medium-low heat. Add beef; cook 7 minutes or until browned. Remove to **CROCK-POT**® slow cooker using slotted spoon.

2. Add tomatoes, carrots, potatoes, celery, onion, apple juice, parsley flakes, basil, salt, garlic, pepper and bay leaves to **CROCK-POT**® slow cooker; stir to blend. Cover; cook on HIGH 6 to 7 hours. Remove and discard bay leaves.

3. Stir water into flour in small bowl until smooth; whisk into **CROCK-POT**® slow cooker. Cover; cook on HIGH 10 to 20 minutes or until sauce is thickened.

Makes 6 servings

Sweet Potato Stew

1 cup chopped onion
1 cup chopped celery
1 cup grated sweet potato
1 cup vegetable broth or water
2 slices bacon, crisp-cooked and crumbled
1 cup half-and-half
　Black pepper
¼ cup minced fresh parsley

1. Place onion, celery, sweet potato, broth and bacon in **CROCK-POT®** slow cooker. Cover; cook on LOW 6 hours.

2. Turn **CROCK-POT®** slow cooker to HIGH. Add enough half-and-half to **CROCK-POT®** slow cooker to reach desired consistency. Cook, uncovered, on HIGH 30 minutes or until heated through.

3. Season to taste with pepper. Stir in parsley.

Makes 4 servings

Spiced Pork and Apple Stew

1 teaspoon canola oil
1¼ pounds cubed lean pork stew meat
1 medium sweet onion, cut into ½-inch-thick slices
2 cloves garlic, minced
1 can (28 ounces) crushed tomatoes
2 large or 3 small red or white potatoes, cut into 1-inch pieces
1½ cups baby carrots, cut into ½-inch pieces

2 small apples, cored and cubed
1 cup chicken broth
2 tablespoons spicy brown mustard
1 tablespoon packed brown sugar
2 teaspoons ground cinnamon
1 teaspoon ground cumin
¼ teaspoon salt
2 tablespoons chopped fresh Italian parsley (optional)

1. Heat oil in large nonstick skillet over medium-high heat. Add pork; brown on all sides. Add onion and garlic; cook and stir 5 minutes. Remove to **CROCK-POT®** slow cooker.

2. Add tomatoes, potatoes, carrots, apples, broth, mustard, brown sugar, cinnamon, cumin and salt to **CROCK-POT®** slow cooker. Cover; cook on LOW 6 to 8 hours or until pork and potatoes are tender. Garnish with parsley.

Makes 8 servings

Mushroom-Beef Stew

1 pound cubed beef stew meat

1 can (10¾ ounces) condensed cream of
   mushroom soup, undiluted

2 cans (4 ounces *each*) sliced mushrooms,
   drained

1 package (1 ounce) onion soup mix

   Hot cooked noodles

Combine beef, soup, mushrooms and dry soup mix in **CROCK-POT®** slow cooker. Cover; cook on LOW 8 to 10 hours. Serve over noodles.

Makes 4 servings

CHICKEN AND TURKEY

Beer Chicken

2 tablespoons olive oil

1 cut-up whole chicken (3 to 5 pounds)

10 new potatoes, halved

1 can (12 ounces) beer

2 medium carrots, thinly sliced

1 cup chopped celery

1 medium onion, chopped

1 tablespoon chopped fresh rosemary

1. Heat oil in large skillet over medium heat. Add chicken; cook 5 to 7 minutes on each side or until browned. Remove to **CROCK-POT®** slow cooker.

2. Add potatoes, beer, carrots, celery, onion and rosemary to **CROCK-POT®** slow cooker. Cover; cook on HIGH 5 hours.

Makes 4 to 6 servings

Creamy Pesto and Sun-Dried Tomato Chicken

2 teaspoons butter

1 teaspoon olive oil

6 boneless, skinless chicken breasts (1½ pounds total)

½ cup sun-dried tomatoes packed in oil, chopped

½ cup pesto, oil drained

½ cup chicken broth

1 package (1 ounce) ranch seasoning mix

¼ cup half-and-half

1. Coat inside of **CROCK-POT**® slow cooker with nonstick cooking spray. Heat butter and oil in large skillet over medium-high heat. Add chicken; brown 3 to 4 minutes on each side.

2. Place chicken, tomatoes, pesto, broth and seasoning mix in **CROCK-POT**® slow cooker. Cover; cook on LOW 6 hours or on HIGH 3 to 4 hours. Stir in half-and-half.

Makes 6 servings

Pineapple and Butternut Squash Braised Chicken

1 medium butternut squash, cut into 1-inch pieces (about 3 cups)

1 can (20 ounces) pineapple chunks, undrained

½ cup ketchup

2 tablespoons packed brown sugar

8 chicken thighs (about 2 pounds)

½ teaspoon salt

¼ teaspoon black pepper

1. Coat inside of **CROCK-POT**® slow cooker with nonstick cooking spray. Combine squash, pineapple with juice, ketchup and brown sugar in **CROCK-POT**® slow cooker. Season chicken with salt and pepper. Place chicken on top of squash mixture.

2. Cover; cook on LOW 5 to 6 hours. Remove chicken to large platter; cover loosely with foil. Turn **CROCK-POT**® slow cooker to HIGH. Cook, uncovered, on HIGH 10 to 15 minutes or until thickened. Serve sauce over chicken.

Makes 4 servings

Coconut-Curry Chicken Thighs

8 chicken thighs (about 2 to 2½ pounds)

½ teaspoon salt

¼ teaspoon black pepper

1 tablespoon olive oil

1 medium onion, chopped

1 medium red bell pepper, chopped

3 cloves garlic, minced

1 tablespoon grated fresh ginger

1 can (13½ ounces) coconut milk

3 tablespoons honey

1 tablespoon Thai red curry paste

2 teaspoons Thai roasted red chili paste

2 tablespoons chopped fresh cilantro (optional)

½ cup chopped cashew nuts (optional)

1. Coat inside of **CROCK-POT**® slow cooker with nonstick cooking spray. Season chicken with salt and pepper. Heat oil in large skillet over medium-high heat. Add chicken; cook 6 to 8 minutes until browned. Remove to **CROCK-POT**® slow cooker.

2. Pour off all but 1 tablespoon of fat from skillet. Heat skillet over medium-high heat. Add onion, bell pepper, garlic and ginger; cook and stir 1 to 2 minutes or until vegetables begin to soften. Remove skillet from heat. Stir in coconut milk, honey, curry paste and chili paste until smooth. Pour coconut mixture over chicken in **CROCK-POT**® slow cooker.

3. Cover; cook on LOW 4 hours. Serve chicken with sauce. Garnish each serving with cilantro and cashews.

Makes 4 servings

Mediterranean Chicken

1 tablespoon olive oil

2 pounds boneless, skinless chicken breasts

1 can (28 ounces) diced tomatoes

2 onions, chopped

½ cup dry sherry

6 teaspoons minced garlic

Juice of 2 lemons

2 cinnamon sticks

1 whole bay leaf

½ teaspoon black pepper

1 pound cooked egg noodles

½ cup feta cheese

1. Heat oil in large skillet. Add the chicken and lightly brown.

2. Combine tomatoes, onions, sherry, garlic, lemon juice, cinnamon sticks, bay leaf and pepper in **CROCK-POT**® slow cooker. Add chicken. Cover; cook on LOW 8 to 10 hours or on HIGH 4 to 5 hours or until done.

3. Remove and discard cinnamon sticks and bay leaf. Serve chicken and sauce over cooked noodles. Sprinkle with cheese just before serving.

Makes 6 servings

Fresh Herbed Turkey Breast

2 tablespoons butter, softened

¼ cup fresh sage, minced

¼ cup fresh tarragon, minced

1 clove garlic, minced

1 teaspoon black pepper

½ teaspoon salt

1 split turkey breast (4 pounds)

1 tablespoon plus 1½ teaspoons cornstarch

1. Combine butter, sage, tarragon, garlic, pepper and salt. Rub butter mixture all over turkey breast.

2. Place turkey breast in **CROCK-POT**® slow cooker. Cover; cook on LOW 8 to 10 hours or on HIGH 4 to 5 hours or until turkey is no longer pink in center.

3. Remove turkey breast to serving platter; cover loosely with foil to keep warm. Slowly whisk cornstarch into cooking liquid; cook on HIGH 10 minutes or until thickened and smooth. Slice turkey breast. Serve with sauce.

Makes 8 servings

Note: Recipe can be doubled for a 5-, 6- or 7-quart **CROCK-POT**® slow cooker.

Indian-Style Curried Drumsticks

12 chicken drumsticks, skin removed
(about 3 pounds)

1 cinnamon stick

2 tablespoons vegetable oil

1 large onion, diced

3 tablespoons tomato paste

1 tablespoon ground cumin

1 tablespoon grated fresh ginger

1 tablespoon minced garlic

2 teaspoons salt

2 teaspoons ground turmeric

1 teaspoon ground coriander

½ teaspoon black pepper

8 medium red potatoes, cut in half (about
1¾ pounds total)

1¼ cups chicken broth

1 cup frozen peas

1. Place drumsticks and cinnamon stick in **CROCK-POT**® slow cooker.

2. Heat oil in medium saucepan over medium heat. Add onion; cook and stir until softened. Add tomato paste, cumin, ginger, garlic, salt, turmeric, coriander and black pepper; cook and stir 2 minutes. Add onion mixture to **CROCK-POT**® slow cooker.

3. Add potatoes and broth to **CROCK-POT**® slow cooker. Cover; cook on LOW 6 hours or until chicken is almost falling off the bone.

4. Remove chicken and potatoes to large serving platter using slotted spoon. Stir peas into **CROCK-POT**® slow cooker. Cover; cook on LOW 5 minutes to warm peas. Serve drumsticks and potatoes topped with curry.

Makes 4 to 6 servings

Chicken Parmesan with Eggplant

6 boneless, skinless chicken breasts

2 eggs

2 teaspoons salt

2 teaspoons black pepper

2 cups seasoned dry bread crumbs

½ cup olive oil

½ cup (1 stick) butter

2 small eggplants, cut into ¾-inch-thick slices

1½ cups grated Parmesan cheese

2¼ cups tomato-basil pasta sauce

1 pound sliced or shredded mozzarella cheese

1. Slice chicken breasts in half lengthwise. Cut each half lengthwise again to get four ¾-inch slices.

2. Combine eggs, salt and pepper in medium bowl. Place bread crumbs in separate medium bowl. Dip chicken in egg mixture; turn to coat. Then coat chicken with bread crumbs, covering both sides evenly.

3. Heat oil and butter in large skillet over medium heat. Add breaded chicken; cook 6 to 8 minutes until browned on both sides. Remove to paper towel-lined plate to drain excess oil.

4. Layer half of eggplant, ¾ cup Parmesan cheese and 1 cup sauce in bottom of **CROCK-POT®** slow cooker. Top with half of chicken, remaining half of eggplant, remaining ¾ cup Parmesan cheese and ¼ cup sauce. Arrange remaining half of chicken on sauce; top with remaining 1 cup sauce and mozzarella cheese. Cover; cook on LOW 6 hours or on HIGH 2 to 4 hours.

Makes 6 to 8 servings

Curry Chicken with Peaches and Raisins

2 peaches, peeled and sliced into ¼-inch slices, reserving 8 slices for garnish

Lemon juice

4 boneless, skinless chicken thighs *or* 2 boneless, skinless chicken breasts

Salt and black pepper

1 tablespoon olive oil

⅓ cup raisins

1 shallot, thinly sliced

1 tablespoon grated fresh ginger

2 cloves garlic, crushed

½ teaspoon curry powder

1 teaspoon ground cumin

½ teaspoon whole cloves

¼ cup chicken broth

1 tablespoon cider vinegar

¼ teaspoon ground red pepper (optional)

1 teaspoon cornstarch (optional)

Fresh cilantro (optional)

Hot cooked rice (optional)

1. Toss reserved slices of peaches with lemon juice to coat and refrigerate. Rinse, dry and season chicken with salt and black pepper.

2. Heat oil in large skillet over medium-high heat. Add chicken and lightly brown, about 3 minutes per side. Remove to **CROCK-POT®** slow cooker. Top with remaining peaches, raisins and shallot.

3. Whisk ginger, garlic, curry powder, cumin, cloves, broth, vinegar and ground red pepper, if desired in small bowl. Pour mixture over chicken. Cover; cook on LOW 5 hours or on HIGH 3 to 3½ hours.

4. Remove chicken to serving dish. Stir cornstarch into sauce to thicken, if desired. Spoon peaches, raisins and sauce over chicken. Top with reserved peaches and cilantro, if desired. Serve over rice, if desired.

Makes 2 servings

Chicken Meatballs in Spicy Tomato Sauce

3 tablespoons olive oil, divided	3 tablespoons tomato paste
1 medium onion, chopped	2 teaspoons salt, divided
6 cloves garlic, minced	1½ pounds ground chicken
1½ teaspoons dried basil	2 egg yolks
¼ teaspoon red pepper flakes	1 teaspoon dried oregano
2 cans (about 14 ounces *each*) diced tomatoes	¼ teaspoon black pepper

1. Heat 2 tablespoons oil in large skillet over medium-high heat. Add onion, garlic, basil and red pepper flakes; cook and stir 5 minutes or until onion is softened. Remove half of mixture to **CROCK-POT®** slow cooker. Stir in diced tomatoes, tomato paste and 1 teaspoon salt.

2. Remove remaining onion mixture to large bowl. Add chicken, egg yolks, oregano, remaining 1 teaspoon salt and black pepper; mix well. Form mixture into 24 (1-inch) balls.

3. Heat remaining 1 tablespoon oil in large skillet. Add meatballs in batches; cook 7 minutes or until browned. Remove to **CROCK-POT®** slow cooker using slotted spoon. Cover; cook on LOW 4 to 5 hours.

Makes 4 servings

Pollo Ranchero (Country Chicken)

1 cut-up whole chicken (2 to 3 pounds)	2 tablespoons seasoned salt
5 cups chopped tomatoes	2 tablespoons onion powder
2 cups water	2 tablespoons garlic powder
1 cup chopped ham	2 tablespoons tomato paste
1 large onion, chopped	Hot cooked rice
2 jalapeño peppers, minced*	
4 sprigs fresh tarragon	

*Jalapeño peppers can sting and irritate the skin, so wear rubber gloves when handling peppers and do not touch your eyes.

Combine chicken, tomatoes, water, ham, onion, jalapeño peppers, tarragon, seasoned salt, onion powder, garlic powder and tomato paste in **CROCK-POT®** slow cooker. Cover; cook on HIGH 3 to 4 hours. Serve over rice.

Makes 4 servings

Shredded Chicken Tacos

2 pounds boneless, skinless chicken thighs

1 cup prepared mango salsa, plus additional for serving

8 (6-inch) yellow corn tortillas, warmed

Optional toppings: shredded pepper jack cheese, sour cream and/or lettuce

1. Coat inside of **CROCK-POT®** slow cooker with nonstick cooking spray. Add chicken and 1 cup salsa. Cover; cook on LOW 4 to 5 hours or on HIGH 2½ to 3 hours.

2. Remove chicken to large cutting board; shred with two forks. Stir shredded chicken back into **CROCK-POT®** slow cooker. To serve, divide chicken evenly among tortillas. Top as desired.

Makes 4 servings

Chicken with Mushrooms

8 boneless, skinless chicken breasts (2 pounds total), cut into pieces

3 cups sliced mushrooms

1 large onion, chopped

1 can (6 ounces) tomato paste

½ cup chicken broth

¼ cup dry red wine

2 tablespoons quick-cooking tapioca

2 cloves garlic, minced

2 teaspoons sugar

2 teaspoons dried basil

Salt and black pepper

Hot cooked noodles (optional)

Grated Parmesan cheese (optional)

Place chicken, mushrooms, onion, tomato paste, broth, wine, tapioca, garlic, sugar, basil, salt and pepper in **CROCK-POT®** slow cooker. Cover; cook on LOW 7 to 8 hours or on HIGH 3 to 4 hours. Serve over noodles, if desired. Garnish with cheese.

Makes 4 servings

Turkey Spinach Lasagna

Nonstick cooking spray

¾ cup chopped onion

2 medium cloves garlic, minced

1 pound ground turkey

1 teaspoon Italian seasoning

¼ teaspoon black pepper

1 container (15 ounces) ricotta cheese

1 cup (4 ounces) Italian shredded cheese blend, divided

12 ounces no-boil lasagna noodles

1 package (10 ounces) frozen chopped spinach, thawed and pressed dry

1 jar (24 to 26 ounces) chunky marinara sauce

½ cup water

1. Spray large skillet with cooking spray; heat over medium heat. Add onion and garlic; cook and stir 4 minutes. Add turkey; cook and stir until no longer pink, stirring to break up meat. Season with Italian seasoning and pepper; remove from heat. Set aside.

2. Combine ricotta cheese and ½ cup Italian cheese in small bowl; mix well.

3. Layer half of uncooked noodles, breaking in half to fit and overlap as necessary, in **CROCK-POT®** slow cooker. Spread half of meat mixture and half of spinach over noodles. Top with half of marinara sauce and ¼ cup water. Gently spread cheese mixture on top. Continue layering with remaining noodles, meat mixture, spinach, marinara sauce and ¼ cup water.

4. Cover; cook on LOW 4 hours. To serve, sprinkle top with remaining ½ cup Italian cheese. Cover; cook on LOW 10 to 15 minutes or until cheese is melted. Divide evenly into eight pieces.

Makes 8 servings

Sesame Chicken

1 cup rice flour

3 tablespoons sesame seeds

½ teaspoon black pepper

6 boneless, skinless chicken breasts (about 2 pounds)

2 tablespoons vegetable oil

1 cup chicken broth

½ cup chopped celery

¼ cup chopped onion

1 teaspoon dried tarragon

2 tablespoons water

2 tablespoons cornstarch

Hot cooked rice (optional)

Squash ribbons (optional)

1. Combine rice flour, sesame seeds and pepper in large bowl; stir to blend. Add chicken; toss to coat.

2. Heat oil in large skillet over medium heat. Add chicken; cook 5 to 7 minutes or until browned on all sides. Remove to **CROCK-POT**® slow cooker.

3. Add broth, celery, onion and tarragon to **CROCK-POT**® slow cooker. Cover; cook on LOW 7 to 8 hours or on HIGH 3 to 4 hours.

4. Stir water into cornstarch in small bowl until smooth; whisk into **CROCK-POT**® slow cooker. Cover; cook on HIGH 15 to 20 minutes or until thickened. Serve with rice and squash ribbons, if desired.

Makes 6 servings

Slow Cooker Chicken and Dressing

4 boneless, skinless chicken breasts
   (about 1 pound)
   Salt and black pepper
4 slices Swiss cheese
2 cans (10¾ ounces *each*) condensed cream of
   chicken, celery or mushroom soup, undiluted

1 can (about 14 ounces) chicken broth
3 cups packaged stuffing mix
½ cup (1 stick) butter, melted

Place chicken in **CROCK-POT®** slow cooker. Season with salt and pepper. Top each breast with cheese slice. Add soup and broth. Sprinkle stuffing mix over top; pour melted butter over all in **CROCK-POT®** slow cooker. Cover; cook on LOW 6 to 8 hours or on HIGH 3 to 4 hours.

Makes 4 servings

Turkey Tacos

1 pound ground turkey
1 medium onion, chopped
1 can (6 ounces) tomato paste
½ cup chunky salsa
1 tablespoon chopped fresh cilantro
½ teaspoon salt
1 tablespoon butter

1 tablespoon all-purpose flour
¼ teaspoon salt
⅓ cup milk
½ cup sour cream
   Pinch ground red pepper
8 taco shells

1. Brown turkey and onion in large skillet over medium heat, stirring to break up meat. Combine turkey mixture, tomato paste, salsa, cilantro and salt in **CROCK-POT®** slow cooker. Cover; cook on LOW 4 to 5 hours.

2. Just before serving, melt butter in small saucepan over low heat. Whisk in flour and salt; cook 1 minute. Whisk in milk; cook and stir over low heat until thickened. Remove from heat. Combine sour cream and ground red pepper in small bowl. Stir into hot milk mixture. Cook over low heat 1 minute, stirring constantly.

3. Spoon ¼ cup turkey mixture into each taco shell; top with sauce.

Makes 8 servings

Tip: When adapting recipes for your **CROCK-POT®** slow cooker, adjust the amount of herbs and spices. Whole herbs and spices increase in flavor while ground spices tend to lose flavor during slow cooking. If you prefer, you can adjust the seasonings or add herbs and spices just before serving.

Herbed Turkey Breast with Orange Sauce

1 large onion, chopped

3 cloves garlic, minced

1 teaspoon dried rosemary

½ teaspoon black pepper

1 boneless, skinless turkey breast (3 pounds)*

1½ cups orange juice

Unless you have a 5-, 6- or 7-quart CROCK-POT® slow cooker, cut any piece of meat larger than 2½ pounds in half so it cooks completely.

1. Place onion in **CROCK-POT**® slow cooker. Combine garlic, rosemary and pepper in small bowl.

2. Cut slices about three fourths of the way through turkey at 2-inch intervals. Rub garlic mixture between slices. Place turkey, cut side up, in **CROCK-POT**® slow cooker. Pour orange juice over turkey. Cover; cook on LOW 7 to 8 hours.

3. Slice turkey. Serve with orange sauce.

Makes 4 to 6 servings

Tip: Don't peek! The **CROCK-POT**® slow cooker can take as long as 30 minutes to regain heat lost when the cover is removed. Only remove the cover when instructed to do so by the recipe.

Indian-Style Apricot Chicken

6 skinless chicken thighs, rinsed and patted dry (about 2 pounds)

¼ teaspoon salt

¼ teaspoon black pepper

1 tablespoon vegetable oil

1 large onion, chopped

2 cloves garlic, minced

2 tablespoons grated fresh ginger

½ teaspoon ground cinnamon

⅛ teaspoon ground allspice

1 can (about 14 ounces) diced tomatoes

1 cup chicken broth

½ package (4 ounces) dried apricots

Pinch saffron threads (optional)

Hot cooked rice (optional)

2 tablespoons chopped fresh Italian parsley (optional)

1. Coat inside of **CROCK-POT**® slow cooker with nonstick cooking spray. Season chicken with salt and pepper. Heat oil in large skillet over medium-high heat. Add chicken; cook 6 to 8 minutes or until browned on all sides. Remove to **CROCK-POT**® slow cooker using slotted spoon.

2. Add onion to skillet; cook and stir 3 to 5 minutes or until translucent. Stir in garlic, ginger, cinnamon and allspice; cook and stir 15 to 30 seconds or until mixture is fragrant. Add tomatoes and broth; cook 2 to 3 minutes or until mixture is heated through. Pour into **CROCK-POT**® slow cooker.

3. Add apricots and saffron, if desired. Cover; cook on LOW 5 to 6 hours or on HIGH 3 to 4 hours. Serve with rice, if desired. Garnish with parsley.

Makes 6 servings

Note: To skin chicken easily, grasp skin with paper towel and pull away. Repeat with fresh paper towel for each piece of chicken, discarding skins and towels.

Easy Parmesan Chicken

8 ounces mushrooms, sliced

1 medium onion, cut into thin wedges

1 tablespoon olive oil

4 boneless, skinless chicken breasts

1 jar (26 ounces) pasta sauce

½ teaspoon dried basil

¼ teaspoon dried oregano

1 whole bay leaf

½ cup (2 ounces) shredded mozzarella cheese

¼ cup grated Parmesan cheese

Hot cooked spaghetti

Chopped fresh basil (optional)

1. Place mushrooms and onion in **CROCK-POT®** slow cooker.

2. Heat oil in large skillet over medium-high heat. Add chicken; cook 5 to 6 minutes on each side or until browned. Place chicken in **CROCK-POT®** slow cooker. Pour pasta sauce over chicken; add dried basil, oregano and bay leaf. Cover; cook on LOW 6 to 7 hours or on HIGH 3 to 4 hours. Remove and discard bay leaf.

3. Sprinkle chicken with cheeses. Cook, uncovered, on LOW 10 minutes or until cheeses are melted. Serve over spaghetti and garnish with fresh basil.

Makes 4 servings

Tip: Dairy products should be added at the end of the cooking time because they will curdle if cooked in the **CROCK-POT®** slow cooker for a long time.

Greek Chicken Pitas
with Creamy Mustard Sauce

Filling

- 1 medium green bell pepper, sliced into ½-inch strips
- 1 medium onion, cut into 8 wedges
- ½ pound boneless, skinless chicken breasts, rinsed and patted dry
- 1 tablespoon extra virgin olive oil
- 2 teaspoons Greek seasoning
- ¼ teaspoon salt

Sauce

- ¼ cup plain yogurt
- ¼ cup mayonnaise
- 1 tablespoon prepared mustard
- 4 whole pita bread rounds
- ½ cup crumbled feta cheese

   Optional toppings: sliced cucumbers, sliced tomatoes and/or kalamata olives

1. Coat inside of **CROCK-POT**® slow cooker with nonstick cooking spray. Place bell pepper and onion in bottom. Add chicken; drizzle with oil. Sprinkle evenly with Greek seasoning and salt. Cover; cook on HIGH 1¾ hours or until chicken is no longer pink in center and vegetables are crisp-tender.

2. Whisk yogurt, mayonnaise and mustard in small bowl until smooth. Remove chicken to large cutting board; slice. Remove vegetables using slotted spoon. Fill pita halves evenly with chicken, yogurt sauce, vegetables and feta cheese. Top as desired.

Makes 4 servings

Coq au Vin with Lima Beans

4 pounds chicken thighs and drumsticks

3 slices bacon, cut into pieces

4 cups chicken broth

1 cup sliced mushrooms

1 cup sliced carrots

1 cup dry red wine

½ cup pearl onions

⅓ cup whiskey

3 to 4 cloves garlic, chopped

2 tablespoons tomato paste

1½ teaspoons herbes de Provence

2 whole bay leaves

Salt and black pepper

1 tablespoon water

2 tablespoons all-purpose flour

1 cup lima beans

Chopped fresh Italian parsley (optional)

Roasted red potatoes, quartered (optional)

1. Coat inside of **CROCK-POT®** slow cooker with nonstick cooking spray. Add chicken and bacon to **CROCK-POT®** slow cooker. Cover; cook on HIGH 45 minutes, turning chicken halfway through cooking time.

2. Turn **CROCK-POT®** slow cooker to LOW. Add broth, mushrooms, carrots, wine, onions, whiskey, garlic, tomato paste, herbes de Provence and bay leaves to **CROCK-POT®** slow cooker. Stir water into flour in small bowl until smooth. Whisk into **CROCK-POT®** slow cooker. Cover; cook on LOW 6 hours. Add beans to **CROCK-POT®** slow cooker during last 10 minutes of cooking. Remove and discard bay leaves. Garnish with parsley. Serve with potatoes, if desired.

Makes 8 to 10 servings

Chicken Fajitas with Barbecue Sauce

1 can (8 ounces) tomato sauce

⅓ cup chopped green onions

¼ cup ketchup

2 tablespoons water

2 tablespoons orange juice

2 cloves garlic, finely chopped

1 tablespoon cider vinegar

1 tablespoon chili sauce

½ teaspoon vegetable oil

Dash Worcestershire sauce

Nonstick cooking spray

10 ounces boneless, skinless chicken breasts, cut into ½-inch strips

2 green or red bell peppers, thinly sliced

1 cup sliced onion

2 cups tomato wedges

4 (6-inch) flour tortillas, heated

1. Combine tomato sauce, green onions, ketchup, water, orange juice, garlic, cider vinegar, chili sauce, oil and Worcestershire sauce in **CROCK-POT**® slow cooker; stir to blend. Cover; cook on HIGH 1½ hours.

2. Spray large skillet with cooking spray; heat over medium heat. Add chicken; cook and stir 5 to 7 minutes.

3. Turn **CROCK-POT**® slow cooker to LOW. Add chicken, bell peppers and sliced onion to **CROCK-POT**® slow cooker; stir to blend. Cover; cook on LOW 3 to 4 hours.

4. Add tomato wedges to **CROCK-POT**® slow cooker. Cover; cook on LOW 30 to 45 minutes or until heated through. Serve with tortillas.

Makes 4 servings

Thai Chicken

2½ pounds chicken pieces
1 cup hot salsa
¼ cup peanut butter
2 tablespoons lime juice
1 tablespoon soy sauce

1 teaspoon minced fresh ginger
   Hot cooked rice (optional)
½ cup peanuts, chopped
2 tablespoons chopped fresh cilantro

1. Place chicken in **CROCK-POT**® slow cooker. Mix together salsa, peanut butter, lime juice, soy sauce and ginger in small bowl; pour over chicken.

2. Cover; cook on LOW 8 to 9 hours or on HIGH 3 to 4 hours. Serve over rice, if desired, topped with sauce, peanuts and cilantro.

Makes 6 servings

Chicken and Biscuits

4 boneless, skinless chicken breasts, cut into 1-inch pieces
1 can (10¾ ounces) condensed cream of chicken soup

1 package (10 ounces) frozen peas and carrots
1 package (7½ ounces) refrigerated biscuits

1. Place chicken in **CROCK-POT**® slow cooker; pour in soup. Cover; cook on LOW 4 hours.

2. Stir in peas and carrots. Cover; cook on LOW 30 minutes or until vegetables are heated through.

3. Meanwhile, bake biscuits according to package directions. Spoon chicken and vegetable mixture over biscuits to serve.

Makes 4 servings

Chicken in Honey Sauce

6 boneless, skinless chicken breasts (about 1½ pounds)

Salt and black pepper

2 cups honey

1 cup soy sauce

½ cup ketchup

¼ cup vegetable oil

2 cloves garlic, minced

Sesame seeds (optional)

1. Place chicken in **CROCK-POT**® slow cooker; season with salt and pepper.

2. Combine honey, soy sauce, ketchup, oil and garlic in medium bowl. Pour over chicken. Cover; cook on LOW 6 to 8 hours or on HIGH 3 to 4 hours.

3. Garnish with sesame seeds before serving. Serve with extra sauce, if desired.

Makes 6 servings

Tip: Recipes often provide a range of cooking times to account for variables, such as the temperature of the ingredients before cooking, the quantity of food in your **CROCK-POT**® slow cooker and the altitude. Cooking times will be longer at higher altitudes.

Chicken Scaloppine in Alfredo Sauce

2 tablespoons all-purpose flour

¼ teaspoon salt

¼ teaspoon black pepper

6 pound boneless, skinless chicken tenderloins (about 1 pound), cut lengthwise in half

1 tablespoon butter

1 tablespoon olive oil

1 cup Alfredo pasta sauce

1 package (12 ounces) uncooked spinach noodles

1. Place flour, salt and pepper in large bowl; stir to combine. Add chicken; toss to coat. Heat butter and oil in large skillet over medium-high heat. Add chicken; cook 3 minutes per side or until browned. Remove chicken in single layer to **CROCK-POT®** slow cooker.

2. Add Alfredo pasta sauce to **CROCK-POT®** slow cooker. Cover; cook on LOW 1 to 1½ hours.

3. Meanwhile, cook noodles according to package directions. Drain; place in large shallow bowl. Spoon chicken and sauce over noodles.

Makes 6 servings

Chicken Enchilada Roll-Ups

6 boneless, skinless chicken breasts (about 1½ pounds)

½ cup plus 2 tablespoons all-purpose flour, divided

½ teaspoon salt

2 tablespoons butter

1 cup chicken broth

1 onion, diced

¼ to ½ cup sliced canned jalapeño peppers

½ teaspoon dried oregano

2 tablespoons whipping cream or milk

6 (7- to 8-inch) flour tortillas

6 thin slices American cheese or American cheese with jalapeño peppers

1. Cut each chicken breast lengthwise into 2 or 3 strips. Combine ½ cup flour and salt in large resealable food storage bag. Add chicken strips and shake to coat with flour mixture. Melt butter in large skillet over medium heat. Brown chicken strips in batches, cooking 2 to 3 minutes per side. Remove to **CROCK-POT®** slow cooker.

2. Add broth to skillet and scrape up any browned bits. Pour broth mixture into **CROCK-POT®** slow cooker. Add onion, jalapeño peppers and oregano. Cover; cook on LOW 7 to 8 hours or on HIGH 3 to 4 hours.

3. Blend remaining 2 tablespoons flour and cream in small bowl until smooth; whisk into chicken mixture. Cook, uncovered, on HIGH 15 minutes or until thickened. Spoon chicken mixture onto center of flour tortillas. Top each with cheese slice. Fold up tortillas and serve.

Makes 6 servings

Old World Chicken and Vegetables

1 tablespoon dried oregano	2 green bell peppers, cut into thin strips
1 teaspoon salt, divided	1 yellow onion, thinly sliced
1 teaspoon paprika	1 cut-up whole chicken (about 3 pounds)
½ teaspoon garlic powder	⅓ cup ketchup
¼ teaspoon black pepper	Hot cooked egg noodles

1. Combine oregano, ½ teaspoon salt, paprika, garlic powder and black pepper in small bowl.

2. Place bell peppers and onion in **CROCK-POT®** slow cooker. Add chicken thighs and legs; sprinkle with half of spice blend. Add chicken breasts; sprinkle with remaining spice blend. Cover; cook on LOW 8 hours or on HIGH 4 hours. Stir in ketchup and remaining ½ teaspoon salt.

3. Serve chicken and vegetables over noodles.

Makes 4 servings

Stuffed Chicken Breasts

6 boneless, skinless chicken breasts	Black pepper
8 ounces feta cheese, crumbled	1 can (about 14 ounces) diced tomatoes
3 cups chopped fresh spinach leaves	½ cup oil-cured olives*
⅓ cup sun-dried tomatoes packed in oil, drained and chopped	Hot cooked polenta
1 teaspoon minced lemon peel	Lemon peel twists (optional)
1 teaspoon dried basil, oregano or mint	*If using pitted olives, add to CROCK-POT® slow cooker in the final hour of cooking.*
½ teaspoon garlic powder	

1. Place 1 chicken breast between two pieces of plastic wrap. Using tenderizer mallet or back of skillet, pound until about ¼ inch thick. Repeat with remaining chicken.

2. Combine feta, spinach, sun-dried tomatoes, lemon peel, basil, garlic powder and pepper in medium bowl.

3. Place chicken breasts, smooth sides down, on work surface. Place 2 tablespoons feta mixture on wide end of each breast. Roll tightly.

4. Place rolled chicken, seam sides down, in **CROCK-POT®** slow cooker. Top with tomatoes and olives. Cover; cook on LOW 5½ to 6 hours or on HIGH 4 hours. Serve over polenta. Garnish with lemon peel.

Makes 6 servings

Easy Cheesy BBQ Chicken

6 boneless, skinless chicken breasts (about 1½ pounds)

1 bottle (26 ounces) barbecue sauce

6 slices bacon, crisp-cooked and cut in half

6 slices Swiss cheese

1. Place chicken in **CROCK-POT**® slow cooker; pour in barbecue sauce. Cover; cook on LOW 8 to 9 hours. (If sauce becomes too thick during cooking, add a little water.)

2. Place 2 bacon halves and 1 cheese slice on each chicken breast in **CROCK-POT**® slow cooker. Turn **CROCK-POT**® slow cooker to HIGH. Cover; cook on HIGH 15 minutes or until cheese is melted.

Makes 6 servings

Tip: To make cleanup easier, coat the inside of the **CROCK-POT**® slow cooker with nonstick cooking spray before adding the ingredients. To remove any sticky barbecue sauce residue, soak the stoneware in hot sudsy water, then scrub it with a plastic or nylon scrubber. Don't use steel wool.

Simple Coq au Vin

4 chicken legs
  Salt and black pepper
2 tablespoons olive oil
8 ounces mushrooms, sliced
1 onion, sliced into rings

½ cup dry red wine
½ teaspoon dried basil
½ teaspoon dried thyme
½ teaspoon dried oregano
  Hot cooked rice

1. Season chicken with salt and pepper. Heat oil in large skillet over medium-high heat. Brown chicken on both sides. Remove chicken to **CROCK-POT**® slow cooker.

2. Add mushrooms and onion to skillet; cook and stir until onions are tender. Add wine, stirring to scrape up any browned bits from bottom of skillet. Add mixture to **CROCK-POT**® slow cooker. Sprinkle with basil, thyme and oregano.

3. Cover; cook on LOW 8 to 10 hours or on HIGH 3 to 4 hours. Serve chicken and sauce over rice.

Makes 4 servings

Chicken Cacciatore

4 teaspoons olive oil
3 pounds boneless, skinless chicken breasts
½ teaspoon salt
¼ teaspoon black pepper
½ medium red bell pepper, sliced
½ medium green bell pepper, sliced
½ medium yellow bell pepper, sliced
1 cup onion, sliced
14 grape tomatoes

1½ cups water
¼ cup all-purpose flour
2 teaspoons garlic powder
1 teaspoon ground cumin
1 teaspoon dried oregano
1 teaspoon paprika
⅛ teaspoon ground red pepper
  Hot cooked noodles or rice (optional)

1. Heat 2 teaspoons oil in large skillet over medium-high heat. Sprinkle chicken with salt and black pepper. Add half of chicken to skillet; cook 4 minutes per side or until browned. Remove to large plate. Repeat with remaining 2 teaspoons oil and chicken.

2. Add bell peppers, onion and grape tomatoes to 4- to 6-quart **CROCK-POT**® slow cooker. Combine water, flour, garlic powder, cumin, oregano, paprika and ground red pepper in medium bowl; mix well. Add to **CROCK-POT**® slow cooker. Top with chicken. Cover; cook on LOW 8 to 9 hours or on HIGH 4 to 4½ hours. Serve over noodles, if desired.

Makes 6 servings

Mediterranean Chicken Breasts and Wild Rice

1 pound boneless, skinless chicken breasts, lightly pounded

Salt and black pepper

1 cup wild rice blend

10 cloves garlic, crushed

½ cup sun-dried tomatoes, packed in oil or dried*

½ cup capers, drained

2 cups water

½ cup lemon juice

¼ cup extra virgin olive oil

*If using dry sun-dried tomatoes, soak in boiling water to soften before chopping.

1. Season chicken with salt and pepper. Place chicken in **CROCK-POT**® slow cooker. Add rice, garlic, tomatoes and capers; stir well.

2. Combine water, lemon juice and oil in small bowl; pour over rice and chicken. Stir once to coat chicken. Cover; cook on LOW 8 hours.

Makes 4 servings

Chicken Tagine with Lemon and Olives

1 onion, finely chopped

4 cloves garlic, minced

Grated peel and juice of 1 lemon

2 teaspoons dried rosemary *or* 2 tablespoons chopped fresh rosemary

1 teaspoon dried thyme *or* 1 tablespoon fresh thyme

4 chicken leg quarters

20 pitted green olives, crushed

2 tablespoons butter, cut into small pieces

2 tablespoons water

2 tablespoons all-purpose flour

1. Combine onion, garlic, lemon peel and juice, rosemary and thyme in **CROCK-POT**® slow cooker. Top with chicken, olives and butter. Cover; cook on LOW 5 to 6 hours.

2. Remove chicken. Turn **CROCK-POT**® slow cooker to HIGH. Stir water into flour in small bowl; whisk into **CROCK-POT**® slow cooker. Cover; cook on HIGH 10 to 15 minutes or until sauce is thickened.

Makes 4 servings

Cornish Hens for Two

1 head garlic, divided

1 lemon, cut in half

2 Cornish game hens (1 pound *each*)

  Salt and black pepper

2 large portobella mushrooms

2 medium onions, thinly sliced

1 can (10½ ounces) cream of chicken soup

2 tablespoons fresh Italian parsley, thyme and/or sage

  Hot mashed potatoes, rice or egg noodles (optional)

1. Coat inside of **CROCK-POT®** slow cooker with nonstick cooking spray. Cut head of garlic in half; separate cloves. Reserve half of whole cloves; mince remaining half of cloves. Place ¼ whole cloves garlic and lemon half into each chicken; season with salt and pepper.

2. Place mushrooms, stem side up, onions and minced garlic in **CROCK-POT®** slow cooker; top with chicken, soup and herbs. Cover; cook on LOW 6 hours or on HIGH 3 hours, turning chicken halfway through cooking time. Serve over mashed potatoes, if desired.

Makes 2 servings

FROM
THE SEA

Miso-Poached Salmon

1½ cups water

2 green onions, cut into 2-inch long pieces plus
   additional for garnish

¼ cup yellow miso paste

¼ cup soy sauce

2 tablespoons sake

2 tablespoons mirin

1½ teaspoons grated ginger

1 teaspoon minced garlic

6 (4 ounces *each*) salmon fillets

Hot cooked rice

1. Combine water, 2 green onions, miso paste, soy sauce, sake, mirin, ginger and garlic in **CROCK-POT**® slow cooker; stir to blend. Cover; cook on HIGH 30 minutes.

2. Turn **CROCK-POT**® slow cooker to LOW. Add salmon, skin side down. Cover; cook on LOW 30 minutes to 1 hour or until salmon turns opaque and flakes easily with a fork. Serve over rice with cooking liquid as desired. Garnish with additional green onions.

Makes 6 servings

Slow Cooker Salmon with Beer

4 salmon fillets (6 ounces *each*)	1 large onion, sliced
Salt and black pepper	2 cloves garlic, minced
1 cup Italian dressing	1 teaspoon lemon peel
3 tablespoons olive oil	½ teaspoon dried basil
1 yellow bell pepper, sliced	2 cups spinach, stems removed
1 red bell pepper, sliced	¾ cup amber ale
1 orange bell pepper, sliced	½ lemon, cut into quarters

1. Season both sides of fillets with salt and black pepper. Place fillets in baking dish; pour Italian dressing over fillets. Cover and refrigerate 30 minutes or up to 2 hours. Discard marinade.

2. Pour oil into **CROCK-POT®** slow cooker; lay salmon fillets on top of oil, stacking as necessary. Top with bell peppers, onion, garlic, lemon peel and basil. Cover with spinach. Pour ale over top of all in **CROCK-POT®** slow cooker. Cover; cook on HIGH 1½ hours.

3. Remove fillets to platter; top with vegetables. Squeeze lemon over salmon.

Makes 4 servings

Slow Cooker Shrimp Jambalaya

1 (8-ounce) box New Orleans style jambalaya mix

2½ cups water

1 can (about 14 ounces) diced tomatoes with green pepper, celery and onion

8 ounces andouille sausage, cut into ¼-inch-thick slices

1 teaspoon hot pepper sauce, plus additional for serving

1½ pounds large raw shrimp, peeled and deveined (with tails on)

1. Coat inside of **CROCK-POT**® slow cooker with nonstick cooking spray. Add jambalaya mix, water, tomatoes, sausage and 1 teaspoon hot pepper sauce; stir to blend. Cover; cook on LOW 2½ to 3 hours until rice is cooked through.

2. Stir in shrimp. Cover; cook on LOW 30 minutes or until shrimp are cooked through. Serve with additional hot pepper sauce.

Makes 8 servings

Seafood Cioppino

1 tablespoon olive oil	16 little neck clams, scrubbed
1 medium fennel bulb, thinly sliced	24 mussels, scrubbed
1 medium onion, chopped	1 pound cod fillet, cut into 8 pieces
4 cloves garlic, minced	8 ounces large raw shrimp, peeled and deveined (with tails on)
1 teaspoon dried basil	½ teaspoon salt
¼ teaspoon saffron threads, crushed (optional)	⅛ teaspoon black pepper
1 can (about 14 ounces) diced tomatoes	
1 (8-ounce) bottle clam juice	

1. Coat inside of **CROCK-POT**® slow cooker with nonstick cooking spray. Heat oil in large skillet over medium-high heat. Add fennel, onion, garlic, basil and saffron, if desired; cook and stir 4 to 5 minutes or until vegetables are softened. Remove onion mixture to **CROCK-POT**® slow cooker. Stir in tomatoes and clam juice.

2. Cover; cook on HIGH 2 to 3 hours. Add clams. Cover; cook on HIGH 30 minutes. Add mussels. Cover; cook on HIGH 15 minutes.

3. Season cod and shrimp with salt and pepper. Place on top of shellfish. Cover; cook on HIGH 25 to 30 minutes until clams and mussels have opened and fish is cooked through. Discard any clams and mussels that have not opened.

Makes 4 servings

Shrimp Creole

¼ cup (½ stick) butter

1 onion, chopped

¼ cup biscuit baking mix

3 cups water

2 cans (6 ounces *each*) tomato paste

1 cup chopped celery

1 cup chopped green bell pepper

2 teaspoons salt

½ teaspoon sugar

2 whole bay leaves

Black pepper

4 pounds large raw shrimp, peeled and deveined

Hot cooked rice

1. Cook and stir butter and onion in medium skillet over medium heat 3 to 5 minutes or until onion is tender. Stir in biscuit mix. Place mixture in **CROCK-POT**® slow cooker.

2. Add water, tomato paste, celery, bell pepper, salt, sugar, bay leaves and black pepper. Cover; cook on LOW 6 to 8 hours.

3. Turn **CROCK-POT**® slow cooker to HIGH. Add shrimp. Cover; cook on HIGH 45 minutes to 1 hour or until shrimp are pink and opaque. Remove and discard bay leaves. Serve over rice.

Makes 8 to 10 servings

Cod Tapenade

4 cod fillets or other firm white fish (2 to 3 pounds total)

Salt and black pepper

2 lemons, thinly sliced

Tapenade (recipe follows)

1. Season cod with salt and pepper.

2. Arrange half of lemon slices in bottom of **CROCK-POT®** slow cooker. Top with cod; cover with remaining lemon slices. Cover; cook on HIGH 1 hour or until fish is just cooked through (actual time depends on thickness of fish). Prepare Tapenade.

3. Remove fish to serving plates; discard lemon. Top with Tapenade.

Makes 4 servings

Tapenade

½ pound pitted kalamata olives

2 tablespoons chopped fresh thyme or Italian parsley

2 tablespoons capers, drained

2 tablespoons anchovy paste

1 clove garlic

¼ teaspoon grated orange peel

⅛ teaspoon ground red pepper

½ cup olive oil

Place olives, thyme, capers, anchovy paste, garlic, orange peel and ground red pepper in food processor or blender; pulse to roughly chop. Add oil; pulse briefly to form a chunky paste.

Makes about 1 cup

Tip: In a hurry? Substitute store-brought tapenade for homemade!

Bacon-Wrapped Scallops

24 sea scallops, side muscle removed	2 tablespoons honey
½ cup Belgian white ale	¼ teaspoon ground chipotle pepper
3 tablespoons chopped fresh cilantro	12 slices bacon, halved

1. Pour ½ inch of water in bottom of **CROCK-POT®** slow cooker. Combine scallops, ale, cilantro, honey and chipotle pepper in medium bowl; stir to coat. Refrigerate 30 minutes.

2. Place 1 scallop on end of 1 bacon half. Roll up jelly-roll style and secure with toothpick. Remove to large baking sheet. Repeat with remaining bacon and scallops. Brush tops of scallops with ale mixture.

3. Heat large skillet over medium heat. Add wrapped scallops; cook 5 to 7 minutes or until bacon is just beginning to brown. Remove to **CROCK-POT®** slow cooker.

4. Cover; cook on LOW 1 hour. Serve warm or at room temperature.

Makes 12 servings

Coconut Shrimp

2 cans (14 ounces *each*) unsweetened coconut
milk, divided

1½ cups uncooked jasmine or white rice

½ cup water

1 teaspoon sugar

1 teaspoon fish sauce

1 tablespoon red curry paste

2 pounds jumbo raw shrimp, peeled and
deveined (with tails on)

2 large or 4 small green onions, chopped

Shredded fresh basil (optional)

1. Coat inside of **CROCK-POT**® slow cooker with nonstick cooking spray. Add 1 can coconut milk, rice, water, sugar and fish sauce to **CROCK-POT**® slow cooker; stir to combine. Cover; cook on LOW 4 to 5 hours or on HIGH 1½ to 2 hours or until rice is just cooked.

2. Stir curry paste and remaining 1 can coconut milk in medium bowl until blended; add to **CROCK-POT**® slow cooker. Stir in shrimp. Cover; cook on HIGH 30 minutes or until shrimp are pink and opaque. Stir in green onions. Garnish with basil.

Makes 6 servings

Southwestern Salmon Po' Boys

1 red bell pepper, sliced

1 green bell pepper, sliced

1 onion, sliced

½ teaspoon Southwest chipotle seasoning

¼ teaspoon salt

¼ teaspoon black pepper

4 salmon fillets (about 6 ounces *each*), rinsed and patted dry

½ cup Italian dressing

¼ cup water

4 large French sandwich rolls, split *or* French bread cut into 6-inch pieces and split

Chipotle mayonnaise*

Fresh cilantro (optional)

*If unavailable, combine ¼ cup mayonnaise with ½ teaspoon adobo sauce or substitute regular mayonnaise.

1. Coat inside of **CROCK-POT**® slow cooker with nonstick cooking spray. Arrange half of sliced bell peppers and onion in bottom.

2. Combine chipotle seasoning, salt and black pepper in small bowl; rub over both sides of salmon. Place salmon on top of vegetables in **CROCK-POT**® slow cooker. Pour Italian dressing over salmon and top with remaining bell peppers and onion. Add water. Cover; cook on HIGH 1½ hours.

3. Toast rolls, if desired. Spread tops with chipotle mayonnaise and garnish with cilantro. Spoon 1 to 2 tablespoons cooking liquid onto roll bottoms. Place 1 salmon fillet on each roll (remove skin first, if desired). Top with vegetable mixture.

Makes 4 servings

Shrimp and Okra Gumbo

1 tablespoon olive oil

8 ounces kielbasa, halved lengthwise and cut into ¼-inch-thick half moons

1 green bell pepper, chopped

1 medium onion, chopped

3 stalks celery, cut into ¼-inch slices

6 green onions, chopped

4 cloves garlic, minced

1 cup chicken broth

1 can (about 14 ounces) diced tomatoes

1 teaspoon Cajun seasoning

½ teaspoon dried thyme

1 pound large raw shrimp, peeled and deveined (with tails on)

2 cups frozen cut okra, thawed

1. Coat inside of **CROCK-POT®** slow cooker with nonstick cooking spray. Heat oil in large skillet over medium-high heat. Add kielbasa; cook and stir 4 minutes until browned. Remove to **CROCK-POT®** slow cooker.

2. Return skillet to medium-high heat. Add bell pepper, chopped onion, celery, green onions and garlic; cook and stir 5 to 6 minutes until vegetables are crisp-tender. Remove to **CROCK-POT®** slow cooker. Stir in broth, tomatoes, Cajun seasoning and thyme.

3. Cover; cook on LOW 4 hours. Stir in shrimp and okra. Cover; cook on LOW 1 hour.

Makes 6 servings

Cheesy Shrimp on Grits

1 cup finely chopped green bell pepper

1 cup finely chopped red bell pepper

½ cup thinly sliced celery

1 bunch green onions, chopped and divided

¼ cup (½ stick) butter, cubed

1¼ teaspoons seafood seasoning

2 whole bay leaves

¼ teaspoon ground red pepper

1 pound medium raw shrimp, peeled and deveined

5⅓ cups water

1⅓ cups quick-cooking grits

2 cups (8 ounces) shredded sharp Cheddar cheese

¼ cup whipping cream or half-and-half

1. Coat inside of **CROCK-POT®** slow cooker with nonstick cooking spray. Add bell peppers, celery, all but ½ cup green onions, butter, seafood seasoning, bay leaves and ground red pepper. Cover; cook on LOW 4 hours or on HIGH 2 hours.

2. Add shrimp. Cover; cook on HIGH 15 minutes.

3. Meanwhile, bring water to a boil in medium saucepan. Add grits; cook according to package directions.

4. Remove and discard bay leaves. Stir in cheese, cream and remaining ½ cup green onions. Cook on HIGH 5 minutes or until cheese melts. Serve over grits.

Makes 6 servings

Serving Suggestion: This dish is also delicious served over polenta.

Tip: Seafood is delicate and should be added to the **CROCK-POT®** slow cooker during the last 15 to 30 minutes of the cooking time on HIGH, and during the last 30 to 45 minutes if you're cooking on LOW. This type of seafood overcooks easily, becoming tough and rubbery.

Salmon Chowder

1 can (about 15 ounces) cream-style corn

1 can (about 14 ounces) chicken broth

8 ounces small red potatoes, chopped

1 red onion, finely chopped

¼ teaspoon salt

½ teaspoon black pepper

1 package (8 ounces) cream cheese

½ teaspoon grated lemon peel

1 salmon fillet (about 1½ pounds), skinned and cut into 6 pieces

⅓ cup chopped fresh dill (optional)

Lemon wedges (optional)

1. Stir corn, broth, potatoes, onion, salt and pepper into **CROCK-POT**® slow cooker. Cover; cook on LOW 4 hours or on HIGH 2 hours or until potatoes are fork-tender.

2. Whisk cream cheese and lemon peel into **CROCK-POT**® slow cooker until smooth. Top with salmon. Cover; cook on LOW 45 minutes to 1 hour or until fillets are just cooked through and flake when tested with a fork. Remove fillets from **CROCK-POT**® slow cooker. Ladle soup into bowls; top each with salmon fillet. Garnish with dill and lemon wedge.

Makes 6 servings

Tuna Casserole

2 cans (10¾ ounces *each*) cream of celery soup

2 cans (5 ounces *each*) tuna in water, drained and flaked

1 cup water

2 carrots, chopped

1 small red onion, chopped

¼ teaspoon black pepper

1 egg

8 ounces hot cooked egg noodles

Plain dry bread crumbs

2 tablespoons chopped fresh Italian parsley

1. Stir soup, tuna, water, carrots, onion and pepper into **CROCK-POT®** slow cooker. Place whole unpeeled egg on top. Cover; cook on LOW 4 to 5 hours or on HIGH 1½ to 3 hours.

2. Remove egg; stir in pasta. Cover; cook on HIGH ½ to 1 hour or until onion is tender. Meanwhile, mash egg in small bowl; mix in bread crumbs and parsley. Top casserole with bread crumb mixture.

Makes 6 servings

Note: This casserole calls for a raw egg. The egg will hard-cook in its shell in the **CROCK-POT®** slow cooker.

Shrimp Jambalaya

1 can (28 ounces) diced tomatoes

1 medium onion, chopped

1 medium red bell pepper, chopped

1 stalk celery, chopped

2 tablespoons minced garlic

2 teaspoons dried parsley flakes

2 teaspoons dried oregano

1 teaspoon hot pepper sauce

½ teaspoon dried thyme

2 pounds large cooked shrimp, peeled and deveined (with tails on)

2 cups uncooked instant rice

2 cups chicken broth

1. Combine tomatoes, onion, bell pepper, celery, garlic, parsley flakes, oregano, hot pepper sauce and thyme in **CROCK-POT**® slow cooker. Cover; cook on LOW 8 hours or on HIGH 4 hours.

2. Stir in shrimp. Cover; cook on LOW 20 minutes.

3. Meanwhile, prepare rice according to package directions, substituting broth for water. Serve jambalaya over rice.

Makes 6 servings

Sweet and Sour Shrimp

1 can (16 ounces) sliced peaches in syrup, undrained

½ cup chopped green onions

½ cup chopped red bell pepper

½ cup chopped green bell pepper

½ cup chopped celery

⅓ cup vegetable broth

¼ cup light soy sauce

2 tablespoons rice wine vinegar

2 tablespoons dark sesame oil

1 teaspoon red pepper flakes

¼ cup water

2 tablespoons cornstarch

1 package (6 ounces) snow peas

1 pound cooked medium shrimp

1 cup cherry tomatoes, cut into halves

½ cup toasted walnut pieces*

Hot cooked rice

To toast walnuts, spread in single layer in heavy skillet. Cook over medium heat 1 to 2 minutes or until nuts are lightly browned, stirring frequently.

1. Place peaches with syrup, green onions, bell peppers, celery, broth, soy sauce, vinegar, oil and red pepper flakes in **CROCK-POT®** slow cooker. Cover; cook on LOW 3 to 4 hours or on HIGH 2 to 3 hours or until vegetables are tender. Stir well.

2. Stir water into cornstarch in small bowl until smooth; whisk into vegetable mixture. Stir in snow peas. Cover; cook on HIGH 15 minutes or until thickened.

3. Add shrimp, tomatoes and walnuts to **CROCK-POT®** slow cooker. Cover; cook on HIGH 5 minutes or until shrimp are pink and opaque. Serve over rice.

Makes 4 to 6 servings

Salmon and Bok Choy

1 cup vegetable broth	¼ cup soy sauce
2 cloves garlic, finely chopped	¼ cup packed brown sugar
2 teaspoons ground ginger	2 tablespoons lemon juice
¼ teaspoon red pepper flakes	½ teaspoon Chinese five-spice powder
3 small heads bok choy, stems and leaves sliced	4 cups cooked brown rice
3 pounds salmon fillets	

1. Combine broth, garlic, ginger and red pepper flakes in **CROCK-POT**® slow cooker. Add bok choy stems. Cover; cook on LOW 4 to 6 hours or on HIGH 1½ hours or until fork-tender.

2. Stir bok choy leaves into **CROCK-POT**® slow cooker; top with salmon. Cover; cook on LOW 30 minutes or until fish is cooked through.

3. Meanwhile, whisk soy sauce, brown sugar, lemon juice and five-spice powder in small saucepan. Bring to a boil. Reduce heat; simmer until reduced to ⅓ cup. Serve salmon and bok choy on rice with sauce.

Makes 8 servings

Braised Sea Bass with Aromatic Vegetables

2 tablespoons butter or olive oil

2 fennel bulbs, thinly sliced

3 large carrots, julienned

3 large leeks, cleaned and thinly sliced

Kosher salt and black pepper

6 sea bass fillets or other firm-fleshed white fish (2 to 3 pounds total)

1. Melt butter in large skillet over medium-high heat. Add fennel, carrots and leeks; cook and stir until beginning to soften and lightly brown. Season with salt and pepper. Arrange half of vegetables in bottom of **CROCK-POT®** slow cooker.

2. Season bass with salt and pepper; place on top of vegetables in **CROCK-POT®** slow cooker. Top with remaining vegetables. Cover; cook on LOW 2 to 3 hours or on HIGH 1 to 1½ hours or until fish is cooked through.

Makes 6 servings

Hoppin' John

1 pound andouille or smoked sausage, sliced	1 box (about 8 ounces) dirty rice mix
2½ cups chicken broth, divided	½ cup salsa
2 cans (about 15 ounces *each*) black-eyed peas, rinsed and drained	½ to ¾ cup lump crabmeat
	Sliced green onions (optional)

1. Cook and stir sausage in large skillet over medium heat 5 minutes or until browned. Drain fat. Remove sausage to **CROCK-POT**® slow cooker with slotted spoon. Return skillet to heat; pour in ½ cup broth. Cook and stir, scraping up any browned bits from skillet. Pour over sausage.

2. Stir peas, rice mix, remaining broth and salsa into **CROCK-POT**® slow cooker. Cover; cook on LOW 3 to 4 hours or until rice is tender. Add crabmeat; stir until well combined. Cover; cook on LOW 5 minutes or until heated through. Garnish with green onions.

Makes 6 servings

Asian Lettuce Wraps

2 teaspoons canola oil

1½ pounds boneless, skinless chicken breasts or pork shoulder, chopped into ¼-inch pieces

2 leeks, trimmed and chopped into ¼-inch pieces

1 cup shiitake mushrooms, stems removed and caps chopped into ¼-inch pieces

1 stalk celery, chopped into ¼-inch pieces

1 tablespoon oyster sauce

1 tablespoon soy sauce

1 teaspoon dark sesame oil

¼ teaspoon black pepper

2 tablespoons water

1 bag (8 ounces) coleslaw or broccoli slaw mix

½ red bell pepper, cut into thin strips

½ pound large raw shrimp, peeled, deveined and cut into ¼-inch pieces

3 tablespoons unsalted dry roasted peanuts, coarsely chopped

Hoisin sauce

12 crisp romaine lettuce leaves, white rib removed and patted dry

Fresh whole chives

1. Heat oil in large skillet over medium-high heat. Add chicken; brown on all sides. Remove to **CROCK-POT®** slow cooker. Add leeks, mushrooms, celery, oyster sauce, soy sauce, sesame oil, black pepper and water to **CROCK-POT®** slow cooker. Toss slaw and bell pepper in medium bowl; place in single layer on top of chicken.

2. Cover; cook on LOW 4 to 5 hours or on HIGH 2 to 2½ hours or until chicken is cooked through. Stir in shrimp during last 20 minutes of cooking. When shrimp are pink and opaque, remove mixture to large bowl. Add chopped peanuts; mix well.

3. To serve, spread about 1 teaspoon hoisin sauce on lettuce leaf. Add 1 to 2 tablespoons meat mixture and tightly roll; secure by tying chives around rolled leaves.

Makes 6 servings

Shrimp Louisiana-Style

1 pound medium raw shrimp, unpeeled (with tails on)

½ cup (1 stick) butter, cubed

⅓ cup lemon juice

1 tablespoon Worcestershire sauce

1 teaspoon seafood seasoning

1 teaspoon minced garlic

½ teaspoon salt

½ teaspoon black pepper

1½ teaspoons grated lemon peel, plus additional for garnish

Hot cooked rice (optional)

1. Coat inside of **CROCK-POT**® slow cooker with nonstick cooking spray. Add shrimp, butter, lemon juice, Worcestershire sauce, seafood seasoning, garlic, salt and pepper; mix well. Cover; cook on HIGH 1¼ hours.

2. Turn off heat. Stir in 1½ teaspoons lemon peel. Let stand, uncovered, 5 minutes. Serve in shallow soup bowls over rice, if desired. Garnish with additional grated lemon peel.

Makes 3 to 4 servings

Mom's Tuna Casserole

2 cans (12 ounces *each*) solid albacore tuna, drained and flaked

3 cups diced celery

3 cups crushed potato chips, divided

6 hard-cooked eggs, chopped

1 can (10½ ounces) condensed cream of mushroom soup, undiluted

1 can (10½ ounces) condensed cream of celery soup, undiluted

1 cup mayonnaise

1 teaspoon dried tarragon

1 teaspoon black pepper

1. Combine tuna, celery, 2½ cups potato chips, eggs, soups, mayonnaise, tarragon and pepper in **CROCK-POT®** slow cooker; stir well. Cover; cook on LOW 5 to 7 hours.

2. Sprinkle with remaining ½ cup potato chips before serving.

Makes 8 servings

Tip: Don't use your **CROCK-POT®** slow cooker to reheat leftover foods. Remove cooled leftover food to a resealable food storage bag or storage container with a tight-fitting lid and refrigerate. Use a microwave oven, the stove top or the oven for reheating.

VEGETARIAN FAVORITES

Farro Risotto with Mushrooms and Spinach

2 tablespoons olive oil, divided

1 onion, chopped

12 ounces cremini mushrooms, stems trimmed and quartered

¾ teaspoon salt

¼ teaspoon black pepper

2 cloves garlic, minced

1 cup farro

1 sprig fresh thyme

4 cups vegetable broth

8 ounces baby spinach

½ cup grated Parmesan cheese

1. Heat 1 tablespoon oil in large skillet over medium heat. Add onion; cook 8 minutes or until tender. Remove to **CROCK-POT®** slow cooker. Add remaining 1 tablespoon oil to same skillet; heat over medium-high heat. Add mushrooms, salt and pepper; cook 6 to 8 minutes or until mushrooms have released their liquid and are browned. Add garlic; cook 1 minute. Stir in farro and thyme; cook 1 minute. Remove mushroom mixture to **CROCK-POT®** slow cooker.

2. Stir broth into **CROCK-POT®** slow cooker. Cover; cook on HIGH 3½ hours until farro is tender and broth is absorbed. Remove thyme sprig. Stir in spinach and cheese just before serving.

Makes 4 servings

Quinoa and Vegetable Medley

2 medium sweet potatoes, cut into ½-inch-thick slices

1 medium eggplant, cut into ½-inch cubes

1 large green bell pepper, sliced

1 medium tomato, cut into wedges

1 small onion, cut into wedges

½ teaspoon salt

¼ teaspoon ground red pepper

¼ teaspoon black pepper

1 cup uncooked quinoa

2 cups vegetable broth

2 cloves garlic, minced

½ teaspoon dried thyme

¼ teaspoon dried marjoram

1. Coat inside of **CROCK-POT**® slow cooker with nonstick cooking spray. Combine potatoes, eggplant, bell pepper, tomato, onion, salt, ground red pepper and black pepper in **CROCK-POT**® slow cooker; toss to coat.

2. Place quinoa in strainer; rinse well. Add quinoa to vegetable mixture in **CROCK-POT**® slow cooker. Stir in broth, garlic, thyme and marjoram. Cover; cook on LOW 5 hours or on HIGH 2½ hours or until broth is absorbed.

Makes 6 servings

Tofu Tikka Masala

1 package (14 to 16 ounces) extra firm tofu, cut into 1-inch pieces

½ cup whole milk yogurt

2 teaspoons salt, divided

1 tablespoon plus 1 teaspoon minced garlic, divided

2½ teaspoons grated fresh ginger, divided

2 tablespoons vegetable oil

1 medium onion, chopped

2 tablespoons tomato paste

1 tablespoon garam masala

1 teaspoon sugar

1 can (28 ounces) crushed tomatoes

½ cup whipping cream

3 tablespoons chopped fresh cilantro

Hot cooked basmati rice (optional)

1. Combine tofu, yogurt, 1 teaspoon salt, 1 teaspoon garlic and 1 teaspoon ginger in large bowl; stir to blend. Cover; refrigerate 1 hour or overnight.

2. Heat oil in large skillet over medium heat. Add onion; cook 8 minutes or until softened. Add remaining 1 tablespoon garlic, remaining 1½ teaspoons ginger, tomato paste, remaining 1 teaspoon salt and garam masala; cook and stir 1 minute. Add sugar and tomatoes; bring to a simmer. Remove onion mixture and tofu to **CROCK-POT®** slow cooker using slotted spoon; stir to combine.

3. Cover; cook on LOW 8 hours. Stir in cream and cilantro. Serve over rice, if desired.

Makes 4 to 6 servings

Fennel Braised with Tomato

2 fennel bulbs

1 tablespoon olive oil

1 onion, sliced

1 clove garlic, sliced

4 tomatoes, chopped

⅔ cup vegetable broth

3 tablespoons dry white wine

1 tablespoon chopped fresh marjoram *or* 1 teaspoon dried marjoram

Salt and black pepper

1. Trim stems and bottoms from fennel bulbs, reserving green leafy tops for garnish. Cut each bulb lengthwise into four wedges.

2. Heat oil in large skillet over medium heat. Add fennel, onion and garlic; cook and stir 5 minutes or until onion is soft and translucent. Remove fennel mixture to **CROCK-POT®** slow cooker. Add tomatoes, broth, wine, marjoram, salt and pepper; stir to blend.

3. Cover; cook on LOW 2 to 3 hours or on HIGH 1 to 1½ hours. Garnish with reserved green leafy tops.

Makes 6 servings

Thai Red Curry with Tofu

1 medium sweet potato, peeled and cut into 1-inch pieces

1 small eggplant, halved lengthwise and cut crosswise into ½-inch-wide halves

8 ounces extra firm tofu, cut into 1-inch pieces

½ cup green beans, cut into 1-inch pieces

½ red bell pepper, cut into ¼-inch-wide strips

2 tablespoons vegetable oil

5 medium shallots (about 1½ cups), thinly sliced

3 tablespoons Thai red curry paste

1 teaspoon minced garlic

1 teaspoon grated ginger

1 can (about 13 ounces) unsweetened coconut milk

1½ tablespoons soy sauce

1 tablespoon packed light brown sugar

¼ cup chopped fresh basil

2 tablespoons lime juice

Hot cooked rice (optional)

1. Coat inside of **CROCK-POT®** slow cooker with nonstick cooking spray. Add potato, eggplant, tofu, beans and bell pepper.

2. Heat oil in large skillet over medium heat. Add shallots; cook 5 minutes or until browned and tender. Add curry paste, garlic and ginger; cook and stir 1 minute. Add coconut milk, soy sauce and brown sugar; bring to a simmer. Pour mixture over vegetables in **CROCK-POT®** slow cooker.

3. Cover; cook on LOW 2 to 3 hours. Stir in basil and lime juice. Serve over rice, if desired.

Makes 4 servings

Black Bean Stuffed Peppers

Nonstick cooking spray

1 medium onion, finely chopped

¼ teaspoon ground red pepper

¼ teaspoon dried oregano

¼ teaspoon ground cumin

¼ teaspoon chili powder

1 can (about 15 ounces) black beans, rinsed and drained

6 large green bell peppers, tops removed

1 cup (4 ounces) shredded Monterey Jack cheese

1 cup tomato salsa

½ cup sour cream

1. Spray medium skillet with cooking spray; heat over medium heat. Add onion; cook and stir 3 to 5 minutes or until golden. Add ground red pepper, oregano, cumin and chili powder; cook and stir 1 minute.

2. Mash half of beans with onion mixture in medium bowl; stir in remaining half of beans. Spoon black bean mixture into bell peppers; sprinkle with cheese. Pour salsa over cheese. Place bell peppers in **CROCK-POT®** slow cooker.

3. Cover; cook on LOW 6 to 8 hours or on HIGH 3 to 4 hours. Serve with sour cream.

Makes 6 servings

Tip: You may increase any of the recipe ingredients to taste except the tomato salsa.

Pesto Rice and Beans

1 can (about 15 ounces) Great Northern beans, rinsed and drained

1 can (about 14 ounces) vegetable broth

¾ cup uncooked converted long grain rice

1½ cups frozen cut green beans, thawed and drained

½ cup prepared pesto

Grated Parmesan cheese (optional)

1. Combine Great Northern beans, broth and rice in **CROCK-POT**® slow cooker. Cover; cook on LOW 2 hours.

2. Stir in green beans. Cover; cook on LOW 1 hour or until rice and beans are tender.

3. Turn off heat. Stir in pesto and cheese, if desired. Let stand, covered, 5 minutes or until cheese is melted.

Makes 8 servings

Tip: Choose converted long grain rice, Arborio rice or wild rice for best results. Long, slow cooking can turn other types of rice into mush. If you prefer to use another type of rice instead of converted, cook it on the stove-top and add it to the **CROCK-POT**® slow cooker during the last 15 minutes of cooking.

Vegetable-Bean Pasta Sauce

2 cans (about 15 ounces *each*) cannellini beans,
   rinsed and drained

2 cans (about 14 ounces *each*) diced tomatoes

16 baby carrots

1 medium onion, sliced

1 can (6 ounces) tomato paste

1 ounce dried oyster mushrooms, chopped

¼ cup grated Parmesan cheese

2 teaspoons garlic powder

1 teaspoon dried basil

1 teaspoon dried oregano

½ teaspoon dried rosemary

½ teaspoon dried marjoram

½ teaspoon dried sage

½ teaspoon dried thyme

¼ teaspoon black pepper

1 package (12 ounces) whole wheat spaghetti
   noodles, cooked and drained

1. Combine beans, tomatoes, carrots, onion, tomato paste, mushrooms, cheese, garlic powder, basil, oregano, rosemary, marjoram, sage, thyme and pepper in **CROCK-POT®** slow cooker; stir to blend.

2. Cover; cook on LOW 8 to 10 hours. Serve over noodles.

Makes 8 servings

Chickpea and Vegetable Curry

1 can (about 13 ounces) unsweetened coconut
   milk

1 cup vegetable broth, divided

2 teaspoons curry powder

¼ teaspoon ground red pepper

2 cups cut fresh green beans (1-inch pieces)

1 can (about 15 ounces) chickpeas, rinsed and
   drained

2 carrots, very thinly sliced

½ cup golden raisins

¼ cup all-purpose flour

2 cups hot cooked couscous

Green onion and toasted sliced almonds
   (optional)

1. Coat inside of **CROCK-POT**® slow cooker with nonstick cooking spray. Combine coconut milk,
¾ cup broth, curry powder and ground red pepper in **CROCK-POT**® slow cooker. Stir in green beans,
chickpeas, carrots and raisins. Cover; cook on LOW 6 to 7 hours or on HIGH 2½ to 3 hours or until
vegetables are tender.

2. Stir remaining ¼ cup broth into flour in small bowl until smooth. Stir into vegetable mixture. Cover;
cook on HIGH 15 minutes or until thickened. Ladle into shallow bowls; top with couscous, green onion
and almonds, if desired.

Makes 4 servings

Ratatouille with Parmesan Cheese

Nonstick cooking spray
1 cup diced eggplant
2 medium tomatoes, chopped
1 small zucchini, diced
1 cup sliced mushrooms
½ cup tomato purée
1 large shallot *or* ½ small onion, chopped
1 clove garlic, minced
¾ teaspoon dried oregano
⅛ teaspoon dried rosemary
⅛ teaspoon black pepper
2 tablespoons shredded fresh basil
2 teaspoons lemon juice
¼ teaspoon salt
Grated Parmesan cheese

1. Spray large skillet with cooking spray; heat over medium-high heat. Add eggplant; cook and stir 5 minutes or until lightly browned. Remove eggplant to **CROCK-POT**® slow cooker.

2. Add tomatoes, zucchini, mushrooms, tomato purée, shallot, garlic, oregano, rosemary and pepper; stir to blend. Cover; cook on LOW 6 hours or on HIGH 3 hours.

3. Stir in basil, lemon juice and salt. Turn off heat; let stand 5 minutes. Top each serving with Parmesan cheese.

Makes 4 servings

Stuffed Manicotti

1 container (15 ounces) ricotta cheese

1½ cups (6 ounces) shredded Italian cheese blend, divided

1 egg

¼ teaspoon ground nutmeg

10 uncooked manicotti shells

2 cans (about 14 ounces *each*) Italian seasoned stewed tomatoes

1 cup spicy marinara or tomato basil pasta sauce

Chopped fresh basil or Italian parsley (optional)

French bread (optional)

1. Combine ricotta cheese, 1 cup Italian cheese, egg and nutmeg in medium bowl; mix well. Spoon mixture into large resealable food storage bag; cut off small corner. Pipe cheese mixture into uncooked manicotti shells.

2. Coat inside of **CROCK-POT**® slow cooker with nonstick cooking spray. Combine tomatoes and pasta sauce in large bowl; stir until blended. Spoon 1½ cups sauce mixture into **CROCK-POT**® slow cooker. Arrange half of the stuffed shells in sauce. Repeat layering with 1½ cups sauce, remaining shells and remaining sauce. Cover; cook on LOW 2½ to 3 hours.

3. Sprinkle remaining ½ cup Italian cheese over top. Turn **CROCK-POT**® slow cooker to HIGH. Cover; cook on HIGH 10 to 15 minutes or until cheese is melted. Garnish with basil. Serve with bread, if desired.

Makes 5 servings

Black Bean, Zucchini and Corn Enchiladas

1 tablespoon vegetable oil

1 medium onion, chopped

2 medium zucchini

2 cups corn

1 large red bell pepper, chopped

1 teaspoon minced garlic

½ teaspoon salt

½ teaspoon ground cumin

¼ teaspoon coriander

1 can (about 14 ounces) black beans, rinsed and drained

2 jars (16 ounces *each*) salsa verde

12 (6-inch) corn tortillas

2½ cups (10 ounces) shredded Monterey Jack cheese

2 tablespoons chopped fresh cilantro

1. Heat oil in large skillet over medium heat. Add onion; cook 6 minutes or until softened. Add zucchini, corn and bell pepper; cook 2 minutes. Add garlic, salt, cumin and coriander; cook and stir 1 minute. Stir in beans. Remove from heat.

2. Pour 1 cup salsa in bottom of **CROCK-POT**® slow cooker. Arrange 3 tortillas in single layer, cutting the tortillas in half as needed to make them fit. Place 2 cups vegetable mixture over tortillas; sprinkle with ½ cup cheese. Repeat layering two more times. Layer with remaining 3 tortillas; top with 2 cups salsa. Sprinkle with remaining 1 cup cheese. Reserve remaining filling for another use.

3. Cover; cook on HIGH 2 hours or until cheese is bubbly and edges are lightly browned. Sprinkle with cilantro. Turn off heat. Let stand 10 minutes before serving.

Makes 6 servings

Hot Three-Bean Casserole

2 tablespoons olive oil

1 cup coarsely chopped onion

1 cup chopped celery

2 cloves garlic, minced

1 can (about 15 ounces) chickpeas, rinsed and drained

1 can (about 15 ounces) kidney beans, rinsed and drained

1 package (10 ounces) frozen cut green beans

1 cup water

1 cup coarsely chopped tomato

1 can (8 ounces) tomato sauce

1 to 2 jalapeño peppers, seeded and minced*

1 tablespoon chili powder

2 teaspoons sugar

1½ teaspoons ground cumin

1 teaspoon salt

1 teaspoon dried oregano

¼ teaspoon black pepper

Fresh oregano (optional)

*Jalapeño peppers can sting and irritate the skin, so wear rubber gloves when handling peppers and do not touch your eyes.

1. Heat oil in large skillet over medium heat. Add onion, celery and garlic; cook and stir 5 minutes or until tender. Place in **CROCK-POT®** slow cooker.

2. Add chickpeas, beans, water, chopped tomato, tomato sauce, jalapeño pepper, chili powder, sugar, cumin, salt, oregano and pepper to **CROCK-POT®** slow cooker; stir to blend. Cover; cook on LOW 6 to 8 hours. Garnish with fresh oregano.

Makes 12 servings

Red Beans and Rice

2 cans (about 15 ounces *each*) red beans, undrained

1 can (about 14 ounces) diced tomatoes

½ cup chopped celery

½ cup chopped green bell pepper

½ cup chopped green onions

2 cloves garlic, minced

1 to 2 teaspoons hot pepper sauce

1 teaspoon Worcestershire sauce

1 whole bay leaf

3 cups hot cooked rice

1. Combine beans, tomatoes, celery, bell pepper, green onions, garlic, hot pepper sauce, Worcestershire sauce and bay leaf in **CROCK-POT**® slow cooker; stir to blend. Cover; cook on LOW 4 to 6 hours or on HIGH 2 to 3 hours.

2. Mash bean mixture slightly in **CROCK-POT**® slow cooker until mixture thickens. Cover; cook on HIGH ½ to 1 hour. Remove and discard bay leaf. Serve bean mixture over rice.

Makes 6 servings

Artichoke Pasta

1 tablespoon olive oil

1 cup chopped sweet onion

4 cloves garlic, minced

1 can (28 ounces) crushed tomatoes

1 can (about 14 ounces) artichoke hearts, drained and cut into pieces

1 cup small pimiento-stuffed olives

¾ teaspoon red pepper flakes

8 ounces hot cooked fettuccine pasta

½ cup grated Asiago or Romano cheese

   Fresh basil leaves (optional)

1. Coat inside of **CROCK-POT**® slow cooker with nonstick cooking spray. Heat oil in small skillet over medium heat. Add onion; cook and stir 5 minutes. Add garlic; cook and stir 1 minute. Combine onion mixture, tomatoes, artichokes, olives and red pepper flakes in **CROCK-POT**® slow cooker.

2. Cover; cook on LOW 7 to 8 hours or on HIGH 3 to 4 hours. Top pasta with artichoke sauce and cheese. Garnish with basil.

Makes 4 servings

Homestyle Mac 'n' Cheese

12 ounces uncooked elbow macaroni (about 3 cups)

2 cans (12 ounces *each*) evaporated milk

1 cup milk

⅓ cup all-purpose flour

¼ cup (½ stick) unsalted butter, melted

2 eggs, lightly beaten

1 teaspoon dry mustard

½ teaspoon salt

¼ teaspoon black pepper

4 cups (16 ounces) shredded sharp Cheddar cheese

Toasted plain dry bread crumbs (optional)

1. Coat inside of **CROCK-POT®** slow cooker with nonstick cooking spray. Bring large saucepan of lightly salted water to a boil. Add macaroni to saucepan; cook according to package directions. Drain. Remove to **CROCK-POT®** slow cooker.

2. Combine evaporated milk, milk, flour, butter, eggs, dry mustard, salt and pepper in large bowl; add to **CROCK-POT®** slow cooker. Stir in cheese until well combined. Cover; cook on LOW 3½ to 4 hours or until cheese is melted and macaroni is heated through. Stir well. Top each serving with bread crumbs, if desired.

Makes 6 to 8 servings

Mushroom and Parmesan Risotto

2 tablespoons extra virgin olive oil	½ cup Madeira wine
8 ounces sliced mushrooms	4½ cups low-sodium vegetable broth
½ cup chopped shallots	⅓ cup grated Parmesan cheese
½ cup chopped onion	2 tablespoons unsalted butter
3 cloves garlic, minced	3 tablespoons chopped fresh parsley
1½ cups uncooked Arborio rice	¼ teaspoon black pepper

1. Heat oil in large nonstick skillet over medium-high heat. Add mushrooms; cook and stir 6 to 7 minutes or until mushrooms have released their liquid and are beginning to brown. Stir in shallots, onion and garlic; cook and stir 2 to 3 minutes or until vegetables begin to soften. Add rice; cook and stir 1 minute. Add Madeira; cook and stir 1 minute or until almost absorbed.

2. Remove mixture to **CROCK-POT**® slow cooker. Add broth. Cover; cook on HIGH 2 hours or until liquid is absorbed and rice is tender.

3. Turn off heat; stir in cheese, butter, parsley and pepper.

Makes 6 servings

Mexican Hot Pot

1 tablespoon canola oil	2 cups corn
1 medium onion, chopped	1 can (about 15 ounces) chickpeas, rinsed and drained
3 cloves garlic, minced	
2 teaspoons red pepper flakes	1 can (about 15 ounces) pinto beans, rinsed and drained
2 teaspoons dried oregano	
1 teaspoon ground cumin	1 cup water
1 can (28 ounces) whole tomatoes, drained and chopped	6 cups shredded iceberg lettuce

1. Heat oil in large nonstick skillet over medium-high heat. Add onion and garlic; cook and stir 5 minutes. Add red pepper flakes, oregano and cumin; mix well.

2. Remove onion and garlic mixture to **CROCK-POT**® slow cooker. Stir in tomatoes, corn, chickpeas, beans and water. Cover; cook on LOW 7 to 8 hours or on HIGH 2 to 3 hours. Top each serving with 1 cup shredded lettuce.

Makes 6 servings

Meatless Sloppy Joes

2 cups thinly sliced onions

2 cups chopped green bell peppers

1 can (about 15 ounces) kidney beans, drained and mashed

1 can (8 ounces) tomato sauce

2 tablespoons ketchup

1 tablespoon yellow mustard

2 cloves garlic, finely chopped

1 teaspoon chili powder

1 tablespoon cider vinegar (optional)

4 sandwich rolls

1. Combine onions, bell peppers, beans, tomato sauce, ketchup, mustard, garlic and chili powder in **CROCK-POT®** slow cooker. Cover; cook on LOW 5 to 5½ hours or until vegetables are tender.

2. Season with cider vinegar, if desired. Serve on rolls.

Makes 4 servings

Spinach Artichoke Gratin

2 cups (16 ounces) cottage cheese

2 eggs

4½ tablespoons grated Parmesan cheese, divided

1 tablespoon lemon juice

⅛ teaspoon ground nutmeg

⅛ teaspoon black pepper

2 packages (10 ounces *each*) frozen chopped spinach, thawed and squeezed dry

⅓ cup thinly sliced green onions

1 package (10 ounces) frozen artichoke hearts, thawed and halved

1. Add cottage cheese, eggs, 3 tablespoons Parmesan cheese, lemon juice, nutmeg and pepper to food processor or blender; process until smooth.

2. Coat inside of **CROCK-POT®** slow cooker with nonstick cooking spray. Combine spinach, cottage cheese mixture and green onions in large bowl. Spread half of mixture in **CROCK-POT®** slow cooker.

3. Pat artichoke halves dry with paper towels. Place in single layer over spinach mixture. Sprinkle with remaining 1½ tablespoons Parmesan cheese. Cover with remaining spinach mixture. Cover with lid slightly ajar to allow excess moisture to escape; cook on LOW 3 to 3½ hours or on HIGH 2 to 2½ hours.

Makes 6 servings

Greek Rice

2 tablespoons butter

1¾ cups uncooked converted long grain rice

2 cans (about 14 ounces *each*) vegetable broth

1 teaspoon Greek seasoning

1 teaspoon ground oregano

1 cup pitted kalamata olives, drained and chopped

¾ cup chopped roasted red peppers

Crumbled feta cheese (optional)

Chopped fresh Italian parsley (optional)

1. Melt butter in large nonstick skillet over medium-high heat. Add rice and sauté 4 minutes or until golden brown. Remove to **CROCK-POT®** slow cooker. Stir in broth, Greek seasoning and oregano.

2. Cover; cook on LOW 4 hours or until liquid is absorbed and rice is tender. Stir in olives and roasted red peppers; cook 5 minutes. Garnish with feta and Italian parsley, if desired.

Makes 6 to 8 servings

Portobello Bolognese Sauce

2 tablespoons extra virgin olive oil

2 cups (6 to 8 ounces) chopped portobello mushrooms

4 cloves garlic, minced

1 jar (24 to 26 ounces) spicy pasta sauce

1 cup thinly sliced carrots

2 tablespoons tomato paste

6 ounces thin spaghetti, uncooked

½ cup grated Parmesan or Romano cheese

¼ cup shredded fresh basil

1. Coat inside of **CROCK-POT®** slow cooker with nonstick cooking spray. Heat oil in large skillet over medium heat. Add mushrooms and garlic; cook 6 minutes or until mushrooms have released their liquid and liquid has thickened slightly.

2. Combine mushroom mixture, pasta sauce, carrots and tomato paste in **CROCK-POT®** slow cooker; mix well. Cover; cook on LOW 5 to 6 hours or on HIGH 2½ to 3 hours or until sauce has thickened and carrots are tender.

3. Cook spaghetti according to package directions. Drain; top with Bolognese sauce, cheese and basil.

Makes 4 servings

Barley and Vegetable Risotto

2 teaspoons olive oil	4½ cups vegetable broth
1 small onion, diced	2 cups packed baby spinach
8 ounces sliced mushrooms	¼ cup grated Parmesan cheese
¾ cup uncooked pearl barley	¼ teaspoon black pepper
1 large red bell pepper, diced	

1. Heat oil in large skillet over medium-high heat. Add onion; cook and stir 2 minutes or until lightly browned. Add mushrooms; cook and stir 5 minutes or until mushrooms have released their liquid and are beginning to brown. Remove to **CROCK-POT**® slow cooker.

2. Add barley and bell pepper to **CROCK-POT**® slow cooker; pour in broth. Cover; cook on LOW 4 to 5 hours or on HIGH 2½ to 3 hours or until barley is tender and liquid is absorbed.

3. Stir in spinach. Turn off heat. Let stand 5 minutes. Gently stir in cheese and black pepper just before serving.

Makes 6 servings

Manchego Eggplant

1 cup all-purpose flour

4 large eggplants, peeled and sliced horizontally into ¾-inch-thick pieces

2 tablespoons olive oil

1 jar (24 to 26 ounces) roasted garlic-flavor pasta sauce

2 tablespoons Italian seasoning

1 cup (4 ounces) grated manchego cheese

1 jar (24 to 26 ounces) roasted eggplant-flavor marinara pasta sauce

1. Place flour in medium shallow bowl. Add eggplants; toss to coat. Heat oil in large skillet over medium-high heat. Lightly brown eggplants in batches 3 to 4 minutes on each side.

2. Pour thin layer of garlic pasta sauce into bottom of **CROCK-POT**® slow cooker. Top with eggplant slices, Italian seasoning, cheese and marinara pasta sauce. Repeat layers until all ingredients have been used. Cover; cook on HIGH 2 hours.

Makes 12 servings

Cuban Black Beans and Rice

3¾ cups vegetable broth

1½ cups uncooked brown rice

1 onion, chopped

1 jalapeño pepper, seeded and chopped*

3 cloves garlic, minced

2 teaspoons ground cumin

1 teaspoon salt

2 cans (about 15 ounces *each*) black beans, rinsed and drained

1 tablespoon lime juice

Sour cream (optional)

Sliced green onions (optional)

Jalapeño peppers can sting and irritate the skin, so wear rubber gloves when handling peppers and do not touch your eyes.

1. Stir broth, rice, onion, jalapeño pepper, garlic, cumin and salt into **CROCK-POT**® slow cooker. Cover; cook on LOW 7½ hours or until rice is tender.

2. Stir beans and lime juice into **CROCK-POT**® slow cooker. Cover; cook on LOW 15 to 20 minutes or until heated through. Top with sour cream and green onions, if desired.

Makes 4 to 6 servings

Chili and Cheese "Baked" Potato Supper

- 4 russet potatoes (about 2 pounds)
- 2 cups prepared meatless chili
- ½ cup (2 ounces) shredded Cheddar cheese
- ¼ cup sour cream (optional)
- 2 green onions, sliced

1. Prick potatoes in several places with fork. Wrap potatoes in foil. Place in **CROCK-POT®** slow cooker. Cover; cook on LOW 8 to 10 hours or on HIGH 4 to 5 hours.

2. Carefully unwrap potatoes and place on serving dish. Place chili in medium microwavable dish; microwave on HIGH 3 to 5 minutes. Split potatoes and spoon chili on top. Sprinkle with cheese, sour cream, if desired, and green onions.

Makes 4 servings

Bean and Vegetable Burritos

- 2 tablespoons chili powder
- 2 teaspoons dried oregano
- 1½ teaspoons ground cumin
- 1 large sweet potato, diced
- 1 can (about 15 ounces) black beans, rinsed and drained
- 4 cloves garlic, minced
- 1 medium yellow onion, halved and thinly sliced
- 1 jalapeño pepper, seeded and minced*
- 1 green bell pepper, chopped
- 1 cup frozen corn
- 3 tablespoons lime juice
- 1 tablespoon chopped fresh cilantro
- ¾ cup (3 ounces) shredded Monterey Jack cheese
- 6 (10-inch) flour tortillas, warmed

*Jalapeño peppers can sting and irritate the skin, so wear rubber gloves when handling peppers and do not touch your eyes.

1. Combine chili powder, oregano and cumin in small bowl. Layer potato, beans, half of chili powder mixture, garlic, onion, jalapeño pepper, bell pepper, remaining half of chili powder mixture and corn in **CROCK-POT®** slow cooker. Cover; cook on LOW 5 hours or until potato is tender. Stir in lime juice and cilantro.

2. Spoon 2 tablespoons cheese into center of each tortilla. Top with 1 cup filling. Fold up bottom edge of tortilla over filling; fold in sides and roll to enclose filling.

Makes 6 servings

Cran-Orange Acorn Squash

5 tablespoons uncooked instant brown rice

3 tablespoons minced onion

3 tablespoons diced celery

3 tablespoons dried cranberries

Pinch ground sage

3 small acorn or carnival squash, cut in half and seeded

1 teaspoon unsalted butter, cubed

9 teaspoons orange juice

½ cup warm water

1. Combine rice, onion, celery, cranberries and sage in small bowl. Stuff each of the squash halves evenly with rice mixture; dot with butter. Pour 1½ teaspoons orange juice over stuffing on each of the squash halves.

2. Stand squash in **CROCK-POT®** slow cooker. Pour water into bottom of **CROCK-POT®** slow cooker. Cover; cook on LOW 2½ hours or until squash are tender.

Makes 6 servings

Italian Eggplant with Millet and Pepper Stuffing

¼ cup uncooked millet

2 small eggplants (about ¾ pound total), unpeeled

¼ cup chopped red bell pepper, divided

¼ cup chopped green bell pepper, divided

1 teaspoon olive oil

1 clove garlic, minced

1½ cups vegetable broth

½ teaspoon ground cumin

½ teaspoon dried oregano

⅛ teaspoon red pepper flakes

Sprigs fresh rosemary (optional)

1. Heat large skillet over medium heat. Add millet; cook and stir 5 minutes. Remove to small bowl; set aside. Cut eggplants lengthwise into halves. Scoop out flesh, leaving about ¼-inch-thick shell. Reserve shells; chop eggplant flesh. Combine 1 tablespoon red bell pepper and 1 tablespoon green bell pepper in small bowl; set aside.

2. Heat oil in same skillet over medium heat. Add chopped eggplant, remaining red and green bell peppers and garlic; cook and stir 8 minutes or until eggplant is tender.

3. Combine eggplant mixture, broth, cumin, oregano and red pepper flakes in **CROCK-POT**® slow cooker. Cover; cook on LOW 4½ hours or until all liquid is absorbed.

4. Turn **CROCK-POT**® slow cooker to HIGH. Fill eggplant shells with eggplant-millet mixture. Sprinkle with reserved bell peppers. Place filled shells in **CROCK-POT**® slow cooker. Cover; cook on HIGH 1½ to 2 hours. Garnish with rosemary.

Makes 4 servings

Vegetarian Lasagna

1 eggplant, sliced into ½-inch rounds	1 teaspoon dried basil
½ teaspoon salt	1 teaspoon dried oregano
3 tablespoons olive oil, divided	2 cups ricotta cheese
1 medium zucchini, thinly sliced	1½ cups (6 ounces) shredded mozzarella cheese
8 ounces mushrooms, sliced	1 cup grated Parmesan cheese, divided
1 small onion, diced	1 package (8 ounces) whole wheat lasagna noodles, cooked and drained
1 can (24 to 26 ounces) pasta sauce	

1. Sprinkle eggplant with salt; let stand 10 to 15 minutes. Rinse off excess salt and pat dry; brush with 1 tablespoon oil. Heat large skillet over medium heat. Add eggplant; cook 3 to 5 minutes or until browned on both sides. Remove to large paper towel-lined plate. Heat 1 tablespoon oil in same skillet over medium heat. Add zucchini; cook 3 to 5 minutes or until browned on both sides. Remove to separate large paper towel-lined plate.

2. Heat remaining 1 tablespoon oil in same skillet over medium heat; cook and stir mushrooms and onion until softened. Stir in pasta sauce, basil and oregano. Combine ricotta cheese, mozzarella cheese and ½ cup Parmesan cheese in medium bowl.

3. Spread ⅓ sauce mixture in bottom of **CROCK-POT**® slow cooker. Layer with ⅓ lasagna noodles, ½ eggplant, ½ cheese mixture. Repeat layers. For last layer, use remaining ⅓ of lasagna noodles, zucchini, remaining ⅓ of sauce mixture and top with remaining ½ cup Parmesan cheese.

4. Cover; cook on LOW 6 hours. Turn off heat. Let stand 15 to 20 minutes before evenly cutting into eight squares.

Makes 8 servings

SENSATIONAL SIDES

Five-Ingredient Mushroom Stuffing

6 tablespoons unsalted butter

2 medium onions, chopped

1 pound sliced white mushrooms

¼ teaspoon salt

5 cups bagged stuffing mix, any seasoning

1 cup vegetable broth

Chopped fresh Italian parsley

1. Melt butter in large skillet over medium-high heat. Add onions, mushrooms and salt; cook and stir 20 minutes or until vegetables are browned and most liquid is absorbed. Remove onion mixture to **CROCK-POT®** slow cooker.

2. Stir in stuffing mix and broth. Cover; cook on LOW 3 hours. Garnish with parsley.

Makes 12 servings

Easy Dirty Rice

½ pound bulk Italian sausage

2 cups water

1 cup uncooked long grain rice

1 large yellow onion, finely chopped

1 large green bell pepper, finely chopped

½ cup finely chopped celery

¼ teaspoon salt

½ teaspoon ground red pepper

½ cup chopped fresh Italian parsley

1. Brown sausage in skillet over medium-high heat 6 to 8 minutes, stirring to break up meat. Remove to **CROCK-POT**® slow cooker using slotted spoon.

2. Stir in water, rice, onion, bell pepper, celery, salt and ground red pepper. Cover; cook on LOW 2 hours. Stir in parsley.

Makes 4 servings

Tip: Try substituting brown rice for the white rice in this recipe. Since it contains the bran and the germ, it is more nutritious than ordinary white rice.

BBQ Baked Beans

3 cans (about 15 ounces *each*) white beans, drained

4 slices bacon, chopped

¾ cup prepared barbecue sauce

½ cup maple syrup

1½ teaspoons dry mustard

Coat inside of **CROCK-POT®** slow cooker with nonstick cooking spray. Add beans, bacon, barbecue sauce, syrup and dry mustard; stir to blend. Cover; cook on LOW 4 hours, stirring halfway through cooking time.

Makes 12 servings

Rustic Potatoes au Gratin

½ cup milk

1 can (10¾ ounces) condensed Cheddar cheese soup, undiluted

1 package (8 ounces) cream cheese, softened

1 clove garlic, minced

¼ teaspoon ground nutmeg

⅛ teaspoon black pepper

2 pounds baking potatoes, unpeeled and cut into ¼-inch-thick slices

1 small onion, thinly sliced

Paprika (optional)

1. Heat milk in small saucepan over medium heat until small bubbles form around edge of pan. Remove from heat. Stir in soup, cream cheese, garlic, nutmeg and pepper until smooth.

2. Layer one fourth of potatoes and one fourth of onion in **CROCK-POT®** slow cooker. Top with one fourth of soup mixture. Repeat layers three times, using remaining potatoes, onion and soup mixture. Cover; cook on LOW 6 to 7 hours until most liquid is absorbed. Garnish with paprika.

Makes 6 servings

Slow-Cooked Succotash

2 teaspoons olive oil

1 cup diced onion

1 cup diced green bell pepper

1 cup diced celery

1 teaspoon paprika

1½ cups frozen corn

1½ cups frozen lima beans

1 cup canned diced tomatoes

2 teaspoons dried parsley flakes *or*
  1 tablespoon minced fresh Italian parsley

Salt and black pepper

1. Heat oil in large skillet over medium heat. Add onion, bell pepper and celery; cook and stir 5 minutes or until vegetables are crisp-tender. Stir in paprika.

2. Stir onion mixture, corn, beans, tomatoes, parsley flakes, salt and black pepper into **CROCK-POT®** slow cooker. Cover; cook on LOW 6 to 8 hours or on HIGH 3 to 4 hours.

Makes 8 servings

Cheesy Polenta

6 cups vegetable broth

1½ cups uncooked medium-grind instant polenta

½ cup grated Parmesan cheese, plus additional for serving

4 tablespoons unsalted butter, cubed

Fried sage leaves (optional)

1. Coat inside of **CROCK-POT**® slow cooker with nonstick cooking spray. Heat broth in large saucepan over high heat. Remove to **CROCK-POT**® slow cooker; whisk in polenta.

2. Cover; cook on LOW 2 to 2½ hours or until polenta is tender and creamy. Stir in ½ cup cheese and butter. Garnish with additional cheese and sage.

Makes 6 servings

Candied Sweet Potatoes

3 medium sweet potatoes (1½ to 2 pounds),
   sliced into ½-inch rounds

½ cup water

¼ cup (½ stick) butter, cubed

2 tablespoons sugar

1 tablespoon vanilla

1 teaspoon ground nutmeg

Combine potatoes, water, butter, sugar, vanilla and nutmeg in **CROCK-POT**® slow cooker; stir to blend. Cover; cook on LOW 7 hours or on HIGH 4 hours.

Makes 4 servings

Curried Cauliflower and Potatoes

3 tablespoons vegetable oil

1 medium onion, chopped

1 tablespoon minced garlic

1 tablespoon curry powder

1½ teaspoons salt, plus additional for seasoning

1½ teaspoons grated ginger

1 teaspoon ground turmeric

1 teaspoon yellow or brown mustard seeds

¼ teaspoon red pepper flakes

1 medium head cauliflower, cut into 1-inch pieces

2 pounds fingerling potatoes, cut in half

½ cup water

1. Heat oil in medium skillet over medium heat. Add onion; cook 8 minutes or until softened. Add garlic, curry powder, 1½ teaspoons salt, ginger, turmeric, mustard seeds and red pepper flakes; cook and stir 1 minute. Remove onion mixture to **CROCK-POT®** slow cooker.

2. Stir in cauliflower, potatoes and water. Cover; cook on HIGH 4 hours. Season with additional salt, if desired.

Makes 4 to 6 servings

Mushroom Wild Rice

1½ cups chicken broth

1 cup uncooked wild rice

½ cup diced onion

½ cup sliced mushrooms

½ cup diced red or green bell pepper

1 tablespoon olive oil

Salt and black pepper

Place broth, rice, onion, mushrooms, bell pepper, oil, salt and black pepper in **CROCK-POT®** slow cooker; stir to blend. Cover; cook on HIGH 2½ hours or until rice is tender and liquid is absorbed.

Makes 8 servings

Mashed Root Vegetables

1 pound baking potatoes, peeled and cut into 1-inch pieces

1 pound turnips, peeled and cut into 1-inch pieces

12 ounces sweet potatoes, peeled and cut into 1-inch pieces

8 ounces parsnips, peeled and cut into ½-inch pieces

5 tablespoons butter

¼ cup water

2 teaspoons salt

¼ teaspoon black pepper

1 cup milk

1. Coat inside of **CROCK-POT**® slow cooker with nonstick cooking spray. Add baking potatoes, turnips, sweet potatoes, parsnips, butter, water, salt and pepper; stir to blend. Cover; cook on HIGH 3 to 4 hours.

2. Mash mixture with potato masher until smooth. Stir in milk. Cover; cook on HIGH 15 minutes.

Makes 6 servings

Collard Greens

1 tablespoon olive oil

3 turkey necks

5 bunches collard greens, stemmed and chopped

5 cups chicken broth

1 small onion, chopped

2 cloves garlic, minced

1 tablespoon cider vinegar

1 teaspoon sugar

Salt and black pepper

Red pepper flakes

1. Heat oil in large skillet over medium-high heat. Add turkey necks; cook and stir 3 to 5 minutes or until brown.

2. Combine turkey necks, collard greens, broth, onion and garlic in **CROCK-POT** slow cooker. Cover; cook on LOW 5 to 6 hours. Remove and discard turkey necks. Stir in vinegar, sugar, salt, black pepper and red pepper flakes.

Makes 6 servings

Poblano Creamed Corn

4 whole poblano peppers

3 tablespoons olive oil

1 package (16 ounces) frozen corn

3 slices American cheese

4 ounces cream cheese

2 tablespoons butter

1½ tablespoons chicken broth

1 tablespoon chopped jalapeño pepper (optional)*

Salt and black pepper

*Jalapeño peppers can sting and irritate the skin, so wear rubber gloves when handling peppers and do not touch your eyes.

1. Preheat oven to 350°F. Spray large baking sheet with nonstick cooking spray. Place poblano peppers on prepared baking sheet; brush with oil. Bake 20 minutes or until outer skins loosen. When cool enough to handle, remove outer skin from 1 poblano pepper and mince. Cut remaining 3 poblano peppers in half and reserve.

2. Combine corn, American cheese, minced poblano pepper, cream cheese, butter, broth, jalapeño pepper, if desired, salt and black pepper in **CROCK-POT**® slow cooker. Cover; cook on LOW 4 to 5 hours. To serve, spoon corn into reserved poblano pepper halves.

Makes 6 servings

Red Cabbage and Apples

1 small head red cabbage, cored and thinly sliced

1 large apple, peeled and grated

¾ cup sugar

½ cup red wine vinegar

1 teaspoon ground cloves

½ cup bacon, crisp-cooked and crumbled (optional)

Fresh apple slices (optional)

Combine cabbage, grated apple, sugar, vinegar and cloves in **CROCK-POT®** slow cooker; stir to blend. Cover; cook on HIGH 6 hours, stirring halfway through cooking time. Sprinkle with bacon, if desired. Garnish with apple slices.

Makes 6 servings

Orange-Spice Glazed Carrots

1 package (32 ounces) baby carrots

½ cup packed light brown sugar

½ cup orange juice

3 tablespoons butter

¾ teaspoon ground cinnamon

¼ teaspoon ground nutmeg

¼ cup cold water

2 tablespoons cornstarch

Orange peel (optional)

1. Combine carrots, brown sugar, orange juice, butter, cinnamon and nutmeg in **CROCK-POT®** slow cooker. Cover; cook on LOW 3½ to 4 hours or until carrots are crisp-tender.

2. Spoon carrots into large serving bowl; keep warm. Turn **CROCK-POT®** slow cooker to HIGH.

3. Stir water into cornstarch in small bowl until smooth; whisk into cooking liquid. Cover; cook on HIGH 15 minutes or until thickened. Spoon over carrots. Garnish with orange peel.

Makes 6 servings

Mashed Rutabagas and Potatoes

2 pounds rutabagas, peeled and cut into
   ½-inch pieces

1 pound potatoes, peeled and cut into ½-inch
   pieces

½ cup milk

½ teaspoon ground nutmeg

2 tablespoons chopped fresh Italian parsley
   Sprigs fresh Italian parsley (optional)

1. Place rutabagas and potatoes in **CROCK-POT**® slow cooker; add enough water to cover vegetables. Cover; cook on LOW 6 hours or on HIGH 3 hours. Remove vegetables to large bowl using slotted spoon. Discard cooking liquid.

2. Mash vegetables with potato masher. Add milk, nutmeg and chopped parsley; stir until smooth. Garnish with parsley sprigs.

Makes 8 servings

Roasted Summer Squash
with Pine Nuts and Romano Cheese

2 tablespoons extra virgin olive oil

½ cup chopped yellow onion

1 medium red bell pepper, chopped

1 clove garlic, minced

3 medium zucchini, cut into ½-inch slices

3 medium summer squash, cut into ½-inch slices

½ cup chopped pine nuts

⅓ cup grated Romano cheese

1 teaspoon Italian seasoning

1 teaspoon salt

¼ teaspoon black pepper

1 tablespoon unsalted butter, cubed

1. Heat oil in large skillet over medium-high heat. Add onion, bell pepper and garlic; cook and stir 10 minutes or until onions are translucent and soft. Remove to **CROCK-POT**® slow cooker.

2. Add zucchini and summer squash. Toss lightly.

3. Combine pine nuts, cheese, Italian seasoning, salt and pepper in small bowl. Fold half of cheese mixture into squash. Sprinkle remaining cheese mixture on top. Dot cheese with butter. Cover; cook on LOW 4 to 6 hours.

Makes 8 servings

Coconut-Lime Sweet Potatoes with Walnuts

2½ pounds sweet potatoes, cut into 1-inch pieces

8 ounces shredded carrots

¾ cup shredded coconut, toasted and divided*

1 tablespoon unsalted butter, melted

3 tablespoons sugar

½ teaspoon salt

⅓ cup walnuts, toasted and coarsely chopped**

2 teaspoons grated lime peel

*To toast coconut, spread evenly on ungreased baking sheet. Toast in preheated 350°F oven 5 to 7 minutes or until light golden brown, stirring occasionally.

**To toast walnuts, spread in single layer in small skillet. Cook and stir over medium heat 1 to 2 minutes or until nuts are lightly browned.

1. Combine potatoes, carrots, ½ cup coconut, butter, sugar and salt in **CROCK-POT®** slow cooker. Cover; cook on LOW 5 to 6 hours. Remove to large bowl.

2. Mash potatoes with potato masher. Stir in walnuts and lime peel. Sprinkle with remaining coconut.

Makes 8 servings

Tarragon Carrots in White Wine

½ cup chicken broth

½ cup dry white wine

1 tablespoon lemon juice

1 tablespoon minced fresh tarragon

2 teaspoons finely chopped green onions

1½ teaspoons chopped fresh Italian parsley

1 clove garlic, minced

1 teaspoon salt

8 medium carrots, cut into matchsticks

2 tablespoons melba toast, crushed

2 tablespoons cold water

1. Combine broth, wine, lemon juice, tarragon, green onions, parsley, garlic and salt in **CROCK-POT®** slow cooker. Add carrots; stir well to combine. Cover; cook on LOW 2½ to 3 hours or on HIGH 1½ to 2 hours.

2. Dissolve toast crumbs in water in small bowl; add to carrots. Cover; cook on LOW 10 minutes or until thickened.

Makes 6 to 8 servings

Corn on the Cob with Garlic Herb Butter

4 to 5 ears of corn, husked

½ cup (1 stick) unsalted butter, softened

3 to 4 cloves garlic, minced

2 tablespoons finely minced fresh Italian parsley

Salt and black pepper

1. Place each ear of corn on a piece of foil. Combine butter, garlic and parsley in small bowl; spread onto corn. Season with salt and pepper; tightly seal foil.

2. Place in **CROCK-POT®** slow cooker, overlapping ears, if necessary. Add enough water to come one fourth of the way up each ear. Cover; cook on LOW 4 to 5 hours or on HIGH 2 to 2½ hours.

Makes 4 to 5 servings

Cheesy Mashed Potato Casserole

4 pounds Yukon Gold potatoes, cut into 1-inch pieces

2 cups vegetable broth

3 tablespoons unsalted butter, cubed

½ cup milk, heated

⅓ cup sour cream

2 cups (8 ounces) shredded sharp Cheddar cheese, plus additional for garnish

½ teaspoon salt

¼ teaspoon black pepper

1. Coat inside of **CROCK-POT®** slow cooker with nonstick cooking spray. Add potatoes and broth; dot with butter. Cover; cook on LOW 4½ to 5 hours.

2. Mash potatoes with potato masher; stir in milk, sour cream, 2 cups cheese, salt and pepper until cheese is melted. Garnish with additional cheese.

Makes 10 to 12 servings

No-Fuss Macaroni and Cheese

2 cups (about 8 ounces) uncooked elbow macaroni

3 ounces light pasteurized processed cheese product, cubed

1 cup (4 ounces) shredded mild Cheddar cheese

½ teaspoon salt

⅛ teaspoon black pepper

1½ cups milk

Combine macaroni, cheese product, cheese, salt and pepper in **CROCK-POT**® slow cooker. Pour milk over top. Cover; cook on LOW 2 to 3 hours, stirring halfway through cooking time.

Makes 8 servings

Rustic Cheddar Mashed Potatoes

2 pounds russet potatoes, diced

1 cup water

2 tablespoons unsalted butter, cubed

¾ cup milk

¾ teaspoon salt

½ teaspoon black pepper

½ cup finely chopped green onions

2 tablespoons shredded Cheddar cheese

1. Combine potatoes, water and butter in **CROCK-POT**® slow cooker. Cover; cook on LOW 6 hours or on HIGH 3 hours. Remove potatoes to large bowl using slotted spoon.

2. Beat potatoes with electric mixer at medium speed 2 to 3 minutes or until well blended. Add milk, salt and pepper; beat 2 minutes or until well blended.

3. Stir in green onions and cheese. Turn off heat. Cover; let stand 15 minutes or until cheese is melted.

Makes 8 servings

Lemon-Mint Red Potatoes

2 pounds new red potatoes	¼ teaspoon black pepper
3 tablespoons extra virgin olive oil	4 tablespoons chopped fresh mint, divided
1 teaspoon salt	2 tablespoons butter
½ teaspoon Greek seasoning or dried oregano	2 tablespoons lemon juice
¼ teaspoon garlic powder	1 teaspoon grated lemon peel

1. Coat inside of **CROCK-POT**® slow cooker with nonstick cooking spray. Add potatoes and oil, stirring gently to coat. Sprinkle with salt, Greek seasoning, garlic powder and pepper. Cover; cook on LOW 7 hours or on HIGH 4 hours.

2. Stir in 2 tablespoons mint, butter, lemon juice and lemon peel until butter is completely melted. Cover; cook on HIGH 15 minutes. Sprinkle with remaining 2 tablespoons mint.

Makes 4 servings

Tip: It's easy to prepare these potatoes ahead of time. Simply follow the recipe and then turn off the heat. Let it stand at room temperature for up to 2 hours. You may reheat or serve the potatoes at room temperature.

Green Bean Casserole

2 packages (10 ounces *each*) frozen green beans

1 can (10¾ ounces) condensed cream of
    mushroom soup, undiluted

1 tablespoon chopped fresh Italian parsley

1 tablespoon chopped roasted red peppers

1 teaspoon dried sage

½ teaspoon salt

½ teaspoon black pepper

¼ teaspoon ground nutmeg

½ cup toasted slivered almonds*

*To toast almonds, spread in single layer in small heavy skillet. Cook and stir over medium heat 1 to 2 minutes or until nuts are lightly browned.

Combine beans, soup, parsley, red peppers, sage, salt, black pepper and nutmeg in **CROCK-POT**® slow cooker; stir to blend. Cover; cook on LOW 3 to 4 hours. Sprinkle with almonds.

Makes 6 servings

Blue Cheese Potatoes

2 pounds red potatoes, peeled and cut into ½-inch pieces

1¼ cups chopped green onions, divided

2 tablespoons olive oil, divided

1 teaspoon dried basil

½ teaspoon salt

¼ teaspoon black pepper

½ cup crumbled blue cheese

1. Layer potatoes, 1 cup green onions, 1 tablespoon oil, basil, salt and pepper in **CROCK-POT®** slow cooker. Cover; cook on LOW 7 hours or on HIGH 4 hours.

2. Gently stir in cheese and remaining 1 tablespoon oil. Cover; cook on HIGH 5 minutes. Remove potatoes to large serving platter; top with remaining ¼ cup green onions.

Makes 5 servings

Parmesan Potato Wedges

2 pounds red potatoes, cut into ½-inch wedges

¼ cup finely chopped yellow onion

1½ teaspoons dried oregano

½ teaspoon salt

¼ teaspoon black pepper

2 tablespoons butter, cubed

¼ cup grated Parmesan cheese

Layer potatoes, onion, oregano, salt and pepper in **CROCK-POT®** slow cooker; dot with butter. Cover; cook on HIGH 4 hours. Remove potatoes to large serving platter; sprinkle with cheese.

Makes 6 servings

Beets in Spicy Mustard Sauce

3 pounds beets, peeled, halved and cut into ½-inch slices

¼ cup sour cream

2 tablespoons spicy brown mustard

2 teaspoons lemon juice

2 cloves garlic, minced

¼ teaspoon black pepper

⅛ teaspoon dried thyme

1. Place beets in **CROCK-POT®** slow cooker. Add enough water to cover by 1 inch. Cover; cook on LOW 7 to 8 hours or until beets are tender.

2. Combine sour cream, mustard, lemon juice, garlic, pepper and thyme in small bowl. Spoon over beets; toss to coat. Cover; cook on LOW 15 minutes.

Makes 4 servings

Lemon and Tangerine Glazed Carrots

6 cups sliced carrots	2 tablespoons grated lemon peel
1½ cups apple juice	2 tablespoons grated tangerine peel
6 tablespoons butter	½ teaspoon salt
¼ cup packed brown sugar	Chopped fresh Italian parsley (optional)

Combine carrots, apple juice, butter, brown sugar, lemon peel, tangerine peel and salt in **CROCK-POT®** slow cooker; stir to blend. Cover; cook on LOW 4 to 5 hours or on HIGH 1 to 3 hours. Garnish with parsley.

Makes 10 to 12 servings

Orange-Spiced Sweet Potatoes

2 pounds sweet potatoes, diced	½ teaspoon ground nutmeg
½ cup packed dark brown sugar	½ teaspoon grated orange peel
½ cup (1 stick) butter, cubed	Juice of 1 medium orange
1 teaspoon ground cinnamon	Chopped toasted pecans*
1 teaspoon vanilla	
½ teaspoon salt	

To toast pecans, spread in a single layer in small skillet. Cook and stir over medium heat 1 to 2 minutes or until nuts are lightly browned.

Combine potatoes, brown sugar, butter, cinnamon, vanilla, salt, nutmeg, orange peel and juice in **CROCK-POT®** slow cooker; stir to blend. Cover; cook on LOW 4 hours or on HIGH 2 hours. Sprinkle with pecans.

Makes 8 servings

Variations: For creamier potatoes, add ¼ cup milk or whipping cream and beat with an electric mixer. Sprinkle with cinnamon-sugar mixture in addition to the pecans.

Scalloped Tomatoes and Corn

1 can (15 ounces) cream-style corn

1 can (about 14 ounces) diced tomatoes

¾ cup saltine or soda cracker crumbs

1 egg, lightly beaten

2 teaspoons sugar

¾ teaspoon black pepper

Chopped fresh tomatoes

Chopped fresh Italian parsley

Combine corn, diced tomatoes, cracker crumbs, egg, sugar and pepper in **CROCK-POT**® slow cooker; mix well. Cover; cook on LOW 4 to 6 hours. Sprinkle with fresh tomatoes and parsley before serving, if desired.

Makes 4 to 6 servings

Simmered Napa Cabbage with Dried Apricots

4 cups napa cabbage or green cabbage, cored, cleaned and sliced thin

1 cup chopped dried apricots

¼ cup clover honey

2 tablespoons orange juice

½ cup dry red wine

Salt and black pepper

Grated orange peel (optional)

1. Combine cabbage and apricots in **CROCK-POT**® slow cooker; toss well.

2. Combine honey and orange juice in small bowl; stir until smooth. Drizzle over cabbage. Add wine. Cover; cook on LOW 5 to 6 hours or on HIGH 2 to 3 hours or until cabbage is tender.

3. Season with salt and pepper. Garnish with orange peel.

Makes 4 servings

SWEET TREATS

Apple-Pecan Bread Pudding

8   cups bread, cubed

3   cups Granny Smith apples, cubed

1   cup chopped pecans

8   eggs

1   can (12 ounces) evaporated milk

1   cup packed brown sugar

½   cup apple cider or apple juice

2   teaspoons ground cinnamon

1   teaspoon ground nutmeg

1   teaspoon vanilla

½   teaspoon salt

½   teaspoon ground allspice

Ice cream

Caramel topping or whipped cream

1. Coat inside of **CROCK-POT®** slow cooker with nonstick cooking spray. Add bread cubes, apples and pecans.

2. Combine eggs, evaporated milk, brown sugar, apple cider, cinnamon, nutmeg, vanilla, salt and allspice in large bowl; mix well. Pour egg mixture into **CROCK-POT®** slow cooker. Cover; cook on LOW 3 hours. Serve with ice cream. Top with caramel sauce.

Makes 8 servings

Citrus Chinese Dates with Toasted Hazelnuts

2 cups pitted dates

⅔ cup boiling water

½ cup sugar

Strips of peel from 1 lemon (yellow part only)

Whipped cream (optional)

¼ cup hazelnuts, shelled and toasted*

To toast hazelnuts, spread in single layer in heavy skillet. Cook over medium heat 1 to 2 minutes or until nuts are lightly browned, stirring frequently.

1. Place dates in medium bowl and cover with water. Soak overnight to rehydrate. Drain, and remove dates to **CROCK-POT®** slow cooker.

2. Add ⅔ cup boiling water, sugar and lemon peel to **CROCK-POT®** slow cooker. Cover; cook on HIGH 3 hours.

3. Remove and discard peel. Place dates in serving dishes. Top with whipped cream, if desired. Sprinkle with hazelnuts.

Makes 4 servings

Pears with Apricot-Ginger Sauce

¼ cup water

4 whole firm pears (about 2 pounds total), peeled with stems attached

1 tablespoon lemon juice

2 tablespoons apricot fruit spread

1 teaspoon grated fresh ginger

½ teaspoon cornstarch

½ teaspoon vanilla

1. Coat inside of **CROCK-POT®** slow cooker with nonstick cooking spray. Add water. Arrange pears stem side up. Spoon lemon juice over pears. Cover; cook on HIGH 2½ hours. Remove pears; set aside.

2. Combine fruit spread, ginger, cornstarch and vanilla in small bowl; stir until cornstarch dissolves. Whisk mixture into water in **CROCK-POT®** slow cooker until blended. Cover; cook on HIGH 15 minutes or until sauce thickens slightly. Spoon sauce over pears.

Makes 4 servings

Rustic Peach-Oat Crumble

8 cups frozen sliced peaches, thawed and juice reserved

¾ cup packed brown sugar, divided

1½ tablespoons cornstarch

1 tablespoon lemon juice (optional)

1½ teaspoons vanilla

½ teaspoon almond extract

1 cup quick oats

¼ cup all-purpose flour

¼ cup granulated sugar

1 teaspoon ground cinnamon

¼ teaspoon salt

½ cup (1 stick) cold butter, cubed

1. Coat inside of 5-quart **CROCK-POT**® slow cooker with nonstick cooking spray. Combine peaches with juice, ½ cup brown sugar, cornstarch, lemon juice, if desired, vanilla and almond extract in medium bowl; toss to coat. Place in **CROCK-POT**® slow cooker.

2. Combine oats, flour, remaining ¼ cup brown sugar, granulated sugar, cinnamon and salt in medium bowl. Cut in butter with pastry blender or two knives until mixture resembles coarse crumbs. Sprinkle over peaches. Cover; cook on HIGH 1½ hours or until bubbly at edge. Remove stoneware from base; cool 20 minutes.

Makes about 8 servings

Tequila-Poached Pears

4 **Anjou pears, peeled**

2 **cups water**

1 **can (11½ ounces) pear nectar**

1 **cup tequila**

½ **cup sugar**

    Grated peel and juice of 1 lime

    Vanilla ice cream (optional)

Place pears in **CROCK-POT®** slow cooker. Combine water, nectar, tequila, sugar, lime peel and lime juice in medium saucepan. Bring to a boil over medium-high heat, stirring frequently. Boil 1 minute; pour over pears. Cover; cook on LOW 4 to 6 hours or on HIGH 2 to 3 hours or until pears are tender. Serve warm with poaching liquid and vanilla ice cream, if desired.

Makes 4 servings

Brownie Bottoms

½ **cup packed brown sugar**

½ **cup water**

2 **tablespoons unsweetened cocoa powder**

2½ **cups packaged brownie mix**

1 **package (2¾ ounces) instant chocolate pudding mix**

½ **cup milk chocolate chips**

2 **eggs, beaten**

3 **tablespoons butter or margarine, melted**

    Whipped cream or ice cream (optional)

1. Coat inside of **CROCK-POT®** slow cooker with nonstick cooking spray. Combine brown sugar, water and cocoa in small saucepan over medium heat; bring to a boil over medium-high heat.

2. Meanwhile, combine brownie mix, pudding mix, chocolate chips, eggs and butter in medium bowl; stir until well blended. Spread batter in **CROCK-POT®** slow cooker; pour boiling sugar mixture over batter.

3. Cover; cook on HIGH 1½ hours. Turn off heat. Let stand 30 minutes. Serve with whipped cream, if desired.

Makes 6 servings

Cherry Rice Pudding

1½ cups milk

1 cup hot cooked rice

3 eggs, beaten

½ cup sugar

¼ cup dried cherries or cranberries

½ teaspoon almond extract

¼ teaspoon salt

1 cup water

Ground nutmeg (optional)

1. Spray 1½-quart casserole with nonstick cooking spray. Combine milk, rice, eggs, sugar, cherries, almond extract and salt in large bowl; stir to blend. Pour into prepared casserole. Cover with buttered foil, butter side down.

2. Place rack in **CROCK-POT**® slow cooker and pour in water. Place casserole on rack. Cover; cook on LOW 4 to 5 hours.

3. Remove casserole from **CROCK-POT**® slow cooker. Let stand 15 minutes before serving. Garnish with nutmeg.

Makes 6 servings

Figs Poached in Red Wine

2 cups dry red wine

1 cup packed brown sugar

12 dried Calimyrna or Mediterranean figs (about 6 ounces)

2 (3-inch) cinnamon sticks

1 teaspoon finely grated orange peel

4 tablespoons whipping cream (optional)

1. Combine wine, brown sugar, figs, cinnamon sticks and orange peel in **CROCK-POT®** slow cooker. Cover; cook on LOW 5 to 6 hours or on HIGH 4 to 5 hours.

2. Remove and discard cinnamon sticks. To serve, spoon figs and syrup into serving dish. Top with spoonful of cream, if desired. Serve warm or cold.

Makes 4 servings

Apple Crumble Pot

Filling

4 Granny Smith apples (about 2 pounds), cored and *each* cut into 8 wedges

⅔ cup packed dark brown sugar

½ cup dried cranberries

2 tablespoons biscuit baking mix

2 tablespoons butter, cubed

1½ teaspoons ground cinnamon

1 teaspoon vanilla

¼ teaspoon ground allspice

Topping

1 cup biscuit baking mix

½ cup rolled oats

⅓ cup packed dark brown sugar

3 tablespoons cold butter, cubed

½ cup chopped pecans

1. Coat inside of **CROCK-POT®** slow cooker with nonstick cooking spray. For filling, combine apples, ⅔ cup brown sugar, cranberries, 2 tablespoons baking mix, butter, cinnamon, vanilla and allspice in **CROCK-POT®** slow cooker; toss gently to coat.

2. For topping, combine 1 cup baking mix, oats and ⅓ cup brown sugar in large bowl. Cut in 3 tablespoons butter with pastry blender or two knives until mixture resembles coarse crumbs. Sprinkle evenly over filling in **CROCK-POT®** slow cooker. Top with pecans. Cover; cook on HIGH 2¼ hours or until apples are tender. *Do not overcook.*

3. Turn off heat. Let stand, uncovered, 15 to 30 minutes before serving. Top with whipped cream, if desired.

Makes 6 to 8 servings

Bittersweet Chocolate-Espresso Crème Brûlée

½ cup chopped bittersweet chocolate

5 egg yolks

1½ cups whipping cream

½ cup granulated sugar

¼ cup espresso

¼ cup Demerara or raw sugar

1. Arrange five 6-ounce ramekins or custard cups inside **CROCK-POT®** slow cooker. Pour enough water to come halfway up sides of ramekins (taking care to keep water out of ramekins). Divide chocolate among ramekins.

2. Whisk egg yolks in small bowl; set aside. Heat small saucepan over medium heat. Add cream, granulated sugar and espresso; cook and stir until mixture begins to boil. Pour hot cream in thin, steady stream into egg yolks, whisking constantly. Pour through fine mesh strainer into clean bowl.

3. Ladle into prepared ramekins over chocolate. Cover; cook on HIGH 1 to 2 hours or until custard is set around edges but still soft in centers. Carefully remove ramekins; cool to room temperature. Cover and refrigerate until serving.

4. Spread tops of custards with Demerara sugar just before serving. Serve immediately.

Makes 5 servings

Chai Tea Cherries 'n' Cream

2 cans (15½ ounces *each*) pitted cherries in
  pear juice

2 cups water

½ cup orange juice

1 cup sugar

4 cardamom pods

2 cinnamon sticks (broken in half)

1 teaspoon grated orange peel

¼ ounce coarsely chopped candied ginger

4 whole cloves

2 whole black peppercorns

4 green tea bags

1 container (6 ounces) black cherry yogurt

1 quart vanilla ice cream

  Sprigs fresh mint (optional)

1. Drain cherries, reserving juice. Combine reserved pear juice, water and orange juice in **CROCK-POT**® slow cooker. Mix in sugar, cardamom pods, cinnamon sticks, orange peel, ginger, cloves and peppercorns. Cover; cook on HIGH 1½ hours.

2. Remove spices with slotted spoon and discard. Stir in tea bags and reserved cherries. Cover; cook on HIGH 30 minutes.

3. Turn off heat. Remove and discard tea bags. Remove cherries from liquid; set aside. Let liquid cool until just warm. Whisk in yogurt until smooth.

4. To serve, divide warm cherries and yogurt sauce among wine or cocktail glasses. Top each serving with ice cream; swirl lightly. Garnish with mint.

Makes 8 servings

Fudge and Cream Pudding Cake

2 tablespoons unsalted butter

1 cup all-purpose flour

½ cup packed light brown sugar

5 tablespoons unsweetened cocoa powder, divided

2 teaspoons baking powder

½ teaspoon ground cinnamon

⅛ teaspoon salt

1 cup light cream

1 tablespoon vegetable oil

1 teaspoon vanilla

1½ cups hot water

½ cup packed dark brown sugar

Whipped cream or ice cream (optional)

1. Coat inside of 5-quart **CROCK-POT**® slow cooker with butter. Combine flour, light brown sugar, 3 tablespoons cocoa, baking powder, cinnamon and salt in medium bowl. Add cream, oil and vanilla; stir well to combine. Pour batter into **CROCK-POT**® slow cooker.

2. Combine hot water, dark brown sugar and remaining 2 tablespoons cocoa in medium bowl; stir well. Pour sauce over cake batter. *Do not stir.* Cover; cook on HIGH 2 hours.

3. Spoon pudding cake onto plates. Serve with whipped cream, if desired.

Makes 8 to 10 servings

Peach Cobbler

2 packages (16 ounces *each*) frozen
    peaches, thawed and drained

½ cup plus 1 tablespoon sugar, divided

2 teaspoons ground cinnamon,
    divided

½ teaspoon ground nutmeg

¾ cup all-purpose flour

6 tablespoons butter, cubed

   Whipped cream (optional)

1. Combine peaches, ½ cup sugar,
1½ teaspoons cinnamon and nutmeg in
CROCK-POT® slow cooker; stir to blend.

2. Combine flour, remaining 1 tablespoon
sugar and remaining ½ teaspoon
cinnamon in small bowl. Cut in butter with
pastry blender or two knives until mixture resembles coarse crumbs. Sprinkle over peach mixture.
Cover; cook on HIGH 2 hours. Serve with whipped cream, if desired.

Makes 4 to 6 servings

Tip: To make cleanup easier when cooking sticky or sugary foods, spray the inside of the
CROCK-POT® slow cooker with nonstick cooking spray before adding ingredients.

Five-Spice Apple Crisp

3 tablespoons unsalted butter, melted

6 Golden Delicious apples, peeled and
    cut into ½-inch-thick slices

2 teaspoons lemon juice

¼ cup packed brown sugar

¾ teaspoon Chinese five-spice powder *or*
    ½ teaspoon ground cinnamon and
    ¼ teaspoon ground allspice, plus additional
    for garnish

1 cup coarsely crushed Chinese-style almond
    cookies or almond biscotti

1. Butter inside of 5-quart **CROCK-POT**® slow cooker with melted butter. Add apples and lemon juice;
toss to combine. Sprinkle apples with brown sugar and ¾ teaspoon five-spice powder; toss again.
Cover; cook on LOW 3½ hours.

2. Spoon into bowls. Sprinkle cookies over apples. Garnish with additional five-spice powder.

Makes 4 servings

Brioche and Amber Rum Custard

2 tablespoons unsalted butter, melted

3½ cups whipping cream

4 eggs

½ cup packed dark brown sugar

⅓ cup amber or light rum

2 teaspoons vanilla

1 loaf (20 to 22 ounces) brioche bread, torn into pieces *or* 5 large brioche, cut into thirds*

½ cup coarsely chopped pecans

Caramel or butterscotch topping (optional)

*If desired, trim and discard heels.

1. Butter inside of **CROCK-POT**® slow cooker with melted butter. Combine cream, eggs, brown sugar, rum and vanilla in large bowl; stir well.

2. Mound one fourth of brioche pieces in bottom of **CROCK-POT**® slow cooker. Ladle one fourth of cream mixture over brioche. Sprinkle with one third of pecans. Repeat layers with remaining brioche, cream mixture and pecans until all ingredients are used.

3. Cover; cook on LOW 3 to 3½ hours or on HIGH 1½ to 2 hours or until custard is set and toothpick inserted into center comes out clean.

4. Serve warm. Drizzle with caramel or butterscotch topping, if desired.

Makes 4 to 6 servings

Pumpkin-Cranberry Custard

1 can (30 ounces) pumpkin
  pie filling

1 can (12 ounces) evaporated
  milk

1 cup dried cranberries

4 eggs, beaten

1 cup whole gingersnap
  cookies (optional)

Combine pumpkin, evaporated
milk, cranberries and eggs in
CROCK-POT® slow cooker;
stir to blend. Cover; cook on
HIGH 4 to 4½ hours. Serve with
gingersnaps, if desired.

Makes 4 to 6 servings

Poached Autumn Fruits with Vanilla-Citrus Broth

2 Granny Smith apples, peeled, cored and
  halved (reserve cores)

2 Bartlett pears, peeled, cored and halved
  (reserve cores)

1 orange, peeled and halved

⅓ cup sugar

5 tablespoons honey

1 vanilla bean, split and seeded (reserve seeds)

1 cinnamon stick

  Vanilla ice cream (optional)

1. Place apple and pear cores in **CROCK-POT**® slow cooker. Squeeze juice from orange halves into
CROCK-POT® slow cooker. Add orange halves, sugar, honey, vanilla bean and seeds and cinnamon
stick. Add apples and pears. Pour in enough water to cover fruit. Stir gently to combine. Cover; cook
on HIGH 2 hours or until fruit is tender.

2. Remove apple and pear halves; set aside. Strain cooking liquid into large saucepan. (Discard
solids.) Simmer gently over low heat until liquid is reduced by half and thickened.

3. Dice apple and pear halves. Add to saucepan to rewarm fruit. To serve, spoon fruit with sauce into
bowls. Top with vanilla ice cream, if desired.

Makes 4 to 6 servings

Mixed Berry Cobbler

1 package (16 ounces) frozen mixed berries

½ cup granulated sugar

2 tablespoons quick-cooking tapioca

2 teaspoons grated lemon peel

1½ cups all-purpose flour

½ cup packed light brown sugar

2¼ teaspoons baking powder

¼ teaspoon ground nutmeg

½ cup milk

⅓ cup butter, melted

Vanilla ice cream or whipped cream (optional)

1. Coat **CROCK-POT**® slow cooker with nonstick cooking spray. Stir together berries, granulated sugar, tapioca and lemon peel in medium bowl. Remove to **CROCK-POT**® slow cooker.

2. For topping, combine flour, brown sugar, baking powder and nutmeg in medium bowl. Add milk and butter; stir just until blended. Drop spoonfuls of dough on top of berry mixture. Cover; cook on LOW 4 hours. Turn off heat. Uncover; let stand about 30 minutes. Serve with ice cream, if desired.

Makes 8 servings

Tip: Cobblers are year-round favorites. Experiment with seasonal fresh fruits, such as pears, plums, peaches, rhubarb, blueberries, raspberries, strawberries, blackberries or gooseberries.

Coconut Rice Pudding

2 cups water

1 cup uncooked converted long grain rice

1 tablespoon unsalted butter

  Pinch salt

2¼ cups evaporated milk

1 can (14 ounces) cream of coconut

½ cup golden raisins

3 egg yolks, beaten

  Grated peel of 2 limes

1 teaspoon vanilla

  Toasted shredded coconut (optional)*

To toast coconut, spread evenly on ungreased baking sheet. Toast in preheated 350°F oven 5 to 7 minutes or until light golden brown, stirring occasionally.

1. Place water, rice, butter and salt in medium saucepan. Bring to a boil over high heat, stirring frequently. Reduce heat to low. Cover; cook 10 to 12 minutes. Remove from heat. Let stand, covered, 5 minutes.

2. Meanwhile, coat inside of **CROCK-POT®** slow cooker with nonstick cooking spray. Add evaporated milk, cream of coconut, raisins, egg yolks, lime peel and vanilla; mix well. Add rice; stir until blended.

3. Cover; cook on LOW 4 hours or on HIGH 2 hours. Stir every 30 minutes, if possible. Pudding will thicken as it cools. Garnish with shredded coconut.

Makes 6 servings

Cherry Delight

1 can (21 ounces) cherry
  pie filling
1 package (about
  18 ounces) yellow
  cake mix
½ cup (1 stick) butter,
  melted
⅓ cup chopped walnuts

Place pie filling in
CROCK-POT® slow cooker.
Combine cake mix and
butter in medium bowl.
Spread evenly over pie filling.
Sprinkle with walnuts. Cover;
cook on LOW 3 to 4 hours or
on HIGH 1½ to 2 hours.

Makes 8 to 10 servings

Fresh Bosc Pear Granita

1 pound fresh Bosc pears, peeled, cored and
  cubed
1¼ cups water
¼ cup sugar
½ teaspoon ground cinnamon

1 tablespoon lemon juice
Fresh raspberries (optional)
Lemon slices (optional)
Fresh mint leaves (optional)

1. Place pears, water, sugar and cinnamon in **CROCK-POT**® slow cooker. Cover; cook on HIGH
2½ to 3½ hours or until pears are very soft and tender. Stir in lemon juice.

2. Remove pears and syrup to blender or food processor; blend until smooth. Strain mixture,
discarding any pulp. Pour liquid into 11×9-inch baking pan. Cover tightly with plastic wrap. Place pan
in freezer.

3. Stir every hour, tossing granita with fork. Crush any lumps in mixture as it freezes. Freeze 3 to
4 hours or until firm. You may keep granita in freezer up to 2 days before serving; toss granita every
6 to 12 hours. Garnish with raspberries, lemon slices and mint.

Makes 6 servings

Christmas Plum Pudding

2½ cups milk	2 teaspoons ground cloves
4 eggs, slightly beaten	2 teaspoons ground mace
10 slices white bread, cut into 2-inch cubes	½ cup orange juice
2¼ cups all-purpose flour	1 tablespoon vanilla
2¼ cups packed brown sugar	3 cups raisins
1 tablespoon ground cinnamon	2 cups dried plums
2 teaspoons baking soda	1 cup dried candied fruit mix

1. Coat inside of **CROCK-POT**® slow cooker with nonstick cooking spray. Combine milk and eggs in large bowl. Add bread; set aside to soak.

2. Combine flour, brown sugar, cinnamon, baking soda, cloves and mace in large bowl. Add orange juice and vanilla; stir until smooth. Add raisins, plums and candied fruit; stir until blended.

3. Place bread in **CROCK-POT**® slow cooker. Pour fruit mixture over bread. Cover; cook on LOW 6 to 7 hours or on HIGH 2 to 4 hours. Serve warm.

Makes 10 servings

Triple Chocolate Fantasy

2 pounds white almond bark, broken into pieces

1 bar (4 ounces) sweetened chocolate, broken into pieces*

1 package (12 ounces) semisweet chocolate chips

3 cups coarsely chopped pecans, toasted**

Use your favorite high-quality chocolate candy bar.

**To toast pecans, spread in single layer in heavy skillet. Cook and stir over medium heat 1 to 2 minutes or until nuts are lightly browned.*

1. Place bark, sweetened chocolate and chocolate chips in **CROCK-POT**® slow cooker. Cover; cook on HIGH 1 hour. *Do not stir.*

2. Turn **CROCK-POT**® slow cooker to LOW. Cover; cook on LOW 1 hour, stirring every 15 minutes. Stir in nuts.

3. Drop mixture by tablespoonfuls onto baking sheet covered with waxed paper; cool. Store in tightly covered container.

Makes 36 pieces

Variations: Here are a few ideas for other imaginative items to add in along with or instead of the pecans: raisins, crushed peppermint candy, candy-coated baking bits, crushed toffee, peanuts or pistachio nuts, chopped gum drops, chopped dried fruit, candied cherries, chopped marshmallows or sweetened coconut.

Strawberry Rhubarb Crisp

Fruit

- 4 cups sliced fresh hulled strawberries
- 4 cups diced rhubarb (about 5 stalks), cut into ½-inch dice
- 1½ cups granulated sugar
- 2 tablespoons lemon juice
- 1½ tablespoons cornstarch, plus water (optional)

Topping

- 1 cup all-purpose flour
- 1 cup old-fashioned oats
- ½ cup granulated sugar
- ½ cup packed brown sugar
- ½ teaspoon ground ginger
- ½ teaspoon ground nutmeg
- ½ cup (1 stick) butter, cut into small pieces
- ½ cup sliced almonds, toasted*

To toast almonds, spread in single layer in heavy skillet. Cook over medium heat 1 to 2 minutes or until nuts are lightly browned, stirring frequently.

1. Coat inside of **CROCK-POT®** slow cooker with nonstick cooking spray. Place strawberries, rhubarb, granulated sugar and lemon juice in **CROCK-POT®** slow cooker; mix well. Cook on HIGH 1½ hours or until fruit is tender.

2. If fruit is dry after cooking, add a little water. If fruit has too much liquid, mix cornstarch with a little water and stir into liquid. Cook on HIGH an additional 15 minutes or until cooking liquid is thickened.

3. Preheat oven to 375°F. Combine flour, oats, sugars, ginger and nutmeg in medium bowl. Cut in butter using pastry blender or two knives until mixture resembles coarse crumbs. Stir in almonds.

4. Remove lid from **CROCK-POT®** slow cooker and gently sprinkle topping onto fruit. Remove stoneware to oven. Bake 15 to 20 minutes or until topping begins to brown.

Makes 8 servings

Spicy Fruit Dessert

2 cups canned pears, drained and diced

2 cups carambola (star fruit), sliced and seeds removed

1 can (6 ounces) frozen orange juice concentrate

¼ cup orange marmalade

¼ teaspoon pumpkin pie spice

Pound cake or ice cream

Whipped cream (optional)

Combine pears, carambola, orange juice concentrate, marmalade and pumpkin pie spice in **CROCK-POT**® slow cooker. Cover; cook on LOW 4 to 6 hours or on HIGH 2 to 3 hours or until cooked through. Serve warm over pound cake with whipped cream, if desired.

Makes 4 to 6 servings

Fruit and Nut Baked Apples

4 large baking apples, such as Rome Beauty or Jonathan

1 tablespoon lemon juice

⅓ cup chopped dried apricots

⅓ cup chopped walnuts or pecans

3 tablespoons packed brown sugar

½ teaspoon ground cinnamon

2 tablespoons unsalted butter, melted

½ cup water

Caramel ice cream topping (optional)

1. Scoop out center of each apple, leaving 1½-inch-wide cavity about ½ inch from bottom. Peel top of apple down about 1 inch. Brush peeled edges evenly with lemon juice. Mix apricots, walnuts, brown sugar and cinnamon in small bowl. Add butter; mix well. Spoon mixture evenly into apple cavities.

2. Pour water in bottom of **CROCK-POT**® slow cooker. Place 2 apples in bottom of **CROCK-POT**® slow cooker. Arrange remaining 2 apples above but not directly on top of bottom apples. Cover; cook on LOW 3 to 4 hours or until apples are tender. Serve warm or at room temperature with caramel ice cream topping, if desired.

Makes 4 servings

Tip: Ever wonder why you need to brush lemon juice around the top of an apple? Citrus fruits, like lemons, contain an acid that keeps apples, potatoes and other white vegetables from discoloring once they are cut or peeled.

Mexican Chocolate Bread Pudding

1½ cups whipping cream

4 ounces unsweetened chocolate, coarsely chopped

½ cup currants

2 eggs, beaten

½ cup sugar

1 teaspoon vanilla

¾ teaspoon ground cinnamon

½ teaspoon ground allspice

⅛ teaspoon salt

3 cups Hawaiian-style sweet bread, challah or rich egg bread, cut into ½-inch cubes

Whipped cream (optional)

Chopped macadamia nuts (optional)

1. Heat cream in large saucepan. Add chocolate; stir until melted.

2. Combine currants, eggs, sugar, vanilla, cinnamon, allspice and salt in medium bowl. Add currant mixture to chocolate mixture; stir well to combine. Pour into **CROCK-POT®** slow cooker.

3. Gently fold in bread cubes using plastic spatula. Cover; cook on HIGH 3 to 4 hours or until knife inserted near center comes out clean.

4. Serve warm or chilled. Top with whipped cream and sprinkle with nuts, if desired.

Makes 6 to 8 servings

Pumpkin Custard

1 cup solid-pack pumpkin

½ cup packed brown sugar

2 eggs, beaten

½ teaspoon ground ginger

½ teaspoon grated lemon peel

½ teaspoon ground cinnamon, plus additional for garnish

1 can (12 ounces) evaporated milk

1. Combine pumpkin, brown sugar, eggs, ginger, lemon peel and ½ teaspoon cinnamon in large bowl. Stir in evaporated milk. Divide mixture among six ramekins or custard cups. Cover each cup tightly with foil.

2. Place ramekins in **CROCK-POT**® slow cooker. Pour water into **CROCK-POT**® slow cooker to come about ½ inch from top of ramekins. Cover; cook on LOW 4 hours.

3. Use tongs or slotted spoon to remove ramekins from **CROCK-POT**® slow cooker. Sprinkle with additional ground cinnamon. Serve warm.

Makes 6 servings

Variation: To make Pumpkin Custard in a single dish, pour custard into 1½-quart soufflé dish instead of ramekins. Cover with foil and place in **CROCK-POT**® slow cooker. (Place soufflé dish on two or three 18×2-inch strips of foil in **CROCK-POT**® slow cooker to make removal easier, if desired.) Add water to come 1½ inches from top of soufflé dish. Cover and cook as directed.

METRIC CONVERSION CHART

VOLUME MEASUREMENTS (dry)

1/8 teaspoon = 0.5 mL
1/4 teaspoon = 1 mL
1/2 teaspoon = 2 mL
3/4 teaspoon = 4 mL
1 teaspoon = 5 mL
1 tablespoon = 15 mL
2 tablespoons = 30 mL
1/4 cup = 60 mL
1/3 cup = 75 mL
1/2 cup = 125 mL
2/3 cup = 150 mL
3/4 cup = 175 mL
1 cup = 250 mL
2 cups = 1 pint = 500 mL
3 cups = 750 mL
4 cups = 1 quart = 1 L

VOLUME MEASUREMENTS (fluid)

1 fluid ounce (2 tablespoons) = 30 mL
4 fluid ounces (1/2 cup) = 125 mL
8 fluid ounces (1 cup) = 250 mL
12 fluid ounces (1 1/2 cups) = 375 mL
16 fluid ounces (2 cups) = 500 mL

WEIGHTS (mass)

1/2 ounce = 15 g
1 ounce = 30 g
3 ounces = 90 g
4 ounces = 120 g
8 ounces = 225 g
10 ounces = 285 g
12 ounces = 360 g
16 ounces = 1 pound = 450 g

DIMENSIONS

1/16 inch = 2 mm
1/8 inch = 3 mm
1/4 inch = 6 mm
1/2 inch = 1.5 cm
3/4 inch = 2 cm
1 inch = 2.5 cm

OVEN TEMPERATURES

250°F = 120°C
275°F = 140°C
300°F = 150°C
325°F = 160°C
350°F = 180°C
375°F = 190°C
400°F = 200°C
425°F = 220°C
450°F = 230°C

BAKING PAN SIZES

Utensil	Size in Inches/Quarts	Metric Volume	Size in Centimeters
Baking or Cake Pan (square or rectangular)	8×8×2	2 L	20×20×5
	9×9×2	2.5 L	23×23×5
	12×8×2	3 L	30×20×5
	13×9×2	3.5 L	33×23×5
Loaf Pan	8×4×3	1.5 L	20×10×7
	9×5×3	2 L	23×13×7
Round Layer Cake Pan	8×1½	1.2 L	20×4
	9×1½	1.5 L	23×4
Pie Plate	8×1¼	750 mL	20×3
	9×1¼	1 L	23×3
Baking Dish or Casserole	1 quart	1 L	—
	1½ quart	1.5 L	—
	2 quart	2 L	—